Style and Difference

A Guide for Writers

Donna Gorrell
St. Cloud State University

Houghton Mifflin Company

Boston • New York

Publisher: Patricia A. Coryell
Executive Editor: Suzanne Phelps Weir
Development Manager: Sarah Helyar Smith
Assistant Editor: Anne Leung
Senior Project Editor: Tracy Patruno
Senior Manufacturing Coordinator: Marie Barnes
Senior Marketing Manager: Cindy Graff Cohen
Marketing Associate: Wendy Thayer

Cover image: © Patrick Bennett/CORBIS

Printed in the U.S.A.

Library of Congress Control Number: 2003110146

ISBN: 0-618-38159-7

23456789-QF-09 08 07 06 05

Contents

Preface   ix

Introduction: Style, Situation, and Difference   1

Part One *Style*   8

1 Coordinate Balanced Ideas   14

2 Subordinate Cumulative Ideas   19

3 Vary Your Sentences   24

4 Vary Your Sentences—Again   35

5 Pack Your Sentences with Parallelism   44

6 Make Your Point with Emphasis and Rhythm   50

7 Modify with Style   60

8 Connect Your Thoughts Coherently   68

9 Be Concise   76

10 Make Your Voice Heard   85

11 Figure Your Language for Vivid Writing   93

12 Omit *and*, Repeat *and*   100

Part Two **_Difference_**   104

13 Use Passive Verbs   107

14 Begin Your Sentences with *and* (*but, or, nor, for, yet, so*)   113

15 Begin Your Sentences with *because* (*since, while*)   119

16 Fragment Your Sentences   125

17 Splice with Commas   133

18 Refer with a Singular *they*   139

19 Say *I* (*we, you*)   146

20 Contract Your Words   153

21 Split Your Infinitives   158

22 Use *which* for *that*   163

23 End Your Sentences with Prepositions   168

24 Repeat, Repeat, Repeat   173

Part Three **_Punctuation and Style_**   180

25 Control Your Commas   184

26 End with Periods Etc.   192

27 Dash with Dashes   199

28 Point with Colons   204

29 Separate with Semicolons   208

30 Possess with Apostrophes   213

31 Connect with Hyphens   218

(handwritten annotations: "useful for me!", "check my writing")

| Part Four | *A Few Good Rules* | 224 |

32 Make Your Verbs Agree with Your Subjects 227

33 Be Sure Your Pronouns Refer to Something 234

34 Make Your Pronouns Agree 241

35 Just in Case—Pronouns Again 248

36 Don't Dangle Your Modifiers 255

| Part Five | *Writers on Style* | 263 |

Richard A. Lanham, Frank Smith, William Zinsser,
Winston Weathers and Otis Winchester, Annie Dillard,
Comte de Buffon, Louis Milic, Keith Hjortshoj,
Monroe C. Beardsley, Walker Gibson, Aristotle, Quintilian,
William Strunk Jr., and E. B. White

Glossary of Terms 275

Works Cited and Quoted 281

Index 291

Preface

Teachers of writing know that published writers, while usually observing established rules and conventions, also freely disregard those rules and conventions when it fits their needs. Writers of both fiction and nonfiction—of scholarly as well as general articles and books—do write fragments, splice sentences with commas, begin sentences with *and*, end them with prepositions, use passive voice, say *I*, contract words, and so on. Yet all too often teachers advise against these elements of style, usually because student writers are unskilled at using them. Their fragments are incomplete ideas, their spliced sentences are ambiguous, too many of their sentences begin with *and* or *but*, and their modifiers dangle.

Instead of prohibiting these usages, *Style and Difference* advises students how to apply them adeptly. With the aid of examples from over one hundred contemporary published writers, this textbook shows that style can differ from as well as conform to the established conventions and rules of writing. *Difference*, in the title of this book, refers to a welcome departure from the norm—another way to approach the art of writing with style. Overall, this book develops the idea that style is difference, and while style acknowledges what we call the conventions of

how is this possible

writing, it also departs from those conventions. Without difference, there is no style.

Our collected wisdom tells us that students need to learn the rules before they can be taught how to break them. I question whether this is true. Consider how many times they've heard the rules, how many papers they've written, how many corrections they've received. Instead of directing attention once again to the rules, most of which are not rules anyway but just acquired conventions of usage, we can do more to advance our students' writing if we make an end run around those rules. I believe that students can relearn or review the usage conventions just as well from the back door as from the front—perhaps even better. A well-crafted comma splice can sharpen awareness of ambiguous ones. The pronoun *I* in a piece of scholarly writing can elucidate its effects. Flexibility in applying rules and conventions of usage can lead to a better understanding of why we have them and how writers adjust their styles according to the situation. Of course, we realize there are still teachers who don't see these conventions as the "odd bits of misinformation" that my old Pence and Emery book calls them. To cover such cases, class discussions about the local academic situation might clarify some of the specific concerns about style in writing.

what do in class

Style and Difference gives practical advice on how students can produce writing with style (and with the correctness that matters) for both academic and professional purposes. Chapter after chapter, they can see how other writers apply various elements of style. How they establish sentence rhythm and emphasis. How they achieve sentence variety. How they connect their thoughts, write concisely, and figure their language. Also how they use contractions and fragments and passive voice. Plus that often overlooked aspect of style, how they use punctuation to say exactly what they want to say. And finally, with a bit of grammar, how published writers do make verbs agree with subjects and pronouns agree with antecedents.

doesn't seem right

The Introduction discusses style as a matter of options determined by situational features such as audience, occasion, and purpose. It suggests that awareness not only of the constraints but also of the freedoms in given situations can liberate writers to experiment with style. Part one, Style, discusses and illustrates customary matters of style such as sentence variety, figurative language, emphasis, and rhythm, showing how writers can shape, color, and depart from the expected in their writing. Part two, Difference, moves to twelve reversals of our prosaic conventions, recommending, for example, "Begin Your Sentences with *and*" and "Fragment Your Sentences." Part three, Punctuation and Style, moves back to the more conventional, giving some practical advice about how choices in punctuation affect style—in chapters such as "Dash with Dashes" and "Point with Colons." Part IV, A Few Good Rules, dips into some ticklish applications of grammar like making verbs agree with problematic subjects and wrestling with pronoun difficulties of reference, agreement, and case. The chapters in Parts two, three, and four close with bulleted summaries and practices that amplify and apply the principles discussed and illustrated in the chapters. Some of the practices ask students to analyze excerpts on various features of style, while others ask students to discuss how particular details contribute to broader features such as coherence or emphasis. Some practices ask students to observe styles in their academic reading, and most encourage students to experiment with ways of altering style. In short, the practices enable students to *practice* style—individually, in small groups, or as an entire class.

Part five, Writers on Style, has thirteen quoted pieces that express views on writing style from contemporary and not-so-contemporary writers such as Frank Smith, Walker Gibson, Annie Dillard, William Zinsser, and Quintilian. These last pieces lend themselves to class discussions on theoretical issues such as whether style is conscious or unconscious, whether differences of style are differences in meaning, and how style relates to identity.

Finally, a glossary at the end of the book defines the key terms that are boldfaced throughout the text.

Because I believe that students learn writing most easily and naturally through exposure to good writing, all chapters—both conventional and contra-conventional—are abundantly illustrated with examples from contemporary nonfiction. Excerpts range widely—from *A World Lit Only by Fire* by William Manchester, *Against the Gods: The Remarkable Story of Risk* by Peter L. Bernstein, *Gather Together in My Name* by Maya Angelou, *A History of Pi* by Petr Beckmann, *A History of Reading* by Alberto Manguel, and *The New Meaning of Treason* by Rebecca West, to name a very few. We have Rachel Carson, John Kenneth Galbraith, Stephen Jay Gould, Steven Pinker, Barbara Tuchman, C. V. Wedgwood, Edward O. Wilson, and many other familiar and not-so-familiar authors.

Importantly, I make the point that writing that is published for a general audience is not as different as one would think from that written for readers in the academy. In a search through scholarly journals in my own discipline, I've found some of the same "broken rules" as I discovered in writing scrutinized by a publisher's copy editor. I've included some of these examples—from journals written, edited, and read by teachers of writing—to show that our academic writing does indeed look very much like published nonfiction. If we can get our students to aim for writing comparable to that of John McPhee, Lewis Thomas, William Manchester, or Rachel Carson (or ourselves), their academic writing will likely meet our expectations.

The chapters can be used in sequences other than their order here. I think there's a logic to the way the book is organized, but when I used an early draft in an undergraduate writing course, I selected among the chapters, assigning one or two or three at a time, maybe pairing "Coordinate Balanced Ideas" with "Pack Your Sentences with Parallelism" (or maybe with "Splice with Commas"), or perhaps "Make Your Point with Emphasis and Rhythm" with "Repeat, Repeat, Repeat." The readings in Part five, Writers on Style, lend themselves to discussions about style that are appropriate at any time during the term. Imagine beginning the course with a discussion of Walker Gibson's sobering reminder that a reader can walk out on a writer at any moment—or with William Zinsser's advice that there is no style store.

Supplements for student and instructor. For students, the website for *Style and Difference,* which can be found at *<http://www.college.hmco.com/english/students>* provides useful links to grammar websites, selected resources on style, and a sample student paper on style analysis.

For instructors, the website, which can be found at *<http://www.college.hmco.com/english/instructors>*, contains sample syllabi, selected resources on style, and passworded access to suggested answers to practices, a discussion of Part five questions, and suggested writing assignments.

Acknowledgments. Although this book originated in my head, and I am ultimately responsible for everything I've said about style, I owe a debt of gratitude to the involvement of many other people. To the company of reviewers I am grateful for their insightful and practical commentaries that enabled me to arrive at this edition:

Larry Beason, University of South Alabama

Claire M. Busse, LaSalle University

Harry Crisp, University of Arkansas, Little Rock

Lynee Lewis Gaillet, Georgia State University

Philip Gaines, Montana State University

Karen Gocsik, Dartmouth College

Vicki K. Janik, State University of New York, Farmingdale

April Langley, University of Missouri, Columbia

Linda C. Mitchell, San Jose State University

Joel Margulis, San Francisco State University

Joe Moxley, University of South Florida

Vara S. Neverow, South Connecticut State University

David H. Payne, University of Georgia

Elizabeth Rankin, University of North Dakota

David Thomas Sumner, Linfield College

Karen Kurt Teal, University of Washington and Edmonds Community College

The help from these reviewers would not have been available to me but for the arrangements made by the editors and production staff at Houghton Mifflin. For that and all the assistance I have received from them, I am inexpressively grateful. Working with them has been a truly gratifying experience. In particular let me thank Suzanne Phelps Weir for believing in my project in the first place. And for innumerable editorial and production details that have been done so well, I'm grateful to Sarah Helyar Smith, Laura Barthule, Anne Leung, Tracy Patruno, Merrill Peterson, and all the Houghton Mifflin staff who were involved in many ways I can't even comprehend.

Closer to home, let me acknowledge all the students in my style and rhetoric classes who have helped me think about style; my colleagues at St. Cloud State University for their interest and encouragement; Luke Eidenschink for his marvelous pen-and-ink conceptions of style in barns; and finally and always, for his support for the entire project, Ken Gorrell.

Donna Gorrell
St. Cloud State University

Style and
Difference

Style, Situation, and Difference

Style is about difference. When we refer to style in clothing, automobiles, houses, barns—or writing!—the essential factor is that the thing is different from all others in its class. The person who dresses with style wears clothing different from what others wear. Automobile manufacturers strive for designs that *differ* in certain ways from others—and they produce cars with style. We, all of us probably, like to think that our homes and rooms reflect a style that is distinctly ours: the way we arrange our furniture, what we hang on our walls, how we treat our windows. Even barns—it's the different one that has style. Whether we're urban, suburban, or rural, we all have an idea of what the basic barn looks like: red, rectangular, and big. But think again. All barns are not red and rectangular with those ridged gambrel roofs. Round or octagonal or nonagonal, or with a cupola on top or a window the shape of a star—these are the features that might catch our eye. These are the features that give the humble barn its style.

Fashion, on the other hand, is sameness, conformity—to be in fashion you have to wear or do or be the latest—conforming to what the people you identify with are wearing or doing or being. To be fashionable is to be correct, to follow the rules. But to have style—you sometimes need to break the rules. Having style is knowing what the rules are and

comparison to writing

deeper mechanics of writing

1

just how closely you have to follow them in order not to be thought weird and to lose your credibility. Then you let yourself be different. As writers, we tend to be too constricted with how writing *should* be—then wonder if our writing has style, and if not how we can get it.

final question

If we try only to be *correct* when we write—to write like other writers, to be conventional and fashionable—we might get writing like that of everyone else who writes only correctly. Instead of following the rules without regard for whether they're making our writing effective or not, we often need to question the rules. To write with style, we need at times to break the rules. *— will this really work*

This book tells you that most of the rules for writing are not hard and fast and that many of them can be broken—many writers do in fact break them. The trick is knowing when—and how—to break them. To illustrate that point, I've searched scores of books and a few articles for examples of how published writers of contemporary nonfiction have observed, stretched, even broken the rules. The writing is all nonfiction because of its similarities with the kind of writing you need to do in school. It is all factual (and true, as far as I know), most of it written to a general audience like you and me, and stylistically not too casual nor too formal. A few pieces are even drawn from professional academic journals just to further support the point that some of what we call rules are only myths and misinformation that in some situations of academic writing can be disregarded.

what is not too casual formal

Moreover, these writers have written with a certain style. We see, for instance, that Samuel Eliot Morison asks more questions than is normally expected, and John Kenneth Galbraith frequently uses reversed sentence order. Sebastian Junger relies heavily on parallel **phrases** and **clauses**, as well as vivid, metaphoric **verbs**. Junger and Lewis Thomas like to use contractions and sentence **fragments.** You may find it productive to study the style of these and other writers to see how they use various aspects of style. That awareness may lead to some experimentation that develops into something that you feel reflects who you are. Like these other writers, you can *write with style*.

look up

Situations. All writing is situational. Some kinds of rule-breaking may be appropriate for you in a given situation and some not. You probably know that some teachers allow sentence fragments if the idea is complete, **comma splices** that are unambiguous, repetition if it serves a stylistic purpose. Others don't tolerate *and* at the beginning of sentences, **prepositions** at the end, *I* and contractions anywhere. So, even though you know that Aldo Leopold writes comma splices, William Zinsser says *I*, and Lewis Thomas uses contractions, you still need to assess *your* writing situations and determine what features of style are appropriate each time you write. Style is influenced by a number of situational factors: your role as a writer, your reader, your attitude toward your subject, and the occasion of your writing.

You the writer.   Style is not the same as personality, though personality is an aspect of an individual style. Style is more like a persona, or role—or even in the Greek sense "mask"—that you put on for the situation. This is not to say that the assumed style is false, only that it reflects that part of you that fits the situation—much as actors play a given part, say Othello, according to how they see the part, depending on their personalities, backgrounds, interests, culture, and so on. As actors differ in their style of playing a part, so do writers differ in the ways they respond to given situations.

Your **voice** is the sound of your style. Depending on the situation, you make choices—some conscious, some unconscious—about whether you want to sound professional, or friendly, or optimistic, or annoyed, and so on. Your experience as a writer helps you choose the words you write and their arrangement in sentences, decide on features of a more casual or a more formal style, and consider many other features of style that represent you to your reader. Will you begin a sentence with *but* or the more formal *however*? How long will your sentences be? Will you render your ideas in **metaphors** and other **figurative language**? These and other decisions affect your voice as you write.

Notice how Rachel Carson's voice differs in the two examples that follow. The first is from her descriptive book *The Edge of the Sea*, the second from her highly persuasive *Silent Spring*:

> Whenever I go down into this magical zone of the low water of the spring tides, I look for the most delicately beautiful of all the shore's inhabitants—flowers that are not plant but animal, blooming on the threshold of the deeper sea. (13)

> How could intelligent beings seek to control a few unwanted species by a method that contaminated the entire environment and brought the threat of disease and death even to their own kind? Yet this is precisely what we have done. (8)

[marginal annotations: "personality", "style", "voice (sound)", "questions for me", "slant", "?"]

Look at the startling differences in word choices—"magical zone" versus "unwanted species," "blooming on the threshold of the deeper sea" versus "threat of disease and death." The sentence styles differ as well, the first being softly rhythmic, the second a sharp and jangling accusation. Both came from the scientist Carson, but each responds in its own way to her purpose in the given situation: to share experience or to call for change.

Whatever choices you make, they all come from your mind, from your experiences, interests, and biases. So there is always an integral part of your voice that remains *you*, no matter how you alter it to fit the situation. (Read more about voice in chapter 10, "Make Your Voice Heard.")

Your reader. Your reader also has experiences, interests, and biases, and as a writer you make adjustments not only in *what* you say but also in *how* you say it to suit your reader. For school and professional audiences, you probably avoid slang and street expressions, you edit carefully, and you adopt a tone that is serious and respectful of both your subject and your reader. Your style tends toward formality. Yet in many school, social, and professional situations you can be less formal than you may think, more conversational.

The following sentence was written by noted essayist Lewis Thomas in his book about language, *Et Cetera, Et Cetera*, for a general, public audience:

> Switched off in adulthood, I'd guess: I'll never in my life learn to speak French convincingly, having tried too late. (95)

Thomas chooses both contractions and the **pronoun** *I*, plus an opening sentence fragment. Depending on *your* reader in given situations, it might be a good idea—or not—for you to avoid contractions and *I*. Depending on your reader, you might use more—or less—**subordination** in your sentences. Depending on your reader, you might have fewer **dashes** and more **colons** or **semicolons**, or the other way around. Knowing your reader can help you decide whether, and when, to apply given features of style.

How do you get to know your reader? By paying attention. In academic writing, your reader is of course the teacher of whatever class you're writing for. But keep in mind that teachers differ in their expectations. How formal is the language the teacher has used in the syllabus and other course information? What aspects of style does the teacher stress in class? What kind of textbook(s) has the teacher selected for the course? What is the level of formality in the textbooks? In the teacher's class presentations? And as a last resort, though maybe too late, observe what things the teacher has marked on a paper you've already written. The problem may not be as much that you broke a rule as that you didn't do it as expertly as a professional writer would. The sentence may not be clear. Talk with the teacher about it.

Your attitude toward your subject.   Style is a writer's primary way of conveying attitude toward a subject, so attitude influences style. In the foregoing sentences by Rachel Carson, consider the two different attitudes toward her subjects: the first quietly admiring, the second sharply criticizing. Writers need to be careful that their style reflects the attitude they want to convey. Observe how word choice in the following sentence expresses Edith Hamilton's attitude:

> The Greek mind was free to think about the world as it pleased, to reject all traditional explanations, to disregard all the priests taught, to search unhampered by any outside authority for the truth.
>
> —*The Greek Way* (28)

Hamilton's affirmative words—*free, pleased,* and *unhampered*—convey her admiration for the ancient Greeks, and her repetitive sentence structure adds **emphasis**. A very different attitude is expressed in the following sentence:

> By the time Fischer left for Nepal in the spring of 1996, he'd begun to garner more of the recognition that he thought was his due.
>
> —Jon Krakauer, *Into Thin Air* (64)

Just the insertion of "he thought" alters the attitude, telling readers that Krakauer does not agree with Fischer. Another writer, Paul Fussell, conveys cynicism in his book *Doing Battle: The Making of a Skeptic,* as in this short sentence:

> By this time, the extirpation of Boy Fussell was almost complete. (171)

The sentence does exactly what Fussell wants it to do. His choice of *extirpation,* meaning "to destroy by pulling up by the roots," and his formal reference to his naive self combine to convey his negative attitude toward his war experience.

Your occasion for writing.   Writing responds to occasions. In most academic writing, the occasion is an assignment that requires a "paper." It's written for teachers and shows what you know, what you understand, and how well you can express your thoughts. Business occasions have similar purposes in reports, memos, letters, and so on. Various professional situations require publications that show knowledge in a field of study; most of these papers are scholarly, written for professional journals. But some are intended for a general audience. Rachel Carson, Lewis Thomas, and Edith Hamilton are scholars in their own fields, but their books *Silent Spring, Et Cetera, Et Cetera,* and *The Greek Way* are written for the enjoyment of readers like you.

An occasion for writing carries with it certain constraints. Writing for a general audience, Carson does not use the technical terms she would adopt when writing for a science journal. In writing about language, Thomas does not burden his reader with medical terms he might employ when writing as a physician in a medical journal. Edith Hamilton, a world-renowned classicist, refrains from the technical references she might use in the university classroom and instead adjusts her style for a nonscholarly audience.

These writers know the conventions of style. They know that conventions are situational and determined in part by the expectations of their readers. But these writers are not bound needlessly by conventions and expectations, and neither should you be. Like Carson, Thomas, Hamilton, and all the others you read in this book, you can meet reader expectations yet stretch the rules so that you develop a style that is distinctly yours.

Looking ahead.   Your writing style is the subject of this book. The chapters in part one begin by reminding you of those basic elements of style that allow writers to balance, expand, emphasize, connect, and illustrate a piece of writing. The chapters emphasize effective application of stylistic features by writers in fields such as history, science, language, mathematics, and adventure. These features are conventional tools that all writers observe almost every time they write. The chapters in part two discuss deviations from those conventions and show you how writers sometimes break the rules in order to achieve the effects covered in part one—in other words, to balance, expand, emphasize, connect, and illustrate. Part three, acknowledging that punctuation choices affect style, gives a brief overview of usage that shows how selected published writers punctuate. Part four is intended for writers who are still a little unclear about how to use pronouns, verbs, and modifiers in difficult situations; these essential aspects of style are illustrated with published excerpts. Finally, part five invites you to think about and discuss style from the perspectives of several writers writing on style and to come up with your own definitions and descriptions.

Each chapter ends with two features that can assist application of the principles discussed and illustrated: A summary draws the principles together, and "Practice" suggests ways of using them. Throughout the book, boldfaced terms refer you to definitions in the glossary following part five.

As you work toward ways of altering your style, consider carefully. Barns with all their stylistic variations are, above all, constructed like barns so they can fulfill certain purposes. So too with writing. The purposes and constraints of your writing situation affect your decisions about style. Almost always, some rules can be broken. But be warned: Readers who believe that the rules are real will notice when you break one. If you do it with confidence and discrimination, however, some readers will probably realize that you're doing so intentionally and—maybe—excuse the irregularity. Others may decide that you're onto a great stylistic device and adopt it themselves. Other readers won't even notice; they'll just like your style.

Part One

Style

S tyle, paradoxically, is both difference and sameness. We recognize style when we encounter something different, yet we can't appreciate that difference without the sameness. The man or woman who dresses with style has the look of the conventional as well as the *je ne sais quoi*. The something different. Style. When we write, we want to write with style, yet we learn those features of style by observing—and writing like—other writers. Yes, paradoxical. Sameness, difference. Of course, it helps to know what to look for.

The problem with recognizing style is that it's so abstract. Think of someone you know who dresses with style. Can you identify what characteristics make up that style? And how is that person's style of dress different from that of other people you know? Think of someone's home or room decoration that you consider has style. What are its features? How do they differ from those of other homes and rooms? Given the difficulty of identifying features of tangible things like dress and home decoration, how much more difficult is it to identify features of style in something as abstract as writing!

Let's assume that style has certain universal features that can apply specifically to given arenas such as dress or writing. As we try to identify those features, let's start with something really tangible, something we can look at objectively—say, barns. At the beginning of this book I mentioned that people may think of barns as red and rectangular and gambrel-roofed. They're big, have big doors, and are set on a farm in open country. We may not see one every day of our lives, but we know what one looks like. So, if this is the basic, conventional barn, what does it take for a barn to have style, to be different?

How about bigger than ordinary, such as a barn in the Adirondack Mountains that appears to be three times the normal length? Or one in Portage County, Ohio, that is not only longer but also taller and wider than the usual barn. This one also has a banked entrance to the second story and has three cupolas on top. Cupolas do have a function—ventilation—but they don't have to be constructed like church spires, as these are. What about neatness, tidiness, such as those on many Illinois and Iowa farms, where you can find clusters of freshly painted red or white buildings set in the midst of cleanly mown lawns, where corn is as high as you-know-what and you can tell there's a good market for corn. On the other hand, there's a smallish barn near Traverse City, Michigan, that has seen some better days. It might once have been some kind of red, though the vertical boards look weathered now. With its still-intact stone foundation, darkened tin slant roof, lack of windows (light can get in through gaps in the siding), and slender trees growing right up beside the walls, this neglected barn has *style*.

There are other barns with style: the one built in a cross shape with a large central cupola and star-shaped ventilators in the gables (looks like an astrological church!), a small stone bank barn and a slotted stone tobacco barn, both in Pennsylvania, and of course the round, octagonal, or thirteen- or fourteen-sided white or red or unpainted barns that you find sprinkled throughout the Midwest, plus the long, single-story yellow one planted in the Berkshire Mountains, the tiny unpainted one in the shadow of a Utah mountain, and the many-windowed, three-storied brown one in the snow of New Hampshire.

So what gives these barns their style? Basically, barns are functional, and many of their functions are similar: sheltering and feeding farm animals, storing feed and equipment, providing a place out of the weather for farmers to work. Yet they have different ways of meeting those functions. These are the stylistic features. Let me list several that I observe:

❖ Color
❖ Size

- ❖ Shape
- ❖ Foundation
- ❖ Building materials
- ❖ Special design features: cupolas, roof line, direction of siding boards, windows, gables, ventilators, trimmings, surprises
- ❖ Upkeep
- ❖ Setting

Now, bear with me. If we just convert these words to describing writing instead of barns, we can perhaps begin to grasp how the features of style serve the function of conveying our ideas in writing.

Color.   How do we color our writing? With colorful words, of course— figurative language, **modifiers**, emphasis, **rhythm**, punctuation, level of formality, and many other choices that lend vividness to what we say.

Size.   Length of a piece of writing is usually specified by occasion or function, so a shift from the ordinary, as with most stylistic features, makes length too an aspect of style. Think of exceptionally short pieces such as Lincoln's Gettysburg Address or John F. Kennedy's Inaugural Address—as opposed to some other dedications and inaugurals you can think of.

Shape.   We can alter the ordinary shape of a piece of writing with shorter or longer sentences or paragraphs, the connections we make for **coherence**, the rhythm and variety of our sentences, the way we arrange our modifiers, the format of the finished piece.

Foundation.   A well-designed structure always has a foundation, whether it's a barn or an apartment building or a road—or a piece of writing. The foundation lends support, strength, and stability to the structure. In writing, we build our thoughts on a foundational idea or theme, erecting a structure made of logically connected sentences and paragraphs.

Materials.   Our building materials for writing are words and sentences and paragraphs—put together with the nails of punctuation. It is our skill that determines how we use those materials: to establish size, shape, symmetry, economy, precision, coherence, emphasis, **clarity**.

Special design features.   Any of the features illustrated in part two, "Difference," can be classified under special design: fragments, contractions, repetitions, comma splices, and so on. Our choices of punctuation can also be included here; a dash, for example, can present a surprise that a **comma** or a colon wouldn't. Readers do like to occasionally encounter the unexpected: a particularly apt metaphor, an astonishingly long sentence, an abruptly short one, a pertinent question, a perfectly balanced series. But writers need to use special design features with care; attractive as they are, they draw attention to themselves, and too many of them are distracting. (Can you imagine a dozen cupolas?)

Upkeep.   This one's a bit of a stretch, but here we might include revision, editing, anything we can do to make our writing sharp, clear, and direct, a positive representation of ourselves to the world passing by.

Setting.   Writing always is situational. What J.F.K. said in his Inaugural Address was not the same as what he said in his campaign speeches; and even if it were the same, the situation would have made it different. Similarly, your contribution to an online discussion is not the same as one to a print publication or in a term paper. The setting of a research paper is not the same as that of a short narrative. Style says the right thing at the right time in the right way. The situation determines several factors in your writing:

- ❖ *Writer constraints.* The features that make you who you are— your background, education, experience, interests, biases, personality—all contribute to how and what you write. In addition you have a purpose for writing—to persuade, to entertain, to inform, and so on. Your purpose may or may not be the same as your motive or need for writing—to earn some money, to show your brother-in-law you know something about the subject, or whatever.
- ❖ *Reader constraints.* As a writer you have to deal with the same constraints in your reader—except that in the reader they are different from yours. Your reader has individual purposes, motives, and needs for reading, and they're all connected somehow to his or her background, education, experience, interests, biases, and personality—much of which you can only guess at. How your writing looks stylistically to your

reader depends on that reader. (Up above, I implied that I liked that small barn in Michigan; you might not.)

❖ *Occasion constraints.* Your style is influenced also by such things as the exigence for your writing—whatever it is that prompts you to write—plus your subject. The occasion may limit your length, formality, and format—all of which affect your style. Then, too, some occasions will prevent you from breaking some (or any) of the conventions described in part two, "Difference." You may not be able to use a singular *they* even though you may desperately want to.

(See also "Introduction: Style, Situation, and Difference.")

At first glance, all these constraints may seem daunting and prohibitive to your style and self-expression; but I invite you to think again about the barns to see how constraints actually contribute to function and style. Consider the small barn nestled against the side of a Utah mountain and the three-storied snowbound one in New Hampshire. It is precisely because these barns respond to all the constraints—of setting but also of the needs and wishes of the persons using these barns—that their designs have style. Or consider the round or many-sided barns, cleverly designed for livestock to be stabled around the perimeter and their feed stored in the center. Though upsetting our notion of what barns look like, these radical variations make outstanding sense.

Style, as we can see from observing barns, is not something tacked on at the end, as some people envision style in writing. It's not just a matter of going back and fixing commas, changing a word here and there, adding a paragraph. It *is* all of these things, but much, much more. Style is integral to everything you do in writing, from your first thought to your final period—just as a barn's style develops from the twinkle in the farmer's eye to the last stroke of paint. Some of this development is conscious but much of it unconscious. I'd guess that the more skilled the writer, the more unconscious the style. But maybe not. What do you think? How much of your writing—and your preparation for writing—is conscious thought and how much unconscious?

In the discussions that follow, you can see how other writers have dealt with conventions and self-expression, sameness and difference, and how they've worked within their constraints yet expanded on them to shape, color, and depart from the expected.

1

Coordinate Balanced Ideas

*T*his chapter and the one that follows are rather heavy on terminology, but I've placed them near the beginning of the book because I see **coordination** and **subordination** as the two major building blocks of sentences and therefore of style. In other words, we can't very well begin without them. If you have trouble with some of the terms, keep your finger on the glossary (p. 274) and use it when you need to.

Beyond the bare-bones sentence of subject-verb-complement, writers coordinate and subordinate. When they coordinate they add equivalent ideas and parallel grammatical elements; when they subordinate they add nonequivalent ideas and grammatical elements.

COORDINATION   The water of Crater Lake is <u>cold</u> *and* <u>clear</u>.

■ Two words coordinated.

I use this more

Crater Lake <u>is located in Oregon</u> *and* <u>is surrounded by the crater's rocks</u>.

■ Two **phrases** coordinated.

SUBORDINATION   <u>Because the water is so clear</u>, you can see deep <u>into its depths</u>.

■ Subordinated **clause** and phrase.

Some writers prefer one practice over the other; some writers find that one or the other dominates given the function of the piece of writing. But all writers commonly use both coordination and subordination. In fact, we can't write a sentence without one or the other or both. This chapter concentrates on coordination (though we can't avoid subordination). *—> Do we really use both?*

Coordinated independent clauses.   The following sentence by Rachel Carson illustrates two coordinated **independent clauses**. (A vertical line separates the independent clauses.)   *2 ml sentences*

The gases began to liquefy, | and Earth became a molten mass.
—*The Sea around Us* (4)

Although each clause could stand alone, Carson combines them, separating them with a comma and connecting them with *and*. Most coordination is not this basic, however, as the following example shows.

Water fountained from a gap in the river ice, | and that is what he lived on. —John McPhee, *Coming into the Country* (239)

This sentence, like Carson's, has two independent clauses, but it also has an embedded **subordinate clause** ("what he lived on"). The following two sentences from Barbara Tuchman's *The March of Folly* are also far from basic. The first has two coordinated independent clauses with an embedded *that* clause, and the second has three independent clauses separated by semicolons: *no other word to connect use semicolons*

Speculations about a neutralist solution were floating in South Vietnam after Diem's assassination, | and it is possible that Saigon might have come to terms with the insurgents at this point but for the American presence. (311–12)

The Soviet Union had been faced down in the Berlin and Cuban missile crises; | Soviet influence over the European Communist parties was much less; | NATO was firmly established. (313)

As these sentences illustrate, coordination joins similar sentence elements and equivalent ideas. They also show that independent clauses are ordinarily connected by a comma and a **conjunction** (such as *and* or *but*) or by a **semicolon**. But writers don't always follow the rules; sometimes they omit the comma, sometimes the *and*, sometimes the semicolon. Here, Sebastian Junger omits the comma, achieving a smooth-flowing sentence:

> Seventy-footers are roaming around the sea state like surly giants | *and* there's not much Billy can do but take them head-on and try to get over the top before they break. —*The Perfect Storm* (138)

This sentence illustrates another kind of coordination: Junger's second *and* links two **infinitive phrases** ("take them head-on" and "try to get over the top"; *to* ordinarily marks an **infinitive** but is omitted before *take* and *try*). One of these infinitives (*try*) has a second infinitive (*to get*). The following sentence has two coordinated independent clauses plus three coordinated phrases:

> The causes of the accident [at Three Mile Island] seem rather complex, | *but* it certainly involved poor design of some reactor elements, | malfunction of some safety features, | *and* poor judgment on the part of some operators. —Jack J. Kraushaar and Robert A. Ristinen, *Energy and Problems of a Technical Society* (137)

- ■ *Design, malfunction,* and *judgment* are coordinated in the second clause.

Coordinated words, phrases, and subordinate clauses. A common use of coordination is to join sentence elements of less grammatical weight than independent clauses, as we saw in Sebastian Junger's sentence and in Kraushaar and Ristinen's. We can also observe it in the following sentences:

> For decades the Soviet empire was held together by *ideology* and *coercion* and even the *perversity* of the imperial economy.
> —David Remnick, *Resurrection* (15)

- ■ Three **nouns**—*ideology, coercion, perversity*—joined as **objects** of the preposition *by*.

In this age *of* negative discovery, *of* the mechanized observer, *of* machine-created data and ever newer kinds of data, we must note a new kind of momentum. —Daniel J. Boorstin, *Cleopatra's Nose* (11)

- ■ Three prepositional *of* phrases; the third *of* has coordinated objects— *data, kinds of data*.

Remnick and Boorstin show how emphasis can be achieved through building on coordination and placing the most emphatic item at the end of the series. Any sentence element can be coordinated with similar elements, and any number of those elements can be joined together—with or without a **coordinating conjunction**. (See chapter 12, "Omit *and*, Repeat *and*.")

To further illustrate the flexibility and adaptability of coordination, notice how it serves the writers' purposes in the following sentences:

> It [language] binds us, unites us, can join hundreds, thousands, now billions of us together to make a single tremendous creature: a social species. —Lewis Thomas, *Et Cetera, Et Cetera* (106)

- ■ Three verbs (*binds, unites, can join*), then three nouns (*hundreds, thousands, billions*), and finally two nouns (*creature, species*)

> Beneath [the sixteenth-century peasant home's] sagging roof were a pigpen, a henhouse, cattle sheds, corncribs, straw and hay, and, last and least, the family's apartment, actually a single room whose walls and timbers were coated with soot.
> —William Manchester, *A World Lit Only by Fire* (53)

- ■ Series of nouns, plus the droll rephrasing of "last but not least."

> He trained as a combat diver—infiltrating positions, securing beaches, rescuing other combat divers—and then left at 21 to join the Air National Guard. —Junger (187)

- ■ Three **participles** (*infiltrating, securing, rescuing*); *and* is omitted.

So far we've seen coordinated words, phrases, and independent clauses. As a final example of coordination, here's a sentence that joins three subordinate clauses:

> Wherever there were brick bell towers and whitewashed churches, wherever rows of bells hung in ascending niches, wherever the common people could crowd belfries to take turns pulling the ropes, the bells sang. —Jay Winik, *April 1865* (29)

The three *wherever* clauses are joined without a conjunction. Notice that the first clause has coordinated **noun phrases** ("brick bell towers" and "whitewashed churches").

Summary

Let me suggest these guiding principles for using coordination:

- ❖ Coordinate only equivalent grammatical elements: clauses with similar clauses, phrases with similar phrases, words with similar **parts of speech**.
- ❖ Coordinate only equivalent ideas.
- ❖ Use coordination when you want to show that ideas or sentence elements are equal in status.
- ❖ Vary equivalent sentence elements with modifiers (see, in particular, the Boorstin, Remnick, and Winik examples).
- ❖ Join two elements with a coordinating conjunction (*and, but, or, nor, for, so, yet*). In some cases you might replace the conjunction with a comma.
- ❖ Join three or more elements with commas and/or coordinating conjunctions. Use semicolons when you want a stronger break between independent clauses.
- ❖ Use coordination for rhythm, emphasis, and sentence variety.

This subject is dealt with again in chapter 5, "Pack Your Sentences with Parallelism," and chapter 17, "Splice with Commas."

☐ **Practice** ☐

Read the following sentences from Rebecca West's *The New Meaning of Treason,* and mark all instances of coordination at the word, phrase, and clause levels. Then discuss the effectiveness of the sentences in terms of rhythm, emphasis, and sentence variety.

British and American scientists are drawn from the intellectuals of their two countries: that is, from a section of the English middle classes, or from American groups profoundly influenced by the culture of that section. Intellectuals may be defined as persons whose natural endowments and education give them the power to acquire experience of a rich and varied order, usually linked in some degree or other with learning and the arts, and, furthermore, to analyze their experiences and to base generalizations on the results of the analyses conducted by them and their fellows. They are essentially gregarious. They pool their experiences, they conform in their conclusions. (156)

2

Subordinate Cumulative Ideas

*U*nlike coordination, which ties together equal ideas and words, subordination adds unequal ideas and words to a sentence. You can subordinate almost any grammatical element: clauses, phrases, and words.

CLAUSE   Many cities and towns have water problems *because their water systems are outdated.*

PHRASE   The pipes *in many water systems* need *to be changed.*

■ Two phrases.

WORDS   *Water* mains break *frequently.*

■ **Adjective** and **adverb**.

A subordinate element adds detail and always relates to another element in the sentence, usually as a **modifier** (see chapter 7, "Modify with Style"). Writers use subordination to gain various effects.

Subordinate to add details.   Subordination-heavy sentences are probably our most common type of sentence, either spoken or written, though they are more complicated than they may seem at first glance.

In fact, this sentence by Thomas Cahill seems quite ordinary until we examine it more closely:

> In the time-honored fashion of the ancient world, he opens the book at random, intending to receive as a divine message the first sentence his eyes should fall upon. —*How the Irish Saved Civilization* (57)

Cahill's basic sentence about Augustine is "he opens the book." But the sentence begins with two orienting **prepositional phrases** ("In the time-honored fashion" and "of the ancient world") and adds detail at the end with a prepositional phrase ("at random") and a **participial phrase** ("intending . . ."). There is also an infinitive phrase ("to receive . . .") and a subordinate clause ("his eyes should fall upon"). For the reader, comprehending this sentence is much simpler than describing it. This next one too is filled with details, though easily read:

> Armed with his credentials and contracts, full of energy and eager to be off and away, Columbus arrived on May 22, 1492, at Palos de la Frontera. —Samuel Eliot Morison, *Admiral of the Ocean Sea* (101)

Basically this sentence says "Columbus arrived." But Morison piles on modifiers at the beginning—a participial phrase ("Armed . . .") and two coordinated adjective phrases ("full of energy" and "eager to be off")— all of which add details to the **subject**, *Columbus*. The phrase beginning *eager* has an embedded infinitive phrase ("to be off and away"). The sentence ends with two prepositional phrases disclosing time and place.

Subordinate for emphasis.   The preceding sentences haven't been selected to confuse you. In fact, they're not even confusing until we try to take them apart. The fact is that writers use subordination so comfortably that we rarely think about how complicated the usage really is. It's the way we add detail and, often, the way we achieve emphasis. The next sentence (which, because of its coordinated clauses, you saw in chapter 1) shows how subordination delays and emphasizes a very brief independent clause:

> Wherever there were brick bell towers and whitewashed churches, wherever rows of bells hung in ascending niches, wherever the

> common people could crowd belfries to take turns pulling the
> ropes, the bells sang. —Jay Winik, *April 1865* (29)

Essentially, Winik says "the bells sang." Because the *wherever* clauses are
structurally similar, or parallel, the sentence is easily comprehended.
But if we look closer, we see that the first clause has coordinated nouns
(*towers* and *churches*), the second one has two prepositional phrases ("of
bells" and "in ascending niches"), and the third has an infinitive phrase
with an embedded participial phrase ("pulling the ropes"). Not so simple
after all.

As the foregoing examples show, subordination can occur anywhere
in a sentence. Usually it's not a good idea to pile too much at the beginning unless you employ some other means to aid the reading, such
as the **parallelism** in Winik's and Morison's sentences. More often,
subordinate clauses and phrases are stacked up *following* the subject and
verb, making what is called a **cumulative sentence**, as Anne Lamott
illustrates here (and I'll spare you the analysis—I think you'll get the
idea). Notice that she begins with the subject and verb of her main
clause and then cumulates details through subordination:

> People tend to look at successful writers, writers who are getting
> their books published and maybe even doing well financially, and
> think that they sit down at their desks every morning feeling like
> a million dollars, feeling great about who they are and how much
> talent they have and what a great story they have to tell; that
> they take in a few deep breaths, push back their sleeves, roll their
> necks a few times to get all the cricks out, and dive in, typing
> fully formed passages as fast as a court reporter. —*Bird by Bird* (21)

"People tend," she says, and then she piles on the details.

The next and final examples illustrate how subordinate clauses
function as parts of speech: adjective clauses introduced by *who, where,
that*, and *which*, an adverb clause introduced by *while*, and a noun
clause introduced by *that*:

> Greek art is intellectual art, the art of men <u>*who* were clear and
> lucid thinkers</u>, and it is therefore plain art. —Edith Hamilton,
> *The Greek Way* (49)

■ Adjective clause describing "men."

He put it up on a kind of mental shelf <u>*where* he put all kinds of</u> <u>questions he had no immediate answers for.</u> —Robert M. Pirsig, *Zen and the Art of Motorcycle Maintenance* (232)

■ Adjective *where* clause identifying "shelf," an embedded *that* clause beginning *he* (*that* understood, meaning "questions").

There are quite a few other things <u>*that* may sting or burn, like</u> <u>jellyfish and Portuguese men-of-war.</u> —Marston Bates, *The Forest and the Sea* (73)

■ Adjective clause clarifying "things."

<u>*While* the royal family's internal relationships were unraveling,</u> Bismarck was laying the ground for the final transformation of Prussia into the Continent's preeminent power. —Jerrold M. Packard, *Victoria's Daughters* (139)

■ Adverb clause modifying the verb *was laying.*

Between 1994 and mid-2002, the Wildlife Protection Society of India documented the death by poaching of 622 wild tigers, and the WPSI believes <u>*that* this figure represents only a fraction of</u> <u>the total loss.</u> —Peter Matthiessen, "Burning Bright" (137)

■ Noun clause, object of *believes.*

Summary

Since this is a book on style, not grammar, I'll quit here and sum up with a few principles about using subordination:

❖ Subordination applies to almost all grammatical elements: clauses (as adjectives, adverbs, and nouns), phrases (participial, infinitive, prepositional), and words.
❖ Through subordination, writers can direct emphasis.
❖ Subordination allows writers to add details that develop and refine the main idea of a sentence.
❖ When subordinated elements are modifiers, they need to be related unambiguously to the words they modify. Notice in particular the adjective and adverb clauses in the last group of examples and the introductory phrases in Morison's sentence. (See also chapter 7, "Modify with Style," and chapter 4, "Vary Your Sentences—Again.")

❖ End-loaded sentences with the subject and verb near the beginning are ordinarily read more easily than those that begin with many modifiers.

❖ Subordinate elements can be coordinated with one another or subordinated to one another.

□ **Practice** □

Read the following sentences from *The Great Crash 1929* in which John Kenneth Galbraith describes an incident in the stock market panic. Identify subordinate clauses (beginning *who* or *which*) and prepositional phrases; then discuss how they contribute detail and emphasize ideas.

At twelve-thirty the officials of the New York Stock Exchange closed the visitors gallery on the wild scenes below. One of the visitors who had just departed was showing his remarkable ability to be on hand with history. He was the former Chancellor of the Exchequer, Mr. Winston Churchill. It was he who in 1925 returned Britain to the gold standard and the overvalued pound. Accordingly, he was responsible for the strain which sent Montagu Norman to plead in New York for easier money, which caused credit to be eased at the fatal time, which, in this academy view, in turn caused the boom. Now Churchill, it could be imagined, was viewing his awful handiwork. (102–03)

3

Vary Your Sentences

*I*n school we learn that sentences average so-many words in length, that they follow a specified word order, that they make **declarative** statements, and so on. But after school we learn that writers occasionally write very long sentences, or very short sentences, and they frequently interrupt their sentences. They also intersperse declarative statements with questions (whether they want an answer or not), shift their word order, and try a variety of sentence patterns. This chapter shows how writers vary their sentences in three ways. Like other writers, you can—

Write long sentences.

Write short sentences.

Interrupt your sentences.

The next chapter, "Vary Your Sentences—Again," deals with three more ways.

Write long sentences.   Some writers are really adept at writing a long sentence. That is, the sentence is so well put together that you don't realize how long it is unless you go back and look for periods. Do you realize, for example, that the following sentence from John F. Kennedy's Inaugural Address is eighty words long?

Let the word go forth from this time and place, to friend and foe alike, that the torch has been passed to a new generation of Americans, born in this century, tempered by war, disciplined by a hard and bitter peace, proud of our ancient heritage, and unwilling to witness or permit the slow undoing of those human rights to which this nation has always been committed, and to which we are committed today at home and around the world.

When you reflect that sentences average somewhere between fifteen and twenty-five words, you know that this sentence is long. Look how it works, though. Kennedy begins with an **imperative** verb, *Let*, which implies a "you" subject; then follows with the grammatical object, *word*, and the rest of the verb idea, then a passel of modifiers describing *word* and "a new generation of Americans." This principle of front-loading the subject and verb then adding modifiers allows the reader to know what the sentence is about from the beginning before the writer builds on that subject.

Here is one that begins with a parallel series of modifiers describing the subject:

Shackled in ignorance, disciplined by fear, and sheathed in superstition, they [the Europeans] trudged into the sixteenth century in the clumsy, hunched, pigeon-toed gait of rickets victims, their vacant faces, pocked by smallpox, turned blindly toward the future they thought they knew—gullible, pitiful innocents who were about to be swept up in the most powerful, incomprehensible, irresistible vortex since Alaric had led his Visigoths and Huns across the Alps, fallen on Rome, and extinguished the lamps of learning a thousand years before. —William Manchester, *A World Lit Only by Fire* (27)

Following his introductory modifiers, Manchester immediately states his subject and verb ("they trudged"), then proceeds to what have to be called modifiers despite the mass of information packed into them about the period of time immediately preceding the Renaissance.

But writers don't always lead with their subjects and verbs. In the following example, Elizabeth Wurtzel holds onto her verb until nearly the end. See how you react as you read:

The calm before the storm: . . . This simple and commonplace expression, the kind busy people use to describe a rare period of downtime, the kind of saying that seems so obvious, that reminds us to trust the silences no more than we trust the noise, that takes note of the way the signals we receive are often counter-intuitive, that tells us not to get too comfortable with our assumptions— this stupid expression about the weather whose meaning and implications I never gave any thought to at all—suddenly struck me as rich and resonant when I realized it is completely wasted on friends and relatives of suicides. —*Bitch: In Praise of Difficult Women* (159)

Two things save this sentence: Wurtzel repeats the subject, *expression*, before leading on (with another interruption, to be sure) to its verb, *struck*, and she ties her modifiers together with repetitive, parallel structure—the *that* clauses, for example. The structure also has a rhythm that gives the reader pauses for assimilating what has been read so far.

In another kind of long sentence, John McPhee not so much combines modifiers as connects what could be sentences. Notice how he describes a cause-and-effect process, each part separated from the others by a semicolon:

One of the geological curiosities of the Pine Barrens is that rainwater soaking down through fallen pine needles and other forest litter takes on enough acid to leach out iron from the sands below; the dissolved iron moves underground into the streams, where it oxidizes on contact with the air and forms a patch of scum on the surface that is partly rust brown and partly iridescent blue, and resembles an oil slick left by an outboard motor; drifting over to the edges of the streams, this iron-oxide film permeates the sands and gravels of the riverbanks and cements them together into a sandstone composite that has been known for centuries as bog iron.

—*The Pine Barrens* (26–27)

So far we've seen examples of a cumulative sentence (modifiers following the main idea; Manchester), an interrupted sentence (Wurtzel), and an orderly coordination of independent clauses (McPhee). The example that follows illustrates, quite grandly, a **periodic sentence**, which saves the main idea for the end. Don't get impatient for the subject and verb—they're near the bottom.

The changing character of the native population, brought about through unremarked pressures on porous borders; the creation of an increasingly unwieldy and rigid bureaucracy, whose own survival becomes its overriding goal; the despising of the military and the avoidance of its service by established families, while its offices present unprecedented opportunity for marginal men to whom its ranks had once been closed; the lip service paid to values long dead; the pretense that we still are what we once were; the increasing concentrations of the populace into richer and poorer by way of a corrupt tax system, and the desperation that inevitably follows; the aggrandizement of executive power at the expense of the legislature; ineffectual legislation promulgated with great show; the moral vocation of the man at the top to maintain order at all costs, while growing blind to the cruel dilemmas of ordinary life—these are all themes with which our world is familiar, nor are they the God-given property of any party or political point of view, even though we often act as if they were. —Thomas Cahill, *How the Irish Saved Civilization* (29–30)

A writer doesn't want to do too many of these, though the occasional long periodic sentence does lend a lot of weight to an idea. Cahill loads his sentence with nine subject ideas (*character, creation, despising, lip service, pretense, concentrations, aggrandizement, legislation, vocation*), all with modifiers and separated with semicolons. Then, almost at the end, he summarizes those ideas in *these* and states it with the verb ("these are"), then adds more modifiers and another independent clause. (Do you want to know the word count? One hundred seventy-seven.)

Do you need a break? Here's a nice short "long" sentence. It has a parallel series of **verb phrases**, all acting from the same subject:

Thirty tons of water flood the crew mess, continue into the officer's mess, explode a steel bulkhead, tear through two more walls, flood the crew's sleeping quarters, course down a companionway, and kill the ship's engine. —Sebastian Junger, *The Perfect Storm* (151)

Only thirty-six words. The progression of these forceful, metaphoric verbs pulls you along to the ultimate action of the tons of water. Movement is also conveyed in the second sentence of the following example too, here with a progression of prepositional phrases:

Shanghai no longer smells like the Mysterious East. The realization came as a shock to my nostrils, which had expected to be indulged on the long drive out the Nanking Road—past the old British Concession race course, now the People's Park, through leafy tunnels of dappled sunlight from the canopy of plane trees,

and into the vaulted arbor of the Avenue Joffre, once in the
heart of the old French Concession, now called simply Huai Hai
Middle Road. —Sterling Seagrave, *The Soong Dynasty* (1)

Though each prepositional phrase is long because of its modifiers, the
progress is not difficult to follow because each phrase begins with its
own preposition: *past, through,* and *into.*

Another long sentence maker is the list following a colon. Here's
an example:

What was more impressive was the array of politicians and
intellectuals who had agreed to line up under the same banner:
there were leaders from the industrial lobby; communists like
Gennady Zyuganov and Richard Kosolapov; military men
like Viktor Alksnis, Valentin Varennikov, and Albert Makashov;
a KGB general, Aleksandr Sterligov; Russian nationalists like
Vasily Belov, Ilya Konstantinov, and Valentin Rasputin; and
journalist-ideologues like Valentin Chikin of *Sovetskaya Rossiya*
and Aleksandr Prokhanov, the publisher and editor of *Dyen*
('the Day'). —David Remnick, *Resurrection* (49)

As long as the writer keeps the list parallel, the reader can go on for
quite some time absorbing the piled-up information.

How are you doing? Can you take one more? It's one you saw in
chapter 2 on subordination. The sentence begins with a simple subject
and verb ("People tend"), but then it's made long by several features.
The verb *tend* is followed by two infinitive phrases (beginning *to look*
and *think*). *To look* is followed by subordination that describes what
Anne Lamott means by *writers.* What follows *think* (*to* is omitted) is
more complicated: a *that* clause embedded with two parallel *feeling*
phrases (the second one embedded with three parallel clauses, beginning *who, how,* and *what*), and then finally a second *that* clause, this
one with four verb phrases (beginning *take, push, roll,* and *dive*), the last
one including a participial phrase ("typing . . . reporter"). Whew! But
it sounds worse than it is. Read it:

People tend to look at successful writers, writers who are getting
their books published and maybe even doing well financially, and
think that they sit down at their desks every morning feeling like
a million dollars, feeling great about who they are and how much
talent they have and what a great story they have to tell; that

they take in a few deep breaths, push back their sleeves, roll their necks a few times to get all the cricks out, and dive in, typing fully formed passages as fast as a court reporter. —*Bird by Bird* (21)

If you encountered that sentence in Lamott's book, you probably wouldn't even bat an eye. You'd just note the descriptions and the progression of the action, take them all in, pause for a breath at punctuation marks, and go on to the next sentence, never aware that you'd just read ninety-eight words without an intervening period.

What we've seen with all these examples is that long sentences do work. They're readable. They're impressive. They're something you should try. Just remember these points:

❖ Use parallel structure for ideas that are equivalent in thought and grammar. All the preceding examples rely on parallelism for clarity. (See chapter 5, "Pack Your Sentences with Parallelism.")

❖ Use only an occasional long sentence. One every few pages should be enough.

❖ Balance your long sentences with short and average-length sentences. The long sentence we saw by Sebastian Junger is followed by this one: "The *Zarah* is 550 feet long."

❖ In most cases, place your subject and verb near the beginning of the sentence. Once a reader knows who's doing what, the rest is likely to make sense.

❖ Read the sentence aloud to check its rhythm and to see if the breath units (usually between punctuation marks) come frequently enough.

❖ Sometimes repeat the subject, as Wurtzel and Cahill do.

❖ Sometimes repeat structural markers such as prepositions (like Seagrave) and conjunctions or **relative pronouns** (like Wurtzel and Lamott).

Write short sentences.   Like long sentences, short sentences should be written only deliberately. They seem to be most effective as beginnings and endings, to introduce or cap ideas—though writers also sometimes use them in series for narration or description. Here are some paragraph openers:

But the moment passed. —Remnick, *Resurrection* (223)

Some fires are hotter than others. —McPhee, *The Pine Barrens* (112)

The First World War had still not quite begun. —John Keegan,
The First World War (69)

It could be so. —Lewis Thomas, *Et Cetera, Et Cetera* (161)

It did. —John Kenneth Galbraith, *The Great Crash 1929* (103)

Effective beginnings? Notice how each sentence, though brief, is meant to draw together the idea of the previous paragraph and the one that follows. So effectively that, because I've taken the sentences out of context, you probably want to know *what* "could be so" and *what* "did." In a chapter titled "Mathematics and Language," Lewis Thomas ends a paragraph with this sentence:

> The universal language of the future, in the view of the tiny minority who now use it for their lives, will be mathematics. (161)

Then follows his brief qualified agreement ("It could be so") in a paragraph about the lasting nature of mathematics.

Galbraith's paragraph follows one that tells how the Morgans of Wall Street were being replaced by other "equally powerful men" known as "the nation's most powerful financiers." That paragraph ends with this sentence:

> The very news that they would act would release people from the fear to which they had surrendered. (103)

And, he says, "It did," in a paragraph that describes how.

Rebecca West begins paragraphs with short sentences too. Here is how she begins three consecutive paragraphs with four- and five-word sentences:

> This situation is not static. . . .

> This will not happen. . . .

> There is no immediate remedy. —*The New Meaning of Treason* (400–01)

Even chapters begin with concise statements. This is another one from *The First World War*:

> Armies make plans. —Keegan (24)

No doubt about it, a pithy beginning plunges a reader directly into the next thought. But exceptionally short sentences are no more common than exceptionally long ones. Nor should they be. They are effective in their infrequency.

Sometimes, though, writers will bunch a number of short sentences together. Galbraith has a short paragraph made up of mostly short sentences just a few paragraphs beyond the one we've looked at.

> This was it. The bankers, obviously, had moved in. The effect was electric. Fear vanished and gave way to concern lest the new advance be missed. Prices boomed upward. (105)

Forcing readers to stop frequently for periods, Galbraith conveys the erratic excitement of a time when bankers were attempting to check a chain reaction that was inexorably leading to the crash of the stock market. The following passage from a chapter on modern Israel combines two short sentences with a longer one:

> The past lies around every corner. Herod's tomb is next door to one's hotel in Jerusalem. And at Megiddo, the site of Armageddon that dominates old pathways from Egypt to Mesopotamia, archeologists have uncovered the strata of twenty cities, including Solomon's with its stalls for four thousand horses and chariots.
> —Barbara Tuchman, *Practicing History* (125)

Writers are sometimes tempted, when they see two short sentences side by side, to combine them, and at times that's a good idea. Here, however, Tuchman's short sentences are better off short, making clear that the second sentence is one of subsequent illustrations of the topic, not part of the statement of topic.

Brief endings can be emphatic. In a single-sentence paragraph, Jay Winik concludes a section of narrative that describes efforts to avert a civil war:

> It would not be enough. —*April 1865* (21)

He also uses the technique for emphasis at the end of a section of exposition:

> The convenient version of history forgets the unbroken link of secessionist threats emanating from the country's earliest days, just as it intimates that it was only Southerners who flirted with disunion in these perilous later years. Northerners did, too. (22)

Alfred Lansing ends a narrative section about travel in Antarctic ice this way:

> The wind continued into the next day without loosening the pack perceptibly. They waited. —*Endurance* (109)

Although Lansing's two sentences could have been combined, the second is more emphatic as he wrote it.

- ❖ To summarize, you can gain sentence variety with an occasional short sentence.
- ❖ Lead into a new idea with a short sentence.
- ❖ Emphasize an idea with a short sentence.
- ❖ Give immediacy to narration or description with a series of short sentences.
- ❖ Follow a long sentence with a short one, or a short one with a long one.

Interrupt your sentences.   While extremely long and extremely short sentences are almost always a conscious stylistic choice, sentence interruptions may flow naturally from a speaking style. In the following example, Sebastian Junger seems to be speaking to his readers:

> She keeps trying—what else is there to do?—and Stimpson goes back on deck to try to keep the *Satori* pointed into the seas. (154)

Even in Lewis Thomas's sentence below, the interruption has the air of speech:

> I bring up these shoals of numbers and their repeated cycles, when reduced to single digits, not out of vanity (although I admit to some self-indulgence) but rather the opposite: to disclose that I cannot be a mathematician. (167)

The purpose of interruptions is usually to add information:

> Olfaction is a complex cognitive task which we can, within limits, perform—and with considerable accuracy—but which we can describe inadequately at best. —Carl Sagan, *The Dragons of Eden* (165)

- ■ Two interruptions, the first set off with commas, the second with dashes.

Aristotle, the model scientist, the man of cool head and detached observation, unbiased and impersonal, does not display any dispassionate aloofness in his consideration of reason.

—Edith Hamilton, *The Greek Way* (30)

■ Two **appositives** renaming *Aristotle* ("the model scientist" and "the man of cool head") and two adjectives describing him ("unbiased" and "impersonal").

A man I came to despise, a fat first lieutenant who was the battalion intelligence officer, charged me and my platoon with the task of locating a machine gun said to be operating at night just in front of the German line. —Paul Fussell, *Doing Battle* (139)

■ An appositive ("lieutenant" renaming *man*) with a modifying *who* clause.

Despite advice to the contrary, writers obviously don't always avoid long interruptions between essential parts of their sentences such as subjects and verbs, or even between parts of verbs. The Hamilton and Fussell examples separate subjects and verbs, and the Sagan example separates parts of the verb.

How writers punctuate interruptions depends on how much separation and emphasis they want. In the preceding examples, we've seen dashes, parentheses, and commas. Commas usually give the least amount of separation and emphasis, dashes more so. Parentheses give greater separation but usually less emphasis. The following passage illustrates the kinds of breaks achieved with dashes and commas:

[Reed] was so obviously "writable"—if I may invent a word, which is against my principles—that I could not believe that, except for a routine political biography published in 1914 and an uninspired academic study in 1930, nothing had been written about him since his death in 1902. —Tuchman, *Practicing History* (83)

The dashed interruption in Tuchman's sentence adds explanation and commentary; it illustrates how dashes can set off interruptions that have interior commas. The second interruption ("except . . . 1930"), enclosed with commas, emphasizes by correction the force of the final statement.

The next example illustrates interruptions enclosed by commas and parentheses (plus my bracketed enclosure to identify *he*):

> But he [John Paul Jones] did return the plate, every bit of it, after the war was over; as Lord Selkirk (coming down from his high horse) acknowledged and even graciously announced in the Edinburgh newspapers. —Samuel Eliot Morison, *John Paul Jones* (154)

The comma enclosure ("every bit of it") adds information and emphasis, while the parenthetical interruption adds an authorial comment.

Some writers seem to favor interruptions as a means of sentence variety. As long as the reader doesn't get lost between start and finish, these sentences can be a welcome change in rhythm.

❖ Use sentence interruptions for variety, emphasis, rhythm, information, or commentary.

❖ Enclose interruptions with commas for least break, parentheses for most, and dashes for greatest emphasis.

❖ Use punctuation in pairs to begin and end the interruption.

❖ Avoid reader confusion by using dashes for only one purpose in a sentence. See also chapter 27, "Dash with Dashes."

□ **Practice** □

Write a long sentence of at least seventy-five words. Begin with your subject and verb, then add modifiers and additional information but not additional independent clauses. Insert an interruption with dashes or parentheses. Finish up with a short sentence.

4

Vary Your Sentences—Again

*T*his chapter is a continuation of the previous chapter, illus-
trating the means writers draw on to vary their sentences. You
too can—

Ask questions.

Reverse your word order.

Try other sentence patterns.

Ask questions.   For sentence variety, some writers like the occasional
question. Besides bringing about a change in sentence order, a question has the rhetorical advantage of involving a reader directly in con-
structing the next idea. Particularly at the beginning of a paragraph, a
question serves not only as a variation in sentence style but also as an
announcement of topic:

> Why does the spider mite appear to thrive on insecticides?
> —Rachel Carson, *Silent Spring* (253)

> Was there something about medieval Judaism that elicited the
> brutal new hostility? —James Carroll, *Constantine's Sword* (248)

Why do human beings do these things? —Thomas Cahill, *How the
Irish Saved Civilization* (136)

Each of these questions announces a topic, but each functions also as
a **transition** from the preceding paragraph, connecting ideas through
key words: *spider mite, hostility, these things*. Each consequent paragraph
offers an explanation for the statements that went before. Here are two
more opening questions that serve similar functions:

Why did the majority of early Christian churches reject such
writings as *Thomas* and accept other, possibly later accounts—
for example, Matthew, Luke, and John? —Elaine Pagels, *The Origin
of Satan* (73)

What is the specific allure of maps, especially old maps?
—Miles Harvey, *The Island of Lost Maps* (264)

Again, the reader is drawn in, the topic is announced, and the preceding paragraph is connected. Again, the question implies that an explanation will follow.

But not all questions imply explanations. The following question
follows a discussion of income-producing human capital and, to my
reading of it, comes under the category "rhetorical question":

Why else would so many breadwinners spend their hard-earned
money on life-insurance premiums? —Peter L. Bernstein, *Against
the Gods* (110)

Bernstein's question reads more like commentary than query; he doesn't
expect an answer. The following example, which occurs at the end of
a chapter, has a similar purpose, if not being an outright accusation:

When will the public become sufficiently aware of the facts to
demand such action? —Carson, *Silent Spring* (152)

Carson softens the charge only slightly with the words "the public" instead of what she really means—*you*, the reader. In the same book, she
also turns to questions when she wants to suggest ideas that she doesn't
have adequate supporting evidence for:

But what of the opposite end of the food chain—the human being
who, in probable ignorance of all this sequence of events, has
rigged his fishing tackle, caught a string of fish from the waters of

Clear Lake, and taken them home to fry for his supper? What could a heavy dose of DDD, or perhaps repeated doses, do to him? (49)

Even though Carson doesn't have the answers and the evidence, her questions put the controversial ideas into the reader's mind.

Questions can represent the writer's thinking out loud, as in the following excerpt from Miles Harvey's investigation of map thefts:

> But if the commercial aspects of collecting weren't what kept him going, then why did he pursue a map like the Rosselli with such fervor? Its historical import? Sure. Its beauty? Of course. Its rarity? Doubtless. The stature it would bring him? Possibly.
> —*The Island of Lost Maps* (254)

As the writer dialogues with himself, he gains sentence variety and emphasis. A question by Samuel Eliot Morison seems to function in the same way:

> As the Isle and Little Ross faded from Captain Jones's view on that April day in 1778, was he planning to return to Scotland after the war, invest his prize money in land, marry a well-born lass and shine in country society? —*John Paul Jones* (154)

Like the last Harvey example, questions are often followed by fragments, yielding yet another variation in sentence style. In the following example, the question is also a fragment:

> But why Jones? Possibly because Jones is a patronymic, meaning the son of John. —Morison, *John Paul Jones* (24)

Sometimes the questions come at the end of paragraphs:

> But how does one tell how many organisms have escaped through the pores of even the finest nets? —Marston Bates, *The Forest and the Sea* (48)

This ending question is like the one we've seen Carson use to begin a paragraph: both announce a topic and connect paragraphs.

Questions are not difficult to find in published writing. They can have the following functions:

- ❖ Variation from declarative sentences.
- ❖ Transition between paragraphs (and chapters).

- ❖ Announcement of topics of paragraphs (and chapters).
- ❖ Authorial commentary.
- ❖ Authorial reflection.
- ❖ Unsupported suggestions.
- ❖ Appeals to the reader.

Reverse your word order. Normal sentence order in English is subject-verb-complement, as in:

subject	*verb*	*object (complement)*
The writer	has completed	her paper.

A sentence can have modifiers in the form of words, phrases, or clauses that can precede or follow the subject, the verb, or the **complement** (or **direct object**); for example:

> The student writer has now completed her second paper.

But the order is still basically the same—until it's reversed in some way. Two examples:

> Her second paper has the student writer now completed.

> Now has the student writer completed her second paper.

Another way to reverse the order is to ask questions:

> Has the student writer completed her second paper?

Take another look at Rachel Carson's scolding question from the preceding section:

> When will the public become sufficiently aware of the facts to demand such action?

It's not so much a call for an answer as a challenge to act. In reversed sentence order, the verb *will* follows the interrogatory *when*, then comes the subject (*public*) and the rest of the verb (*become*). Another common way to reverse sentence order is to begin with the **expletive** *there*, as in the following sentence:

> There are other ways in which rage merges among girls, though, ways that are roughly girl-specific. —Natalie Angier, *Woman: An Intimate Geography* (266)

You may notice that the effect of starting a sentence this way is to add emphasis to the subject. "Other ways" receives more emphasis as a topic being announced by the delay. To achieve the full force of this construction, of course, a writer needs to use it sparingly. But that advice is true of any inverted sentence pattern.

Besides shifting emphasis, reversal of sentence structure also alters rhythm. Observe the following sentences:

> Rare are the times in a great war when the fortunes of one side or the other are transformed by the sudden accretion of a disequilibrating reinforcement. —John Keegan, *The First World War* (373)

> Highly entertaining and significant are the traces of how the news of Columbus's discovery spread, and what people thought about it. —Samuel Eliot Morison, *Admiral of the Ocean Sea* (362)

In these sentences, Keegan and Morison shift the adjective complements ("Rare" and "Highly entertaining and significant") to the beginning, giving them opening emphasis; each one is then followed by the verb and the subject ("are the times" and "are the traces"). The sentence rhythms would have been a bit more pedestrian without the reversal:

> The times are rare in a great war when the fortunes of one side or the other are transformed by the sudden accretion of a disequilibrating reinforcement.

They also would have been less clear. Morison's sentence edges away from clarity when rewritten to normal word order:

> The traces of how the news of Columbus's discovery spread and what people thought about it are highly entertaining and significant.

The pattern of the following sentence is an interesting variation of the pattern Morison used:

> Dug into the slope a hundred feet below our camp, in an equally precarious setting, were the tents of most of the other teams—including Scott Fischer's group, the South Africans, and the Taiwanese. —Jon Krakauer, *Into Thin Air* (155)

Dug, the first word in Krakauer's sentence, is part of his verb (*were dug*), but he moves it, along with its modifiers, to the beginning to make room at the end for his final modifiers. It's an interesting inversion that allows readers to visualize the scene before moving further into the sentence. John McPhee does something similar in this sentence:

> In the Yukon Flats, beyond the mountains, were thirty-six thousand lakes and ponds, with geese, canvasbacks, scaup, cranes, swans, teal, and widgeons in millions, and mosquitoes in numbers a physicist would understand. —*Coming into the Country* (273)

Here, prepositional phrases allow readers to visualize the scene before arriving at the verb (*were*) and its subject (*lakes and ponds*) then the detail of winged populations. Inversions of this type function well as transitions between sentences or paragraphs.

Notice how the emphatic position of sentence openers is exploited in the following inversions:

> Never was there a time when more people wanted more money more urgently than in those days. —John Kenneth Galbraith, *The Great Crash 1929* (126)

> Seldom is the question asked, What is the relation between the weed and the soil? —Carson, *Silent Spring* (78)

> Not until 1937 did the physical volume of production recover to the levels of 1929, and then it promptly slipped back again.
> —Galbraith (171)

> But never, not in their darkest moments, do they lose their taste for life. —Edith Hamilton, *The Greek Way* (18)

In each case, the negative modifier ("Never," "Seldom," "Not until 1937," "But never") begins the sentence, followed by the verb and then the subject. This use of the opening position gains both emphasis and reader orientation into the sentence.

Writers also employ inversion when they want to make announcements and to achieve a certain formality:

> That the United States could accomplish its aim by superior might no one doubted. —Barbara Tuchman, *The March of Folly* (319)

A *that* clause sometimes serves as the subject of a sentence, but here it begins the sentence as a complement (a direct object) in inverted order, with the subject and the verb way at the end. In normal order the sentence would read: "No one doubted that the United States could accomplish its aim by superior might." Galbraith, too, puts his object first in the second sentence of the following excerpt:

> Preventive incantation required that as many important people as possible repeat as firmly as they could that it [the Crash] wouldn't happen. This they did. (91–92)
>
> ■ In normal order: "They did this."

We've seen that when writers invert their sentences they can achieve the following effects:

❖ Sentence variety.
❖ Variation in rhythm.
❖ Emphatic sentence endings.
❖ Emphatic sentence beginnings.
❖ Clarity in placement of modifiers.
❖ Announcement of topic.
❖ Transition between sentences.

Try other sentence patterns.   Writers of course have numerous ways of varying their sentences, as we've seen in the previous examples. There's another variation, one that has a long history in the English language, one that is in common use but could give fits to sentence diagrammers. I've found several examples:

> The more you go out, the more likely you are never to come back.
> —Sebastian Junger, *The Perfect Storm* (70)

> The thicker the trench system grew, the less likelihood was there of its course being altered even by the weightiest of offensive effort. —Keegan (309–10)

> The more obscure and unfathomable the hatred, and the smaller the national groups involved, the longer and more complex the story seemed to grow. —Robert D. Kaplan, *Balkan Ghosts* (70)

I'll spare you a parsing of these sentences; the basic pattern, though, is paired clauses as we see in Junger's sentence: *the more . . . the more.* The pattern derives from Old English, where *the* was used as an adverb and parts of the sentence were omitted. Junger has an amazing number of them in *The Perfect Storm*.

Another variation is the *what* clause as subject of the sentence:

> What should not be forgotten is that Lincoln was himself an actor, an expert raconteur and mimic, and one who spent hours reading speeches out of Shakespeare to any willing (and some unwilling) audiences. —Garry Wills, *Lincoln at Gettysburg* (36)

Like the *that* variation illustrated in the previous section, this type of sentence makes an emphatic statement.

Emphasis is achieved also, of course, from exclamations, as in this sentence about a mad dog and two boys in a wheat field:

> And for some unknown reason, we had gone out of our way in avoiding him. Good thing! —Edgar Allen Imhoff, *Always of Home* (73)

Finally, here's an impressive example of Barbara Tuchman's use of the introductory *that* clause, this time as subject and with the pattern extended over several sentences:

> That the Russian danger in the world was nevertheless real, that the Communist system was hostile to American democracy and American interests, that Soviet Communism was expansionist and directed toward the absorption of neighboring and other vulnerable states, was undeniable. That it was joined in aggressive partnership with Communist China was a natural conclusion but exaggerated and soon to prove mistaken. That it was right and proper in the national interest for American policymakers to try to contain this inimical system and to thwart it where possible goes without question. That the Communist system threatened American security through Indochina, however, was an extrapolation leading to folly. —*The March of Folly* (249–50)

The repetitive pattern effectively builds up to the forceful concluding statement. Although this type of sentence is somewhat formal, it's an alternative to the overuse of *It* to begin sentences. With *It*, Tuchman's last sentence would read:

> It was an extrapolation leading to folly, however, that the Communist system threatened American security through Indochina.

We can end our discussion of sentence variety by generalizing that alterations of sentence patterns—

❖ Affect our rhythm.
❖ Affect our emphasis.

❖ Often make connections between our sentences.
❖ May improve clarity.

Rhythm, emphasis, coherence, clarity—good reasons for experimenting with variety.

□ **Practice** □

In your reading for school or pleasure, look for sentence variety: questions, reversed word order, and other sentence patterns. Consider why the writer chose the pattern and what effect it had on your reading.

5

Pack Your Sentences with Parallelism

Parallel structure is a feature of coordination (see chapter 1) that enables writers to load their sentences without overburdening readers. It is a way of achieving emphasis and rhythm and coherence, not to mention economy of words, and most writers rely on it whether they realize it or not. Take a look at this sentence from Edith Hamilton's *The Greek Way*:

> The Greek mind was free to think about the world as it pleased, to reject all traditional explanations, to disregard all the priests taught, to search unhampered by any outside authority for the truth. (28)

Describing the Greek mind, Hamilton combines four parallel ideas in four infinitives:

> *to think*
>
> *to reject*
>
> *to disregard*
>
> *to search*

Through the economy of structural repetition, the sentence achieves rhythm, coherence, and clarity.

Conjunctions and commas. In a series like Hamilton's, writers usually introduce the final item with a coordinating conjunction, such as *and*, but many writers often omit it, as Hamilton does here. The next example goes to the other extreme. In its parallel series of infinitives, each is joined with *and* and separated with a comma.

> [Inventions] no longer merely increased man's capacity to make or improve familiar products—to dig, and cut, and shape, and move, and build, and destroy. —Daniel J. Boorstin, *Cleopatra's Nose* (36)

Rhythm is again achieved through repetition, but Boorstin's commas and conjunctions slow our reading and enhance the emphasis on each item begun at the dash. You may have noticed too that, in all the infinitives but the first, the *to* is omitted.

Sebastian Junger in *The Perfect Storm* relies heavily on parallelism to load ideas into sentences and keep the reader moving swiftly through the narrative. Here's an example:

> [The storm trough] follows the Canadian border to Montreal, cuts east across northern Maine, crosses the Bay of Fundy, and traverses Nova Scotia throughout the early hours of October 28th. (103)

The closely coordinated verbs (*follows, cuts, crosses, traverses*) characterize the rapid movement of the storm trough. Junger's last verb is conventionally introduced with *and*. In this next example, he ties together three parallel independent clauses:

> Maybe Billy's got his hands full, or maybe he went below to take a nap, or maybe he simply forgot. (114)

As in Boorstin's sentence, the reading is slowed down when Junger introduces both the second and third clauses with *or* and separates all three with commas. This was a stylistic choice. The ending of the next sentence illustrates a different choice:

> A more likely scenario is that Billy manages to get through the ten o'clock spike in weather conditions but takes a real beating— the windows are out, the electronics are dead, and the crew is terrified. (116)

The arrangement of parallel clauses emphasizes the dramatic end. The sentence also illustrates coordinated verb phrases joined by *but*: "manages . . . but takes."

Parallel periods. Another way to handle parallel clauses is to separate them with periods, a choice that tends to further emphasize each item:

> These unintended, outreaching, everyone-touching consequences were possible because inventors took possession of three new areas. They assumed at least three new roles. They became devisers of new materials. They became makers of new sources of energy. And they crafted new instruments for sharing experience.
>
> —Boorstin (35)

The parallel sentences ("They became . . . They became . . . And they crafted . . .") explain the "three new roles" and "three new areas" in separate, deliberate statements. Boorstin's parallel adjectives in the first sentence (*unintended, outreaching, everyone-touching*) connect what went before (*consequences*) with what follows, causes.

Peter L. Bernstein does something similar in the following excerpt from *Against the Gods*:

> The optimism of the Victorians was snuffed out by the senseless destruction of human life on the battlefields, the uneasy peace that followed, and the goblins let loose by the Russian revolution. Never again would people accept Robert Browning's assurance that "God's in his heaven: / All's right with the world." Never again would economists insist that the fluctuations in the economy were a theoretical impossibility. Never again would science appear so unreservedly benign, nor would religion and family institutions be so unthinkingly accepted in the western world.
>
> World War I put an end to all that. (215–16)

The three sentences beginning with the parallel phrases "Never again," along with the added weight of the doubling in the last of those sentences, all emphasize Bernstein's boldly negative statements about the future after World War I. Also, he introduces his view of the changing world with the parallel noun phrases in his first sentence: "senseless destruction," "uneasy peace," "goblins."

Periods can separate parallel sentence fragments too. David Remnick's fragments amplify the idea introduced in the first sentence:

> In the years after his fall, Mikhail Gorbachev would leave his dacha outside Moscow, fold himself into the backseat of a Volga sedan, and, on the way downtown to his office, survey the contours of the new Russian world. Billboards and beggars. Strip

joints and traffic jams. A small fascist parade. Neon brightness and construction everywhere: a quarter-billion-dollar cathedral rising on the Moscow River embankment, an underground shopping mall burrowing in outside the gates of the Kremlin. —*Resurrection* (3)

Not only are the four fragments parallel ("Billboards . . . Strip joints . . . A small fascist parade. Neon brightness . . ."), but the doubling within three of them packs additional coordination that brackets Remnick's descriptions of the Moscow street scene ("Billboards and beggars." "Strip joints and traffic jams." "Neon brightness and construction . . ."). The opening sentence also has parallelism: three coordinated verbs— *leave, fold, survey*.

Craft. Effective parallelism doesn't just happen; writers work at it. Observe the following carefully crafted sentence:

Had the destruction been complete—had every library been dis-assembled and every book burned—we might have lost Homer and Virgil and all of classical poetry, Herodotus and Tacitus and all of classical history, Demosthenes and Cicero and all of classi-cal oratory, Plato and Aristotle and all of Greek philosophy, and Plotinus and Porphyry and all the subsequent commentary.
—Thomas Cahill, *How the Irish Saved Civilization* (58)

Cahill begins with parallel *had* clauses, the second amplifying the first. But mostly we have to admire the craft of his parallelism that follows the verb *have lost*. These five groups of three, each group consisting of two names and an encompassing *all* phrase (all of them connected with *and*), leave no doubt concerning the potential enormity of the destruc-tion of the Roman Empire. Try reading the sentence aloud to feel the rhythm. Similar parallel structures occur in another excerpt from Cahill:

When we think of peoples as civilized or civilizing, the Egyptians and the Greeks, the Italians and the French, the Chinese and the Jews may all come to mind. The Irish are wild, feckless, and charm-ing, or morose, repressed, and corrupt, but not especially civilized. If we strain to think of "Irish civilization," no image appears, no Fertile Crescent or Indus Valley, no brooding bust of Beethoven. (3)

In this introduction to his book (which, despite the sound of this ex-cerpt, celebrates the unheralded contribution of the Irish to Western civilization—its subtitle is *The Untold Story of Ireland's Heroic Role from the Fall of Rome to the Rise of Medieval Europe*), Cahill uses parallelism to emphasize what he sees as common perceptions. His first sentence has three parallel, paired phrases, and the next has two parallel groups of three, ending with an unexpected *but* phrase. The final sentence emphatically coordinates three *no* phrases.

Parallelism requires and displays craft. It requires that writers be aware of what they are coordinating: noun phrases with noun phrases, subordinate clauses with subordinate clauses, and so on. It requires also that ideas be parallel. Hamilton, for example, coordinates four features of the Greek mind, Boorstin six features of new inventions, Cahill the depth of classical civilization. And parallelism requires awareness of the most effective order for coordinated elements, the final position being the most emphatic, as illustrated in the Junger sentence beginning "A more likely scenario" (p. 45). The final position also lends itself more easily to the addition of modifiers, as we see in Remnick's description of the Moscow streets. Then too, parallelism requires sensitivity to the best choices of punctuation and conjunctions: omission or proliferation of conjunctions; separation with commas, semicolons, or periods.

Parallel structure usually requires some conscious attention, but the effort pays off when the result is a sentence of related ideas presented dramatically yet economically. And rhythmically. And emphatically. Connected ideas are assimilated more easily than disconnected ones. And if the sentence is well constructed, the reader may even pause to admire the craft that made it so.

Summary

- Parallelism is a feature of coordination.
- Parallelism creates rhythm, emphasis, and coherence.
- With parallelism a writer can pack ideas economically into easily assimilated sentences.
- Any grammatical element can be coordinated (made parallel) with equivalent grammatical elements: verbs with verbs, infinitive phrases with infinitive phrases, and so on.
- Grammatical elements joined with a coordinating conjunction (such as *and*, *but*, and *or*) should be parallel in structure and ideas.
- Punctuation and conjunctions between parallel items slow reading but tend to emphasize items.

□ **Practice** □

The following diagrams illustrate parallel structure in two sentences, the first from Sebastian Junger's *The Perfect Storm* and the second from Stephen Jay Gould's *The Lying Stones of Marrakech*. After reading the passages in this form, consider how Junger and Gould constructed their parallels. Junger's sentence is the simpler of the two, with five independent clauses; Gould's has four different pairings. Gould's first pairing is two participial (*-ing*) phrases; the second is two phrases introduced by *as* and connected by *not*. The first *as* phrase has paired nouns (*mountains* and *valleys*), and the second has two noun objects of the preposition *of*. Consider the balance of these pairings: nouns with nouns, participles with participles, independent clauses with independent clauses. Think about whether Junger's last two clauses are parallel to the first three. How do the chosen structures enable the writers to pack information into the sentences? Finally, examine a piece of your own writing to locate a sentence or two with parallel structure. Diagram the parallels and consider the accuracy of their balance. Decide whether you can improve them with revision.

1.   By midafternoon the *Andrea Gail* is ready:

   ‖ The food and bait have been stowed away,

   ‖ the fuel and water tanks have been topped off,

   ‖ spare drums of both have been lashed onto the whaleback,

   ‖ the gear's in good order, <u>and</u>

   ‖ the engine's running well.

—Junger (37)

2.   Galileo shook the earth by

      \ turning his newly invented telescope upon the cosmos

   <u>and</u>\ seeing the moon | as a planet with / mountains

                              <u>and</u> / valleys,

                  <u>not</u> | as the perfect sphere required by

         conventional concepts of | science

                        and | theology.

—Gould (29)

6

Make Your Point with Emphasis and Rhythm

*E*mphasis and rhythm are two sides of the same feature. The rhythm of a sentence consists of stressed and unstressed elements that together create alternating patterns of sound and thought. Although we often think of rhythm in connection with poetry or music, it is also an aspect of prose—a harmonic sequence that readers respond to with unconscious pleasure. Consider how rhythm and emphasis work together in these two sentences:

> If the liberal arts were for the few, philosophy was for the fewer.
> —Thomas Cahill, *How the Irish Saved Civilization* (48)

> Baiting has all the glamour of a factory shift and considerably more of the danger. —Sebastian Junger, *The Perfect Storm* (52)

For emphasis, both writers take advantage of the fact that stress falls naturally at the end of a sentence. But they also increase that emphasis with the rhythm of repetitive sentence structures: Cahill with the alliterative "for the few" and "for the fewer," Junger with "of a factory shift" and "of the danger." Junger also influences the rhythm of his sentence with the adverb *considerably*, which itself receives stress but also magnifies the emphasis on *danger*. Cahill's sentence would have been less effective had he ended with something like "philosophy was for fewer people," Junger's if he'd ended "and is more dangerous."

Writers have various ways of achieving emphasis and rhythm, among them repeating words and sentence structures, shifting weight to the end of a sentence, varying length of sentences, inserting interruptions, employing various sentence transformations, placing important information in main clauses, and using unexpected punctuation or italics.

Repetition.   By its very nature, repetition contributes to rhythm: "singsong," some might say if it's overdone. But a sentence can hold a lot of repetition and still sound good. Look at the repeated words and phrases in this sentence by Thomas Cahill:

> Such an outlook and such a temperament make for wonderful songs and thrilling stories. (97)

Here the repetition of *such* rhythmically stresses both *outlook* and *temperament*, and the parallel noun phrases "wonderful songs" and "thrilling stories" have a similar effect at the end of the sentence.

Rachel Carson uses the end position, plus repetition with a twist, in this sentence:

> The Agriculture Department's mass control program, on the other hand, cost about $3.50 per acre—the most expensive, the most damaging, and the least effective program of all.
> —*Silent Spring* (172)

Repetition of "the most" leads to emphasis at the end when Carson unexpectedly switches to "the least."

Weighted end.   We've seen how Cahill, Junger, and Carson rely on the emphatic weight of sentence endings to make their point. Jay Winik makes similar use of it:

> And for Lincoln himself, the toll on his own psyche, of course, was brutal. —*April 1865* (246)

In addition to stressing the sentence-ending *brutal*, Winik takes advantage of the lesser emphasis that occurs before commas: *himself, psyche,* and *course* are emphasized as well. Some writers increase the end weight with heavier, longer words:

> During this period of history, Crone and cauldron underwent several transformations. —Barbara G. Walker, *The Crone* (118)

Walker's alliterative "Crone and cauldron" contribute to the rhythmic sound of her sentence. Her end word, *transformations*, falls into a class of nouns called **nominalizations**. These are nouns formed from verbs and sometimes adjectives; because of the added endings, they tend to be long. (*Nominalizations* is an example of itself; as nearly as I can tell, it's from the verb *nominalize*, which itself is formed from the noun *nominal*, meaning "noun." *Transformations* derives from the verb *transform*.) Writers often avoid longer nominalizations, preferring instead to express actions in verbs. If Walker had used the verb form, her sentence might have read:

> During this period of history, Crone and cauldron were transformed several times.

And Walker would have lost the emphatic ending.

In addition to lending emphatic weight, nominalizations can be useful as summary words. Walker's sentence, for example, announces the topic of a paragraph that discusses the ways that Crone and cauldron (elements of goddess worship) were transformed in medieval Europe. Nominalizations also effectively summarize preceding ideas:

> The *resentment* against Gorbachev never abated. —David Remnick,
> *Resurrection* (11)

Sometimes these longer words even shorten a sentence:

> The mathematical *expectation* of each man's wealth after the game has been played with this 50–50 set of alternatives is precisely 100 ducats (150 + 50 divided by 2), which is just what each player started with. —Peter L. Bernstein, *Against the Gods* (112)

Bernstein's "expectation" avoids a longer "What could be expected mathematically. . . ."

Passive verbs, another sentence element often avoided in direct, forceful styles, have their uses in establishing emphasis and rhythm. Like nominalizations, they can shift emphatic weight to the end of sentences, as we see in these two examples from *A World Lit Only by Fire* by William Manchester:

> All this meant change, and *was* therefore *resented* by the medieval mind. (229)

> Tried by a jury which included Anne's father, the musician pleaded guilty and, as a commoner, *was* merely *hanged*. (216)

The passive verbs *was resented* and *was hanged* enable Manchester to hold off stating the words he wants the reader to most notice. In the second sentence, he also effectively delays the emphasis by interrupting the flow with "as a commoner"—maybe just to make sure his reader doesn't miss his understated humor.

Varied sentence length.   Sentence ends come more quickly, of course, when sentences are short. Emphasis might then have a hammering effect:

> This was it. The bankers, obviously, had moved in. The effect was electric. Fear vanished and gave way to concern lest the new advance be missed. Prices boomed upward. —John Kenneth Galbraith, *The Great Crash 1929* (106)

Short sentences, especially several in a row like these by Galbraith, tend to sacrifice rhythm for emphasis. But short sentences *are* emphatic. Read this one by John Keegan that comes at the beginning of a chapter in *The First World War* (you've seen it before, in chapter 3); I really like the knowing tone of this sentence:

> Armies make plans. (24)

Every word here is emphasized. Sometimes the short "sentence" isn't really a sentence but a fragment:

> The hatred, the bitterness, the vehemence would not dissipate overnight. Nor would the despondency. —Winik (352)

By omitting *despondency* from his series and giving it end position alone in a fragment, Winik draws attention to this particular emotion experienced at the end of the Civil War. (To read more about short sentences, see chapter 3, "Vary Your Sentences.")

Interruptions. As we saw with Manchester's second sentence (and with Jay Winik's sentence about Lincoln, earlier), another way of capitalizing on the emphatic end position of sentences is to interrupt the flow with nonessential or displaced modifiers:

> Mayday comes from the French *venez m'aider*—come help me!—and essentially means that those on board have given up all hope. —Junger (153)

> There were other flammables aboard—oil, kerosene, priming alcohol, dynamite, cartridges—all menaces to safety if ice sliced into the cargo of benzine, if a spark from the smoking stack fell into spilled fuel. —Lennard Bickel, *Mawson's Will* (40)

> And it was then, for the first time, that people began to realize that all those harsh, incessant noises which had been such a part of their lives—mill whistles, screeching, wagons clattering over cobblestones, coal trains rumbling past day and night—had stopped, absolutely, every one of them. —David G. McCullough, *The Johnstown Flood* (285)

Hope, menaces, had stopped, and *every one*—by interrupting their sentences, these writers altered their sentence rhythms and increased emphasis on the points they need to make. McCullough affects rhythm and emphasis with three interruptions, the first and third set off with commas and the second enclosed by dashes. Bickel's sentence illustrates an appositive list that details and explains the noun it refers to, *flammables.* (You can find additional examples of sentence interruptions in chapter 3, "Vary Your Sentences.")

Sentence transformations. By changing ordinary declarations into some other form, you can affect rhythm and emphasis. We've already seen how one type of sentence transformation—passive verbs instead of active—alters the effect. The two Manchester sentences (p. 53) show how a shift from normally active verbs can take advantage of sentence-ending emphasis. The verb *was resented* shifts the resenter to a prepositional phrase at the end. And the verb *was hanged* itself takes on the emphatic position, omitting the one who performed the hanging as unimportant.

Another kind of transformation alters sentence rhythm by beginning the sentence with a *what* clause:

What [Alfred Russel] Wallace was never to realize was that the mechanism driving all the geology was, in due course, going to be recognized as the then entirely unimaginable process of plate tectonics. —Simon Winchester, *Krakatoa* (67)

And another with *there*:

There is a new canon in today's literature textbooks. Certain writers appear again and again. —Diane Ravitch, *The Language Police* (128)

And another with *it*:

It seems that at some point in the development of every culture, human sacrifice becomes unthinkable, and animals are from then on substituted for human victims. —Cahill (136)

Winchester emphasizes *never to realize* and *plate tectonics*, Ravitch *canon* and *textbooks*. Cahill's beginning shifts emphasis to *culture* and *unthinkable* (both occurring before commas), and his displaced modifier *from then on* permits emphasis on the sentence-ending *human victims*. If he had done the natural thing and put the *from* phrase at the end, he would have lost this important stress:

It seems that at some point in the development of every culture, human sacrifice becomes unthinkable, and animals are substituted for human victims from then on.

Still another kind of transformation takes advantage of the emphatic position at the beginning of a sentence by moving a word there that the writer wants to stress:

So relaxed were these gatherings, so free of the strictures of institutionalized readings, that the listeners (or the reader) could mentally transfer the text to their own time and place.
—Alberto Manguel, *A History of Reading* (119)

But never, not in their darkest moments, do they lose their taste for life. —Edith Hamilton, *The Greek Way* (18)

Manguel's sentence would be less emphatic if it began "These gatherings were so relaxed," although it might still have the weighty ending. Hamilton, besides emphasizing the sentence-opening "But never," intensifies the negative with the interrupting *not* phrase. (Further discussions and examples of sentence transformations can be found in chapter 4, "Vary Your Sentences—Again.")

Emphasis in independent clauses?   Manguel's sentence seems to disprove the convention that main ideas are stated in main clauses, since what he seems to be stressing with his opening words "So relaxed" is actually expressed in his subordinate *that* clause. The convention is fine as a guideline, but one wonders whether published writers pay much attention to it. Take a look at these examples, in which I've italicized the independent clauses:

> *He was succeeded by Heliogabalus,* Caracalla's cousin, a reclusive, fanatical young worshiper of the sun god, a man whom many people regarded as insane. —Elaine Pagels, *The Origin of Satan* (137)

> *Every decade of the nineteenth century was to produce more and more Matthew Arnolds,* who were to feel furiously that by all traditional standards they formed the superior class of the community, the sages and the prophets, and that they were wholly disregarded by a rising class of industrial tyrants. —Rebecca West, *The New Meaning of Treason* (157–58)

> *Radon gas can diffuse into the surrounding air from exposed tailings piles,* although a few feet of earth on the surface of the pile is an effective seal against escape, because the gas has only a 3.82-day half-life and diffuses slowly. —Jack J. Kraushaar and Robert A. Ristinen, *Energy and Problems of a Technical Society* (149)

> As a result of a petition signed by sixteen thousand, *an initiative appeared on the 1974 primary ballot* through which the voters could indicate a wish to move their capital. —John McPhee, *Coming into the Country* (99)

A reading of these examples seems to indicate that other factors influence emphasis at least as much as clause type—sentence ending probably as much as anything. Primarily, the sentences illustrate that writers pile lots of important information into subordinate clauses and phrases.

Punctuation and italics.   Beyond the arrangement of words, writers have a few other tools at their disposal for achieving emphasis and rhythm: punctuation that differs from the expected, and italics. We've already seen the way Sebastian Junger uses dashes to set off—and emphasize—"come help me!" His exclamation point doubles the emphasis. For an example that exploits not only dashes and exclamation points but italics as well, look at this passage:

> And I thought, *It could have worked!* This democracy, this land of freedom and equality and the pursuit of happiness—it could have worked! There was something to it, after all! It didn't have to turn into a greedy free-for-all! We didn't have to make a mess of it and the continent and ourselves! It could have worked!
> —Ian Frazier, *Great Plains* (173–74)

Frazier seems almost to be shouting. The repetition of "It could have worked" in itself is emphatic, and the several structural repetitions establish rhythms that add to that emphasis. The exclamation points may be overdone, though they do seem to fit. Here he is again, this time toned down a little:

> And how great the fur trappers must have felt, sometimes, seeing this land when it was still completely wild! A trapper with a good gun and two mules and a partner to share the watch at night was liable to leave the settlements for the West and never come back. (176)

An exclamation point following a beginning such as "how great" is only expected. The rhythm of the coordination in the second sentence feels right too. Look at one more excerpt punctuated as exclamations. This one seems to indicate alarm:

> Wait! We older ones wanted to cry out, you haven't poured in the lemon juice. Stop! Mistakes are being made! —Anne Lamott, *Bird by Bird* (139)

Finally, see how Peter L. Bernstein uses italics to indicate a surprising announcement:

> For the first time in history Bernoulli is applying measurement to something that *cannot be counted.* —*Against the Gods* (106)

Dashes, exclamation points, and italics are discretionary devices that, because they draw attention to themselves, emphasize the writer's words. And because they are meant to be unexpected, writers employ them infrequently and intentionally. One kind of formatting device that published writers do not seem to use for emphasis is capitalization, either entire words or first letters of words.

Summary

- ❖ Rhythm and emphasis work together in a sentence.
- ❖ Repetition of words or patterns is rhythmic and emphatic.
- ❖ The most emphatic position in sentences is just before the period; other points of emphasis are before other marks of punctuation and at the beginning.
- ❖ Short sentences can be emphatic, either in the midst of longer sentences or in a series of similarly short ones. They tend to sacrifice rhythm for emphasis.
- ❖ Interruptions in sentences tend to alter the rhythm and delay emphasis.
- ❖ Emphasis and rhythm can be manipulated with sentence transformations such as using passive verbs instead of active ones or inverting the sentence in a variety of ways.
- ❖ Dashes, exclamation points, and italics, used with discretion, can emphasize words or sentences.

☐ **Practice** ☐

Thomas Cahill has several methods of achieving rhythm and emphasis in these paragraphs that begin his book of praise, *How the Irish Saved Civilization*. Read the paragraphs, and then identify as many of these methods as you can. Keep in mind that he may be using devices such as italics and capitalization for purposes other than emphasis.

> The word *Irish* is seldom coupled with the word *civilization*. When we think of peoples as civilized or civilizing, the Egyptians and the Greeks, the Italians and the French, the Chinese and Jews may all come to mind. The Irish are wild, feckless, and charming, or morose, repressed, and corrupt, but not especially civilized. If we strain to think of "Irish civilization," no image appears, no Fertile Crescent or Indus Valley, no brooding bust of Beethoven. The simplest Greek auto mechanic will name his establishment "Parthenon," thus linking himself to an imagined ancestral culture. A semiliterate restaurateur of Sicilian origin will give pride of place to his plaster copy of Michelangelo's

David, and so assert his presumed Renaissance ties. But an Irish businessman is far more likely to name his concern "The Breffini Bar" or "Kelly's Movers," announcing a merely local or personal connection, unburdened by the resonances of history or civilization.

And yet . . . Ireland, a little island at the edge of Europe that has known neither Renaissance nor Enlightenment—in some ways, a Third World country with, as John Betjeman claimed, a Stone Age culture—had one moment of unblemished glory. For, as the Roman Empire fell, as all through Europe matted, unwashed barbarians descended on the Roman cities, looting artifacts and burning books, the Irish, who were just learning to read and write, took up the great labor of copying all of western literature—everything they could lay their hands on. These scribes then served as conduits through which the Greco-Roman and Judeo-Christian cultures were transmitted to the tribes of Europe, newly settled amid the rubble and ruined vineyards of the civilization they had overwhelmed. Without this Service of the Scribes, everything that happened subsequently would have been unthinkable. Without the Mission of the Irish Monks, who single-handedly refounded European civilization throughout the continent in the bays and valleys of their exile, the world that came after them would have been an entirely different one—a world without books. And our own world would never have come to be. (3–4)

7

Modify with Style

*M*odifiers serve writers by describing, identifying, qualifying, intensifying, and otherwise altering the nouns and verbs that make up the heart of sentences. Adjectives modify nouns. Adverbs modify verbs, adjectives, other adverbs, and entire sentences. Both adjective and adverb modifiers can take the form not only of single words but of phrases and clauses as well, and all can be compounded. The following sentences illustrate how modifiers work in the three forms. Adjectives are italicized and adverbs underlined.

WORDS   I think we <u>still</u> have a *great* deal to learn about *this* problem of the origin of species, of the origin of <u>reproductively</u> *isolated* populations. —Marston Bates, *The Forest and the Sea* (132)

     ■ Each of these adjectives and adverbs modifies the word it precedes.

In the *Russian* imagination, <u>however</u>, Chechnya is an obsession, an image of *Islamic* defiance, an embodiment of the primitive, the devious, the elusive.
—David Remnick, *Resurrection* (266)

■ *However* modifies the entire sentence. *Russian* and
Islamic modify the words they precede.

PHRASES   The King had never, <u>in the whole course *of his life*</u>,
been a good speaker. —C. V. Wedgwood, *A Coffin for King
Charles* (121)

■ Prepositional phrases; "in the whole course of his life"
is an adverbial modifier of *had been*; "of his life" is an
adjective modifying *course.*

And, *<u>glancing around the cartography department</u>*, I
was amused <u>to observe a state-of-the-art computer *on*</u>
<u>the one desk</u> and a stack *<u>of books about the history of</u>*
<u>cartography on another</u>. —Miles Harvey, *The Island of Lost
Maps* (139)

■ Participial *-ing* phrase modifies *I* and has an embedded
prepositional phrase modifying *glancing.* The infinitive
phrase, beginning *to observe,* modifies the verb *was
amused* and goes to the end of the sentence with five
embedded prepositional phrases.

CLAUSES   They were entering the Sargasso Sea, that great oval-
shaped area of the Western Ocean *that extends roughly
from longitude 32° W to the Bahamas, and from the Gulf
Stream down to Latitude 18° N."* —Samuel Eliot Morison,
Admiral of the Ocean Sea (193)

■ Adjective clause modifying *area*

<u>When at length [the Queen] was able to think and
plan again</u>, her thoughts were wholly for her eldest
son—"le Roi," *as he was henceforward in all her
thoughts and words*. —Wedgwood (189)

■ Adverb clause modifying the verb *were* (or the entire
main clause); adjective clause modifying *le Roi*

(For other discussions of phrases and clauses see chapter 1, "Coordinate Balanced Ideas," and chapter 2, "Subordinate Cumulative Ideas.")

Depending on the way you phrase and place your modifiers, you
can affect the rhythm and emphasis of your sentences, plus gaining
coherence between your sentences. Interrupting modifiers, parallel

series of modifiers, and orienting phrases all can help you make your points with style.

Rhythm and emphasis. Rachel Carson employs a rhythmic parallel series to gain an emphatic end:

> The Agriculture Department's mass control program, on the other hand, cost about $3.50 per acre—*the most expensive, the most damaging, and the least effective program of all.* —Silent Spring (172)

Carson's repeated intensifier *most* leads her reader to the unexpected opposite, *least,* in the last item of the series, all modifying *program.* Repeated phrases with a twist also appear in this sentence by Thomas Cahill:

> If the liberal arts were *for the few*, philosophy was *for the fewer.*
> —*How the Irish Saved Civilization* (48)

Cahill's second prepositional phrase gains emphasis when it echoes and magnifies the first one.

Placement of modifiers affects emphasis by taking advantage of the natural rhythm and stress points in sentences. In these next sentences, by Sebastian Junger and Jay Winik, the inserted intensifier and qualifier direct emphasis to the end of the sentences:

> Baiting has all the glamour of a factory shift and *considerably* more of the danger. —The Perfect Storm (52)

> And for Lincoln himself, the toll on his own psyche, *of course*, was brutal. —*April 1865* (246)

By altering the rhythm of their sentences with the addition of *considerably* and *of course*, these writers have directed more emphasis to their final words. Try reading the sentences without the italicized modifiers. How are rhythm and emphasis affected? In the next three sentences, all of them recounting the harrowing experiences of Ernest Shackleton and his crew, Alfred Lansing capitalizes on the emphatic end position by putting his modifiers there:

> It was a chance, a freak. A hard northerly gale—then *quite cold.*
> —*Endurance* (30)

> This, then, was the Drake Passage, the most dreaded bit of ocean on the globe—and *rightly so.* (225)

About noon a raw and penetrating mistlike rain began to fall,
and the wind slowly started to move around toward the north—
dead ahead. (226)

Sentence *beginnings,* too, can emphasize modifiers. Here Edith
Hamilton reverses the order of her sentence to place the negative adverb *never* at the beginning and then further emphasizes the negation
with an intensifying *not* phrase:

> But *never, not in their darkest moments,* do they lose their taste for
> life. —*The Greek Way* (18)

In this next sentence, William Manchester writes about Ferdinand
Magellan. You'll agree, I'm sure, that Manchester carries description to
the limit in his emphatic beginning:

> *Proud of his lineage, meticulous, fiercely ambitious, stubborn, driven,*
> *secretive,* and *iron-willed,* the capitan-general, or admiral, is
> possessed by an inner vision which he shares with no one.
> —*A World Lit Only by Fire* (224)

To get the full effect of Manchester's emphatic beginning, try moving
the modifiers to another position in the sentence—say, after *admiral.*
Both rhythm and emphasis are affected. (You can read more about
rhythm and emphasis in chapter 6, "Make Your Point with Emphasis
and Rhythm.")

Coherence.   Opening modifiers do more than affect rhythm and emphasis; they can also connect sentences. Those that orient readers to
time and place are particularly useful. See how David Remnick connects
three sentences to each foregoing one by means of orienting modifiers.

> *The next day, in the Duma cafeteria,* Zhirinovsky and his aides
> tried to cut into the chow line. *When one deputy, the businessman*
> *Mark Goryachev, protested,* Zhirinovsky said that when he won
> the presidency—an event he now counted as inevitable—he
> would throw him in jail. *At which point,* Goryachev punched the
> president-presumptive in the face. (95)

Remnick begins with time and place orienters; the second and third
sentences identify temporal sequences—the second with a *when* clause,
the third with a prepositional phrase.

This use of orienting modifiers is a point of style that writers often delay thinking about until they're revising. Because in speech we often put time and place modifiers at the end of our sentences (as in "I found my wallet *the next day*"), we sometimes do the same when we write. But published writers show us how effective these phrases can be as sentence openers. Remnick's first sentence would have lost its connection with the one that went before if he had placed his orienting modifiers at the end. Here are two more examples that orient readers to new information while connecting to what had just been stated:

> *Troubled by his role and the smell of the swamp he was getting into*, Kennedy resorted to another fact-finding mission, the now traditional Washington substitute for policy. —Barbara Tuchman, *The March of Folly* (309)

> *Arriving at the bottom of Khumbu icefall on Monday morning, May 13*, I came down the final slope to find Ang Tshering, Guy Cotter, and Caroline Mackenzie waiting for me at the edge of the glacier.
> —Jon Krakauer, *Into Thin Air* (267)

These two participial phrases that open their sentences relate to previous ideas—for Tuchman to a problem discussed earlier ("the swamp"), for Krakauer to a previous place and date.

Sentence-opening modifiers come with a caution: Watch out for danglers. Sentence-opening adjective phrases act just like any adjectives do: they attach themselves to the closest noun—usually the subject of the sentence. In Manchester's sentence about Magellan, the modifiers attach themselves, rightly, to *capitan-general*. In Tuchman's it is *Kennedy*, and in Krakauer's it is *I*. A less careful writer might have written Tuchman's sentence like this:

> Troubled by his role and the smell of the swamp he was getting into, another fact-finding mission seemed the last resort for Kennedy.

Here the phrase beginning *troubled* tries to attach itself to *mission*, the subject in this revision. (You can read more about **dangling modifier**s in chapter 36, "Don't Dangle Your Modifiers," and more about coherence in chapter 8, "Connect Your Thoughts Coherently.")

Appositives and absolutes. Another common (and useful) means of adding descriptive or identifying information is the appositive, which is not a modifier at all but actually a noun that renames a noun. Look back to Morison's identifying modifiers in his sentence on page 61. They build on an appositive, *area*, that renames *Sargasso Sea*. Likewise, in Tuchman's sentence about John F. Kennedy, the phrase "the now traditional Washington substitute for policy" is an appositive (with its own modifiers), the noun *substitute* renaming *mission*. The following sentence by Robert D. Kaplan has an appositive phrase to amplify and further describe *mass murder*:

> The increasingly authoritarian nature of the Young Turk regime culminated with their 1915 mass murder of an estimated 1.5 million Armenians, *the century's first holocaust. —Balkan Ghosts* (63)

Appositive phrases might be viewed as reduced adjective clauses—all the information of a *who, which*, or *that* clause with the pronoun and verb omitted. Kaplan's appositive phrase filled out as a clause would make the sentence read:

> The increasingly authoritarian nature of the Young Turk regime culminated with their 1915 mass murder of an estimated 1.5 million Armenians, *which was the century's first holocaust.*

Tuchman might have ended: "which was the now traditional Washington substitute for policy." Appositives make writing more concise while at the same time adding information. Writers aiming for a clear, direct style will usually omit phrases like *which was* and *which are*, opting for the appositive instead.

Another means for gaining conciseness while loading a sentence with information is the **absolute phrase**. It's like a whole new sentence but without a verb. Observe in this brief example how absolutes work:

> *The portrait finished*, he went. —Henry Adams, *The Education of Henry Adams* (236)

If the absolute phrase had a verb, it would be a sentence: "The portrait was finished." Written as an absolute, it supplies information to the main statement in a concise way. Here are two more examples:

> Safe now, *the crushing strain of the preceding days lifted from my shoulders*, I cried for my lost companions, I cried because I was grateful to be alive, I cried because I felt terrible for having survived while others had died. —Krakauer (267)

> She [Queen Anne] and Rochford were decapitated within a few
> minutes of each other, *the queen, by precedence of rank, meeting the
> blade first.* —Manchester (217)

An absolute phrase is a noun plus modifiers, those modifiers usually
including participles. In Adams's sentence the participle is *finished*, in
Krakauer's it's *lifted*, and in Manchester's it's *meeting*. With the addition
of *was*, each absolute could have become a sentence.

Summary

- ❖ Modifiers take the form of words, phrases, and clauses.
- ❖ Adjectives modify nouns; adverbs modify verbs, adjectives,
  other adverbs, and entire sentences.
- ❖ Modifiers can function singly, in pairs, and in series.
- ❖ Modifiers can be placed to enhance rhythm and increase
  emphasis.
- ❖ Time, place, and other orienting modifiers at the beginning of
  sentences can connect sentences to preceding ones.
- ❖ Appositive and absolute phrases add information to sentences
  with a minimum of words.

□ Practice □

Study the italicized phrases in the following three sentences and their influence on coherence. Then try to locate in a piece of your own writing
any phrases of time or place that would be more effective moved from end
to beginning of their sentences.

1. "*On a distant ridge of trees*, a somber crow looked down into her
   nest and saw melting balls of ice mixed with egg embryos."
   —Franklin Russell, *Watchers at the Pond* (184)

2. "*At the back of that big house,* a wooden staircase led down from
   the first-floor landing to the yard. " —Doris Lessing, *Particularly Cats* (24)

3. "*At the eastern end of town* all that remained between Jackson
   and Clinton [streets] was a piece of St. John's Convent. *At the
   corner of Jackson and Locust* the blackened rafters of St. John's
   Church were still smoking, and *where the Quinn house had
   stood, fifty feet away,* there was now only a jumble of rubbish."
   —David G. McCullough, *The Johnstown Flood* (184–85)

The next three sentences have absolute phrases, each of which could be expanded to a sentence if given a verb. If you understand how absolutes work, check your writing, and if you have any sentence with *was, were, is,* or *are* that is closely related to another sentence, see if you can revise it as an absolute phrase inserted in the other sentence.

4.   "*The decision taken*, they spent the night of December 5th preparing lists of those who were to be excluded." —Wedgwood, *A Coffin for King Charles* (33)

■ As a sentence: "The decision was taken."

5.   "*The returns in*, the President-elect went vacationing to Bermuda."
—Gene Smith, *When the Cheering Stopped* (28)

■ As a sentence: "The returns were in."

6.   "It is a fearful thing to lead this great peaceful people into war, into the most terrible and disastrous of all wars, *civilization itself seeming to be in the balance.*" —President Woodrow Wilson, quoted by Smith (30)

■ As a sentence: "Civilization itself is seeming to be in the balance."

The next two sentences have appositives. Observe how they efficiently add information to sentences. Can you use appositives to rename and amplify nouns in any of your sentences?

7.   "Those who defined the instruments of timekeeping—*Christiaan Huygens, William Clement, Robert Hooke, and John Harrison among others*—do not enter our history books until recent centuries."
—Daniel J. Boorstin, *Cleopatra's Nose* (32)

■ Appositive renames *Those.*

8.   "His wife—*a Saxon, too*—talked little." —Kaplan (176)

■ Appositive renames *wife.*

8

Connect Your Thoughts Coherently

Whether readers encounter a piece of writing that moves smoothly from one thought to the next, we say it has "flow." We get an image of water moving rapidly over a rocky streambed, or of traffic going from Point A to Point B with no snarls and delays. The term seems to work. From a writer's perspective, though, the word is not so clear. From this perspective, talk of flow is not very helpful: How can you *get* flow anyway? What can you do to get words to move like water over rocks? It doesn't just happen, not like turning on the tap. Instead, creating a piece of writing that reads easily is work. It's a matter of *making connections*. When thoughts are connected, writing is coherent. It flows.

Connecting words. Writers have various tools for connecting their thoughts. The easiest and most obvious is one we've described elsewhere: coordinating conjunctions such as *and* and *but*. Here are examples I quote in chapter 14, "Begin Your Sentences with *and (but, or, nor, for, yet, so)*":

> We have already seen a splendid example of shape-shifting in Amhairghin's foundation lyric: he is first an estuary, then a wave, then the pounding of the sea, then an ox, then a hawk, and so on. *And* though a contemporary reader might take all

this as metaphor, the Irish believed that gods, druids, poets, and others in touch with the magical world could be literal shape-shifters. —Thomas Cahill, *How the Irish Saved Civilization* (128–29)

If their route was to be over the ice, the sledge drivers would harness their teams with all possible speed while the other men gathered stores and equipment, struck the tents, and then stood by the sledges. *Or* if, as they hoped, they could escape by water, they were to ready the boats. —Alfred Lansing, *Endurance* (79)

Professional writers seem, in fact, to prefer these short connectors to the longer, more formal, **transitional adverbs** such as *however* and *therefore*. But not entirely:

In the Russian imagination, *however*, Chechnya is an obsession, an image of Islamic defiance, an embodiment of the primitive, the devious, the elusive. —David Remnick, *Resurrection* (266)

Transitional words, whether conjunctions or adverbs, are most effective at or near the beginning of the sentence. So too are phrases of time and place. Notice how John M. Barry begins the next three sentences.

In New Orleans rainwater must be pumped *up*, over the levees, into either the river or Lake Pontchartrain, both of which are often higher than much of the city. *In 1913* an engineer named Albert Baldwin Wood designed and built pumps capable of moving 47,000 cubic feet of water a second, roughly half the low-water flow of the Mississippi itself, through subterranean canals buried under the "neutral ground," the city's term for the tree-lined islands that transform so many New Orleans streets into boulevards. *These remarkable pumps* were copied around the world, and still operate today. —*Rising Tide* (228)

At the beginning of his first two sentences, Barry orients the reader to time and place. His first sentence would be much less connected had he begun it "Rainwater must be pumped *up* in New Orleans" (incidentally, the italics on *up* are Barry's). The first words of his last sentence are an excellent example of a restated idea as discussed later in this chapter.

Consistent subjects. The job of transitional words and phrases is to relate ideas. They're kind of like the filling between layers of a cake: it holds the cake together and adds a little something in flavor and texture but is not the cake itself—a chocolate cake doesn't get its name from its filling. So, even though transitions smooth out the reading, real coherence is integral to the subject. Notice in the next example how Jon Krakauer maintains a consistent subject throughout the paragraph:

> An idealistic, melancholic *Englishman* named Maurice Wilson had not been so fortunate when *he*'d attempted a similarly reckless ascent thirteen years before Denman. Motivated by a misguided desire to help his fellow man, *Wilson* had concluded that climbing Everest would be the perfect way to publicize his belief that the myriad ills of humankind could be cured through a combination of fasting and faith in the powers of God. *He* hatched a scheme to fly a small airplane to Tibet, crash-land it on the flanks of Everest, and proceed to the summit from there. The fact that *he* knew absolutely nothing about either mountaineering or flying didn't strike him as a major impediment.
>
> —Into Thin Air (89)

Need we say that this writing *flows*? Observe again how a consistent subject connects ideas:

> Long the subject of ridicule and persecution, derided as cults, *alternative religions* are finally being taken seriously. The *study of new religious movements*—NRMs for short—has become a growth industry. *NRM scholars* come from a variety of backgrounds, but *many* are sociologists and religious historians. *All* are sympathetic to the idea that *new religious movements* should be respected, protected and studied carefully. *They* tend to avoid the words "cult" and "sect," because of the polemical connotations; as a result *NRM scholars* are often caricatured in anti-cult circles as "cult apologists." *They* examine such matters as how new movements arise; what internal dynamics are at work as the movements evolve; how they spread and grow; how societies react to them; and how and why they move toward the mainstream." —Toby Lester, "Oh, Gods!" (38)

Lester and Krakauer illustrate how pronouns, synonyms, and related words can effectively link ideas to previously stated noun subjects.

Repetition of key words.   Repetition, in fact, is one of the writer's most effective tools for making connections. It works because each mention reminds the reader of what has just been read and then leads to a new statement. Notice how repetition connects known to new in the following example:

> *We poison* the caddis flies in a stream and the salmon runs dwindle and die. *We poison* the gnats in a lake and the *poison* travels from link to link of the food chain and soon the birds of the lake margins become *its* victims. *We spray* our elms and the following springs are silent of robin song, not because *we sprayed* the robins directly but because the *poison* traveled, step by step, through the now familiar elm leaf–earthworm–robin cycle. These are matters of record, observable, part of the visible world around us. They reflect the web of life—or death—that scientists know as ecology.
> —Rachel Carson, *Silent Spring* (189)

By repeating the word *poison* plus synonyms and pronouns, Carson leads you from known information to her new and final statement. She also uses another writer's tool to keep you with her—parallelism, a form of repetition—by beginning her first three sentences in a similar way. For another example of how parallelism helps a reader put ideas together, look back to the last sentence of Toby Lester's paragraph. It links several ideas with connected parallel clauses beginning *how, what, how, how,* and *how and why.* (To read more about the uses of repetition, see chapter 24, "Repeat, Repeat, Repeat.")

Restating ideas.   The word *flow* perhaps best suits the method of coherence in which the beginning of each sentence restates the last idea of the previous sentence. Look back to John M. Barry's final sentence on page 69 and notice how the beginning words, "These remarkable pumps," summarize the idea of the preceding sentences and make a smooth move into the new statement. Rachel Carson connects the idea of cold in these sentences:

> The *Humboldt Current*, sometimes called the Peru, flows northward along the west coast of South America, carrying waters almost as cold as the Antarctic from which it comes. But *its chill* is actually that of the deep ocean, for the current is reinforced by almost continuous upwelling from lower oceanic layers. It is because of the *Humboldt* that penguins live almost under the equator, on the Galapagos Islands. In these *cold waters*, rich in minerals, there is an abundance of sea life perhaps unparalleled anywhere else in the world. —*The Sea around Us* (144)

In Carson's second sentence, "its chill" restates the preceding main idea, and in the third sentence her reference to "the Humboldt" again summarizes the idea of cold water, a thought repeated again in the final sentence. Each time, the new idea in a sentence comes after a connection has been made with the preceding one. This is an effective method for gaining coherence, but, like all the methods described here, it can become tiresome if used to the exclusion of other methods.

Forecasting.   Many paragraphs begin with a sentence that forecasts the sense of what follows. When readers are thus oriented, they make connections between otherwise perhaps disparate ideas. Peter L. Bernstein relies on a common forecasting method in this paragraph:

> *There are three reasons* why regression to the mean can be such a frustrating guide to decision-making. *First*, it sometimes proceeds at so slow a pace that a shock will disrupt the process. *Second*, the regression may be so strong that matters do not come to rest once they reach the mean. Rather, they fluctuate around the mean, with repeated, irregular deviations on either side. *Finally*, the mean itself may be unstable, so that yesterday's normality may be supplanted today by a new normality that we know nothing about. It is perilous in the extreme to assume that prosperity is just around the corner simply because it always has been just around the corner. —*Against the Gods* (172)

The announced "three reasons" followed by *first, second,* and *finally* hold Bernstein's paragraph together, along with his repetition of the key words *mean* and *regression.*

Forecasting sentences, often called topic sentences, are common when writers are conveying information. See how the method works in this paragraph by Jay Winik recounting one of the last days of the Civil War:

> *The situation was ugly.* The citizens of Amelia County had already been cleaned out by Confederate impressment crews and the exigencies of war. Lee's forage wagons came back virtually empty: there were no pigs, no sheep, no hogs, no cattle, no provender. And there would be no breakfast that morning for the men. Growing increasingly anxious, Lee knew that his only option now was to rouse his army and begin a hard, forced march toward Danville—where a million and a half rations were stored.
> —*April 1865* (128)

Winik's first sentence prepares the reader for an unpleasant situation. His synonymous words for food also hold the paragraph together.

Connected ideas.   Unfortunately, some writers practice all of these coherence devices and still end up with writing that can be described, among other ways, as "clunky." Rather than flowing smoothly with thoughts connected logically and clearly to one another, it bumps along, and the reader is left having to make the connections. What happens sometimes is that the writer omits a connecting *idea*. Consider Toby Lester's paragraph again (p. 70). What if he had omitted his fourth sentence, the one that gives you the principles guiding the NRM scholars? In that case, you would have been trying to relate the sentence that says they "tend to avoid the words 'cult' and 'sect'" with the one telling you about the scholars' backgrounds. You could have eventually gathered the gist of the omitted sentence, but you would have had to work harder.

Or consider this example:

> Make a habit of reading what is being written today and what has been written before. Writing is learned by imitation. If anyone asked me how I learned to write, I'd say I learned by reading the men and women who were doing the kind of writing *I* wanted to do and trying to figure out how they did it. But cultivate the best models. —William Zinsser, *On Writing Well* (36)

Zinsser might have omitted his second sentence, leaving you to connect the third to the first—which you could have done. But by stating the principle of the paragraph in the second sentence he makes the connection for you. When writers omit essential connecting sentences, it's not because they do so intentionally. More likely, the idea is in their heads but, in the process of moving forward in the writing, they've overlooked it. It is this lack of coherence that for readers is the most troublesome.

Summary

Writers connect their thoughts by—

- ❖ Beginning sentences with coordinating conjunctions (*and, but, or, nor, for, so, yet*).
- ❖ Using transitional adverbs (such as *however, therefore, then*) at or near the beginning of their sentences.

❖ Putting phrases of time and place at the beginning of their sentences.

❖ Repeating key words, plus synonyms and pronouns.

❖ Using parallel structure with related ideas.

❖ Beginning sentences with words summarizing ideas already stated.

❖ Forecasting the topics of paragraphs.

❖ Not omitting essential relating ideas.

□ **Practice** □

Read the following passages and, referring to the summary list, decide what methods these writers used to achieve "flow." In the third paragraph try omitting the fourth sentence to see how essential it is to connecting the sentence that follows.

1. "The reaction of many people to the thought of having to store radioactive waste for such a long period is one of complete skepticism, and much of the public resistance to nuclear power centers on the radioactive waste disposal problem. Many people concerned with nuclear reactors who have investigated the isolation of high level radioactive waste for long periods of time feel that it is a solvable problem. There do not seem to be any major technical barriers that stand in the way, but because of public concern, political barriers have arisen in recent years. The federal agencies charged with the problem have been lax in not settling on some scheme long ago that could have been put in practice, at least on an experimental basis and in a reversible manner, so that public confidence would not now be so completely lacking." —Jack J. Kraushaar and Robert A. Ristinen, *Energy and Problems of a Technical Society* (145)

2. "All this ferment led to that rarest of cultural phenomena, an intellectual movement which alters the course of both learning and civilization. Pythagoreans had tried it, four hundred years before the birth of Christ, and failed. So, in the third and fourth centuries AD, had Manichaeans, Stoics, and Epicureans. But the humanists of the sixteenth century were to succeed spectacularly—so much so that their triumph is unique. They would be followed by other ideologies determined to shape the future—seventeenth-century rationalism, the eighteenth-century Enlightenment, Marxism in

the nineteenth century, and, in the twentieth, by pragmatism, determinism, and empiricism. Each would alter the stream of great events, but none would match the achievements of Renaissance humanists." —William Manchester, *A World Lit Only by Fire* (106)

3.   "As the nineteenth century closed, the dream of objective truth was rekindled by two philosophies. The first, European in origin, was positivism, the conviction that the only certain knowledge is the exact description of what we perceive with our senses. The second, American in origin, was pragmatism, the belief that truth is what consistently works in human action. *From the outset both positions were symbiotic with science.* They drew major strength from the spectacular advances in the physical sciences then underway, which vindicated them by the varied actions— electromagnetic motors, X-rays, reagent chemistry—that exact, practical knowledge made possible." —Edward O. Wilson, *Consilience: The Unity of Knowledge* (61)

9

Be Concise

*I*t's called *padding*. It's like that fluffy, fuzzy stuff between layers of down coats. It can keep you warm on a winter's day, but if you let it out to blow in the air there's hardly anything there. Feathers. They're good for coats and comforters but not for writing.

Some people pad their writing intentionally. That may be because they haven't thought through their subject adequately so don't have much to say; they need filler. Or it may be because they think that fluffing up their sentences and paragraphs will make their ideas look more important. Here's an example of the second possibility, written by an elementary school principal and sent to parents regarding schoolyard conduct (you get extra points if you read the entire thing):

> As you know we have been working throughout the year to analyze some of the issues relative to playground behavior and to lay the groundwork for behavioral expectations. The majority of children in M_____ consistently demonstrate respect for peers and adults, good decision-making skills, and the ability to interact with others in positive and productive ways. There are, however, children who from time to time encounter difficulty on the playground and would benefit from knowing that communication from school to home will be a constant occurrence. . . . As we

develop plans for next year, it is my hope to have some structures in place to address these issues. In the interim, we are going to institute a recess report form to be utilized for the remainder of this school year. . . . This will give us a reasonable block of time to evaluate the effectiveness of the reports and the level of effectiveness in decreasing situations which are problematic. . . . If you should receive a report regarding a situation which involved your child, please discuss it with him/her and reinforce the need to make appropriate choices on the playground. It is also important that as parents, you support the efforts of the recess aides to make the playground a safe and enjoyable place for all students. . . . Again, please know that the teachers and I appreciate your support of the responsibilities and duties of the recess aides and your willingness to support our efforts to address the situations which arise on the playground in a timely and effective manner.

—Quarterly Review of Doublespeak

Despite all these words and a few "difficulties" in phrasing (and as you can see from the ellipses, *Doublespeak* even omitted some), the principal never gets around to saying directly that some of the children are misbehaving as a result of insufficient parental guidance!

Most of us, I think, don't write this way intentionally. Perhaps we're trying for a style more formal than one we're accustomed to and so rely too frequently on drawn-out phrases like "in the event that" and "at the present time," or **redundancies** like "various differences" and "return back," or longer words such as "prevarications" or "equivocations" instead of something short like "lies." Whether we're trying for extended length or not, rough drafts tend to have more words than necessary (more punctuation too!). Those extra words get there while we think through a subject. We just keep on writing words and more words, and when we don't go back to remove them we pass them on to our readers. Contrary to some of our expectations, those extra words don't make our writing appear more professional. Just the opposite, in fact. To write like professionals, we need to take the time to delete excessive verbiage.

Those needless words come in many forms, some of which are redundancies; hidden subjects, objects, and verbs; and **metadiscourse**.

Redundancies.   Words are redundant if they say the obvious, either something already stated or something any intelligent reader could assume. Repetition itself is not bad; in fact in chapter 24, "Repeat, Repeat,

Repeat," you can see how repeated words and structures, in the right hands, can have a positive effect on rhythm, emphasis, clarity, and coherence. Observe this example from that chapter:

> Not that any of this would help Gorbachev. He was *despised* by the communists, *who* regarded him as no better than the CIA; *despised* by the "great power" nationalists, *who* believed he was responsible for the humiliation of a great power and its army; and *despised* as well by liberal democrats, *who* felt he had never fully shed his allegiance to the nomenklatura that raised him.
> —David Remnick, *Resurrection* (7)

David Remnick strengthens rather than weakens his sentence by repeating the verb *despised* and the clauses beginning *who*.

It's when words are repeated mindlessly and needlessly that they become redundancies, as in these examples:

> She gets her information from different books and articles that she has read on the different insecticides.

> In the modern world of today, the Republic of the Philippines has a population of nearly 60 million people, half of whom are engaged in the area of agriculture.

Now this is padding! The first sentence contains *different* twice when neither one is necessary, and then adds the redundant clause "that she has read." Revised, the sentence could read:

> She gets her insecticide information from books and articles.

The second sentence is loaded with redundancies. The phrase "In the modern world of today" is not needed since the present **tense** of the verb *has* establishes the time. The words *population* and *people* say the same thing, so one could be deleted. And the fluffy phrase "in the area of" is just filler. The sentence could be revised to read:

> The Republic of the Philippines has a population of nearly 60 million, half of whom are engaged in agriculture.

Here's another example:

> Authors use an array of different perspectives to get their main objectives across, especially when the writers are writing about an issue that they hold dear to their hearts.

Here it is again with the redundancies struck out:

> Authors use an array of ~~different~~ perspectives to get their ~~main~~ objectives across, especially when ~~the writers are~~ writing about an issue ~~that they hold~~ dear to their hearts.

At the same time, we do need to acknowledge that redundancies occur in published writing, usually to good effect, as in this sentence:

> Children have cultures, too, which absorb parts of the adult culture *and also* develop values and norms of their own.
>
> —Steven Pinker, *The Blank Slate* (390)

Ordinarily *also* is not needed with *and*, although when it does occur it tends to emphasize what follows. Emphasis seems to be Pinker's intention.

Hidden subjects, objects, and verbs.   When I find wordiness in the writing of my students, much of it is of the types just illustrated. But the most persistent, and perhaps the most invisible, is that caused when empty words replace subjects and verbs. To illustrate:

> At the beginning of this ad, it shows the new Infiniti for 2004.

The real subject of this sentence, its topic, is "the beginning of this ad," but it's been tucked into a prepositional phrase and the empty pronoun *it* takes its place. What the writer meant to say was—

> The beginning of this ad shows the new Infiniti for 2004.

Here's another example:

> By making these rude and derogatory statements only degrades McCoy's intellectual sensibility.

This sentence has no real subject, only a long *by* phrase that purports to be a subject. We can remove *by*, allowing the rest of the phrase to serve as subject, like this:

> Making these rude and derogatory statements only degrades McCoy's intellectual sensibility.

Or better yet, more direct and concise:

> These rude and derogatory statements only degrade McCoy's intellectual sensibility.

This version is probably the clearest expression of what the writer meant. So it happens with most writers: through revision we say it better.

I've come to believe that one of the most overused words in the English language is *use*, or its extended form *use of*. It's a difficult one to avoid, as my last sentence shows, and it seems ubiquitous. Observe:

> She uses these fears to try and persuade people not to use these harmful and dangerous chemicals.

In this sentence the word, repeated, has two different implications, even though each alone is reasonable. A quick reference to a thesaurus might be called for. Maybe substitute "draws on these fears"? And we don't really need both *harmful* and *dangerous*, do we? And could we omit *try and* before *persuade*?

Then there's *use of*, often empty of meaning, filling up spaces:

> The *use of* this ethical high ground presents the author as someone who can be trusted to deliver the facts.

> This lack of established authority created a challenge for the author to find an effective balance in her *use of* style.

In the first sentence, *use* substitutes for the real subject, "ethical high ground." By deleting "The use of" we clarify meaning:

> This ethical high ground presents the author as someone who can be trusted to deliver the facts.

In the second sentence, *use of* appears in a prepositional phrase; get rid of it and we have one less prepositional phrase, not to mention a sharper sentence:

> This lack of established authority created a challenge for the author to find an effective balance in her style.

Let's take the revision one step further:

> This lack of established authority challenged the author to find an effective balance in her style.

Verbs can be hidden by needless words too. Read this sentence again, taken from the *Doublespeak* article:

> There are, however, children who from time to time encounter difficulty on the playground and would benefit from knowing

that communication from school to home will be a constant occurrence.

At the end of this sentence, the principal probably meant to say that parents and school should be communicating constantly. Instead, he puts communicating in a noun (*communication*) and has to add another noun (*occurrence*) to say that it would be happening. Try a revision:

Some children, however, misbehave on the playground and would benefit from knowing that the school is reporting regularly to the parents.

The following sentence could be briefer and more forceful, too, if the verbs were brought out from hiding:

Resulting from this book, heightened awareness came forth and new laws and practices were put into effect.

One verb is disguised as an adjective, *heightened*, and another has been stated as a noun, *effect*. The sentence might perhaps have been written:

This book heightened awareness [of the problem?] and resulted in new laws and practices.

Metadiscourse.   Writers give their readers cues for how to read and interpret sentences. These words and phrases are sometimes termed *metadiscourse*, or **discourse** about discourse, or words that tell readers how to read the words. They may take the form of transitional adverbs such as *however* and *therefore*; they may take the form of adverbial qualifiers and intensifiers such as *nearly* and *indeed*; they may indicate time and place; they may be modifiers that express the writer's attitude toward the subject. Metadiscourse serves a necessary function, as the following sentences illustrate:

Strictly speaking, pidgin is *not really* a language; it is made up of *convenient* words borrowed from all the available language sources and then strung together in more or less random order.
—Lewis Thomas, *Et Cetera, Et Cetera* (96)

Soil experts, *likewise*, would have a *hard* life without the Sand Counties. Where else would their podzols, gleys, and anaerobics find a living? —Aldo Leopold, *A Sand County Almanac* (102)

Lewis Thomas cues the reader by qualifying his definition: *strictly speaking* and *not really*. Then with his adjective modifier *convenient* he expresses his opinion about the borrowed words. Leopold, with *likewise*, tells the reader that a similar statement is coming; the adjective *hard* expresses his idea of *life*.

Qualifiers, intensifiers, and other modifiers can be specific aids to reading. They can tell a reader what's coming next, summarize what has gone before, express the writer's opinion about the subject, and soften or emphasize words. Their skillful application is an important tool for writers. Notice how Thomas Cahill connects this sentence to the preceding one and then expresses his opinion:

> *Such* an outlook and *such* a temperament make for *wonderful* songs and *thrilling* stories. —*How the Irish Saved Civilization* (97)

The two *such* phrases look back, and the adjectives *wonderful* and *thrilling* tell the reader how Cahill views the songs and stories. Another example, this one by Erik Larson describing a hurricane's eye, illustrates more clearly how metadiscourse orients the reader:

> *At the very center of the eye*, the air is often utterly calm. Sailors *throughout history* have reported seeing stars at night, blue sky during the day. *Often, however,* the eye is neither clear nor cloudy, but filled with a liquid light that amplifies the stillness, as if the world were suddenly fused in wax. The sea, *however,* is anything but calm. Freed abruptly from the wind, waves from all quadrants of the eyewall converge at the center, where they collide and compound to form sudden mountains of undirected energy.
> —*Isaac's Storm* (133)

The first sentence orients the reader to the subject, and the second indicates a historical note. *Often* and *however* in the third sentence presage contrasting information. The fourth sentence is pivotal in contrasting the calmness of the air with the violence of the sea. Larson's word choices—*utterly, liquid, collide, compound, sudden mountains*—give an ominous tone to his description.

As helpful—and essential—as metadiscourse is, all too often it is not much more than empty words that don't qualify or intensify or modify anything. These are words like *basically, very, really, actually,* and *generally.* The list could go on, but you get the idea. They're fine occasionally, for emphasis or rhythm, but be careful that they don't become just weakening filler. Watch also for those two shifty -*y* words that masquerade as qualifiers but in fact reverse meaning: *virtually* and *arguably*. "She is arguably the most qualified lawyer in town" means that she is probably *not* the most qualified lawyer in town. The same goes for *virtually*. However, if someone is "literally on his deathbed," be assured that he is indeed about to leave this world.

The trick for taking advantage of metadiscourse is to know how much to use, what to use, and when to use it. Less experienced writers often use too much, as in these examples:

> In my opinion, I think Boorstin presents a more convincing argument.

> Personally, I think the author is rhetorically effective in his observations.

How much more effective might it be for the writer to state

> Boorstin presents a more convincing argument.

> The author is rhetorically effective in his observations.

Both revisions are still clearly the writers' opinions. Instead of empty metadiscourse, the writers could express their opinions through apt word choice, as in this forcefully stated paragraph by a student writer discussing a portion of Rachel Carson's *Silent Spring*:

> In "Needless Havoc," Carson directs just enough sarcasm at her adversaries to reveal them as the profiteering, ignorant conglomerates they are while maintaining her grave sense of urgency. Her wit is evident from the opening pages. For example, on page 85 she speaks of man's "crusade against insects," likening chemical companies' eagerness to kill insects to a poorly waged war. This remark portrays chemical manufacturers as not only ridiculous in their conquest, but blatantly overzealous as well. The caustic rhetoric continues as Carson speaks of wildlife that was "sacrificed in the campaign against an insect" (94). The brutal connotations of the word "sacrificed" sharpen the blade of Carson's attack, showing advocates of chemical spraying as barbarians who possess no remorse when eradicating living beings. Her well-timed sense of humor plays an important part in strengthening her arguments. —Chris Hanson

There's no *I think* here, no *certainly* or *really* or *basically*. Instead, Chris expresses his opinion with forceful modifiers, nouns, and verbs that carry the weight of his ideas: "profiteering ignorant conglomerates," "grave sense of urgency," "poorly waged war," "blatantly overzealous," "caustic rhetoric," "brutal connotations," "sharpen the blade," "well-timed sense of humor."

Summary

One of the main differences between professional writing and that of less experienced writers is that professional writers generally avoid redundancies, hidden subjects, objects, and verbs, and unnecessary metadiscourse. To make your writing more concise and more direct, keep in mind that—

❖ Rough drafts tend to be wordy.
❖ Redundant words restate the obvious.
❖ The overuse of *use* weakens writing.
❖ Doubled words draw attention to themselves.
❖ The grammatical subject of a sentence should ordinarily express the topical subject.
❖ Actions are more forceful when stated as verbs, not as adjectives or nouns.
❖ Metadiscourse can tell readers how to read the surrounding words.
❖ Qualifiers, intensifiers, and other modifiers require skillful use.

☐ **Practice** ☐

Revise the paragraph from *Quarterly Review of Doublespeak* on page 76 to make it state the message concisely and directly.

10

Make Your Voice Heard

Many people write about voice, but none agree on exactly what it is. When do we refer to voice instead of style, for example, or to voice instead of tone or persona or role? Unfortunately, I have the same problem: I can tell you how I think of voice, but my explanation will probably be no more complete than someone else's. What I'll do is show you some examples of writing where I see a clear voice and let you make your own assumptions. But I'll make a few too.

To start, let's look again at those two sentences by Rachel Carson that you read in the introduction to this book:

> Whenever I go down into this magical zone of the low water of the spring tides, I look for the most delicately beautiful of all the shore's inhabitants—flowers that are not plant but animal, blooming on the threshold of the deeper sea. —*The Edge of the Sea* (13)

> How could intelligent beings seek to control a few unwanted species by a method that contaminated the entire environment and brought the threat of disease and death even to their own kind? Yet this is precisely what we have done. —*Silent Spring* (8)

What gives the second sentence an angry voice compared to the peaceful one of the first sentence? Word choice? Sentence style? Subject matter?

All of these, probably. But significantly, even though they are different both sentences are Carson's voice. Each conveys an aspect of her identity, helps you to know who she is. Think of how you recognize a familiar voice on the telephone; it doesn't matter whether the person is angry or sad, coaxing or complaining—something in the voice identifies the person.

Understand that everyone has a voice. You have an oral voice, you have a written voice. Your written voice, like your oral voice, is how you sound to an audience. It is affected by choices—what words you use, how you arrange them in sentences, whether you adopt features of a more casual or a more formal style, how, in fact, you apply all the features of style. And the choices you make depend on the situation—do you want to sound professional, or friendly, or optimistic, or annoyed, and so on. How will your audience perceive what you say?

Your choices depend on your purpose for writing: to inform, to persuade, to express displeasure, to amuse, to explore ideas, and so on. This purpose determines your attitude, or tone, which is part of your voice. Whatever the variables, there is always an integral part of your written voice that remains *you,* no matter how you alter it to fit the situation. Like the two Carson sentences, the choices you make all come from the same mind, the same experiences, interests, biases.

Four informal voices.   Listen for the voices in these four excerpts from books written for a general audience, and look for stylistic features that make each voice distinctive:

> I felt very aggressive about the whole thing; alas, not being a toddler, I couldn't go and kick anybody in the kneecap. Which is the sort of thing that toddlers do, whatever their sex. They kick, they hit, they scream, they throw objects around, they act like pills past their expiration date. —Natalie Angier, *Woman: An Intimate Geography* (263–64)

> Thirty tons of water flood the crew mess, continue into the officer's mess, explode a steel bulkhead, tear through two more walls, flood the crew's sleeping quarters, course down a companionway, and kill the ship's engine. —Sebastian Junger, *The Perfect Storm* (151)

> The tall and dark-brown woman (whose movement never seemed to start or stop) was trailed one step by the pudgy little butter-yellow baby lurching, falling, now getting himself up, at

moments rocking on bowed legs, then off again in the wave of Momma. I never saw her turn to stop to right him, but she would slow her march and resume when he was steady again.

—Maya Angelou, *Gather Together in My Name* (74)

But Edie was exquisitely beautiful, all big baby browns with indelibly dilated pupils that made her eyes look like black spots Dalmatianed against eggshell-pale skin—a contrast so absolute that it evoked both the astonished openness and sweet opaqueness of a deer caught in headlights. —Elizabeth Wurtzel, *Bitch: In Praise of Difficult Women* (196)

Can you hear the voices? These four writers are comfortable enough with the English language, with their subjects, and with their own identity that they can stretch the rules to fit what they want to say, the way they want to say it. Angier uses a sentence fragment followed by a sentence of five independent clauses separated by commas. Junger ties together seven verb phrases. Angelou, in a voice affectionately describing her little son and her grandmother, inserts a parenthetical remark and ties together five phrases that fit the action. And Wurtzel piles on modifiers after her initial subject-verb statement.

But the most striking feature of these examples, what really makes the voices stand out, is the writers' choices of words and figurative language. Angier with her palpable "kick anybody in the kneecap" and her original but perhaps confusing **simile** "like pills past their expiration date." Junger with those powerful metaphoric verbs: *flood, continue, explode, tear, flood, course, kill.* Angelou with her descriptive *pudgy* and *butter-yellow.* And Wurtzel's surfeit of figures: **metonymy** and **alliteration** in "big baby browns," simile in "like black spots," metaphors in "Dalmatianed against eggshell-pale skin" and "a deer caught in headlights."

Tone of voice in three less casual styles.   The foregoing examples show informal voices in tones meant to amuse as well as to inform the reader. They are justifiable voices, filled with little surprises in word choice and sentence style. But other voices are justifiable too. Here's one that might be termed academic style. It's from an introductory physics textbook:

Every civilization has had as one of its first goals the achievement of fast and reliable transportation. Well before recorded history, animals provided swifter and stronger land transport than did the human foot, and rafts and boats of all descriptions made waterways favorite avenues of commerce. History shows that success in trading and even in warfare has generally been governed by the quality of transportation. We now mark in our memories many ancient civilizations by the lingering artifacts of their transportation systems—canals, roadways, sea-lanes, and even heavily worn footpaths. —Jack J. Kraushaar and Robert A. Ristinen, *Energy and Problems of a Technical Society* (328)

The voice here is more formal than the voices of the earlier examples though certainly not in a dry, stuffy, or even impersonal tone. It's the informed voice of two writers who are at ease with their subject and a nontechnical but academic audience. Their word choices, though not startling, are interesting: *swifter, the human foot, avenues of commerce, mark in our memories, lingering artifacts, heavily worn footpaths.*

More unexpected than the vocabulary are the rhythm and emphasis of the sentences. The first sentence is arranged so that the final emphasis is on the subject of the paragraph: transportation. The same thing happens in the second sentence, where emphasis falls on the synonymous "avenues of commerce." This emphasis would not have happened if the orienting phrase "Well before recorded history" had not begun the sentence. Instead, the sentence has a pleasing rhythm, helped along with the inverted clause "than did the human foot" and the compounded "swifter and stronger" and "rafts and boats." In the third sentence the insertion of *even* affects the rhythm and emphasis, and the sentence ends with the key word *transportation*. The final sentence establishes a relationship with the reader and ends with an explanatory series arranged in rhythmic order.

The sentences in Kraushaar and Ristinen's paragraph average twenty-three words, which is about a normal length. But observe the sentence below, which does some of the same things stylistically but totals more than ninety words.

Shackled in ignorance, disciplined by fear, and sheathed in superstition, [the Europeans] trudged into the sixteenth century in the clumsy, hunched, pigeon-toed gait of rickets victims, their vacant faces, pocked by smallpox, turned blindly toward the future they thought they knew—gullible, pitiful innocents who were about to be swept up in the most powerful, incomprehensible, irresistible vortex since Alaric had led his Visigoths and Huns across the

Alps, fallen on Rome, and extinguished the lamps of learning a thousand years before. —William Manchester, *A World Lit Only by Fire* (27)

Manchester's word choices, like Kraushaar and Ristinen's, are interesting, maybe sometimes surprising, but, taken individually, not too unexpected. It's in combination that they incrementally make an overall decisive statement. The cumulative description of those early sixteenth-century Europeans is told in an empathetic, knowledgeable tone of voice that probably would have been less effective had Manchester broken the sentence into more normal lengths.

In another example, military historian John Keegan writes with another learned voice to engage the nonscholarly reader:

The First World War was a tragic and unnecessary conflict. Unnecessary because the train of events that led to its outbreak might have been broken at any point during the five weeks of crisis that preceded the first clash of arms, had prudence or common goodwill found a voice; tragic because the consequences of the first clash ended the lives of ten million human beings, tortured the emotional lives of millions more, destroyed the benevolent and optimistic culture of the European continent and left, when the guns at last fell silent four years later, a legacy of political rancour and racial hatred so intense that no explanation of the causes of the Second World War can stand without reference to those roots. —*The First World War* (3)

Keegan uses rather unsurprising words in the long sentence fragment, but his emphasis and rhythm boldly carry the reader forward to his conclusion. His explanation of the tragedy of the conflict is a series of rhythmic verb phrases ("ended . . . , tortured . . . , destroyed . . . , left . . . ") that culminate in his emphatic ending.

What this analysis has so far shown is that style is integral to voice. The "academic you" writes to sound informed but not stuffy, interesting but not offhand. It's your combined choices of words, sentence structure, even punctuation that together represent a particular voice. Add in attitude toward the subject and the reader, and you have tone. But there's still that *je ne sais quoi*—that thing we can't put words to. Because, whether casual or academic, written or spoken, your voice somehow still represents who you are—or sometimes who you *want* to be or sometimes who you *pretend* to be.

Timbre. So let's take that analysis a step further, beyond style and attitude. Each written voice—like the spoken voice—has a certain resonance, a certain timbre, a certain something that identifies the person. Think again of the telephone voice you identify: what tells you that this is someone you know? Something beyond tone of voice, right? Whether in speaking or writing, you can only somewhat adjust the way your voice resonates in given situations. If on the telephone you sound angry instead of accommodating, your listener still knows it's you talking. If you make particular stylistic choices in writing a doctoral dissertation or a formal report, you achieve an appropriate formality but still maintain something of yourself that differs from how someone else would write.

Voices resonate differently. The Kraushaar and Ristinen example resonates, as does the Angier one, but they sound different. The following example resonates, but in a droning way:

> In the country of Italy, for example, cooperative organizations based on agriculture were set up by farmers in an effort to give them insurance against whatever bad weather would come their way; under this plan, the farmers who lived in areas that had a good season for growing crops would agree to make compensation to those other farmers who lived in areas where the weather had been of a less favorable kind.

This voice is turgid, inflated with stylistic elements that, when overused, slow down the reading for any reader unfortunate enough to have to read them. We find nominalizations (*organizations, insurance, compensation*), passive voice ("were set up by farmers"), prepositional phrases ("In the country," "of Italy," "on agriculture," and so on), plus many unnecessary words. These are not bad elements of style—in their place and in moderation they're useful. Even words that are not needed for meaning might be desirable for the sake of rhythm. That tedious sentence was my rewriting of the one below, which has a sharp and lucid voice.

> In Italy, for example, farmers set up agricultural cooperatives to insure one another against bad weather; farmers in areas with a good growing season would agree to compensate those whose weather had been less favorable. —Peter L. Bernstein, *Against the Gods* (93)

Bernstein's writing, like that of Keegan, Manchester, and Kraushaar and Ristinen, shows that an informative, objective style doesn't have to sound dull and tedious.

That certain something.   So now, what would you say voice is? Can you define it? Maybe it's analogy time again, time to go back to the barns. Earlier in this book, we established that barns have style as determined by various features: size, location, color, shape, type of doors and ventilators, and so on. We can look at a barn and define its style in terms of its features: a modern, octagonal barn; a stone tobacco barn; a big white ramped barn. But just by looking at a picture or by driving past we can't define its *voice*. It's not that barns don't have a voice; anything that has a style has a voice. But to know what that voice, that identity, is, you need to *go inside*. There all your senses take over. Yes, of course it smells like a barn, but you also hear and see—and feel. You can tell what the barn does and doesn't do. What it holds and doesn't hold. What kind of *life* there is inside—from the Holsteins in the stalls to the sparrows in the rafters.

Or here's a closer analogy. In the music world there's such a thing as voice too. Take a builder of pipe organs. In the final stages, a technician tunes the organ, makes fine adjustments in the pipes so they play the right notes, so a C-sharp is a true C-sharp, for example. But then the technician makes further, finer adjustments. These are to *voice* the organ, to give it the exact resonance, or timbre, that to the experienced ear *identifies the maker*. The organ now is beyond being right, it is itself. It's like Wynton Marsalis playing Bach's Brandenburg Concerto no. 2: many musicians can play the piece right, but only Marsalis can play it like Marsalis. Moreover, when Marsalis plays Hovhannes's "Prayer of St. Gregory" or any jazz piece, it's still the Marsalis voice though a very different tone.

We've come to the point where we can say that your voice and your style are aspects of your identity. Together they reveal something of who you are. And they are inseparable. Your voice is part of your style, but your choices of style, along with tone and timbre, determine the sound of your voice. In addition, we have to admit to that all-important *je ne sais quoi* that is yours alone, that certain something that we still haven't named. What it comes down to, I think, is what we decided in the barn: "hearing" voice is feeling. And, like the organ or the Brandenburg, it's knowing what to listen for.

Summary

❖ Voice is how your writing sounds to a reader.

❖ Everyone who writes has a written voice, though some voices sound better or more familiar than others.

❖ Voice is determined by who you are, but it may also be affected by who you want to be or who you're pretending to be.

❖ Voice can be altered to suit a situation, but only somewhat.

❖ Voice is part of style; it uses style.

❖ Voice consists of stylistic features plus tone and timbre.

❖ Word choice contributes to tone of voice, or attitude.

❖ Sentence structure and punctuation contribute to voice.

❖ Timbre, or resonance, is an identifying feature of voice.

❖ Situation determines the appropriateness of voice.

❖ Voice is more than being right; it is being *just right.*

☐ **Practice** ☐

1. Do a style analysis of Peter L. Bernstein's sentence on page 90 and my rewrite of it.

   ❖ What stylistic features make his sentence "sharp and lucid"?

   ❖ What stylistic features make mine "dull and tedious"?

   ❖ Characterize Bernstein's voice. What is its tone, or attitude? Do you consider the voice appropriate for academic and professional writing?

2. In what ways does William Manchester's excerpt on page 88 do "some of the same things stylistically" as that of Kraushaar and Ristinen on page 87?

3. Write a description of your written voice. What are its features? How does it relate to your style? To your identity? How do you adjust it to suit the situation?

11

Figure Your Language for Vivid Writing

Back in the sixteenth century, an English writer named John Lyly wrote a novel about a character named Euphues who used such an excess of figurative language that his name came to describe an affectedly elegant style: euphuism. It's not that the figures were so bad. Lyly gave us vivid expressions such as "Where there's smoke there's fire" and "Still waters run deep." What gained him his immortality was his *excessive* nonliteral language—"too much of a good thing," as he might say.

Figurative language has a history older than Euphues and older even than the English language. It goes back at least as far as Aristotle, who instructed his rhetoric students about the stylistic reasons for using metaphors, similes, and those other figures that have Greek-sounding names, such as **anaphora**, metonymy, **anastrophe**, **asyndeton**, and **polysyndeton**. They give "clearness, charm, and distinction" to style, he said. They're as ancient as the history of Greece and Rome but as timely as tomorrow's presidential address.

Because figurative language is nonlinear and nonliteral, it adds an extra layer of meaning to the denotation of words. It invites readers to make connections to other experiences, other knowledge, even other emotions. A reference to "monstrous waves," for example, evokes not only an image of big waves but also an impression of something frightening and unnatural. A statement that "The redhead left the room" invites the reader to visualize a whole person.

Metaphor.   The most common figure is the metaphor. It's so common, in fact, that most times we don't even notice it. Many of our verbs are actually metaphors. Consider these examples:

> I *telescoped* my energy on the gliding steps of the flash, with no less purpose than a ballet student mastering a tour jete.
> —Maya Angelou, *Gather Together in My Name* (100)

> That Rome should ever *fall* was unthinkable to Romans.
> —Thomas Cahill, *How the Irish Saved Civilization* (12)

> The rains continued. Storms *hung* over the region. On September 13, the Neosho River *roared* through southeastern Kansas, killing five, causing millions of dollars in damages. In Illinois a flood *rammed* a tree through an oil pipeline, setting it ablaze, spreading fire on the water. —John M. Barry, *Rising Tide* (174)

In each case you grasp a nonliteral meaning of the italicized verb. As implied comparisons between literal meanings and implied meanings, metaphors extend the range of our stylistic choices. Notice what John Keegan does with this sentence:

> He was *sowing the seed* that would *reap* another four million German corpses. —*The First World War* (6)

You would not read this sentence literally, though you do get Keegan's meaning. The metaphor allows you to respond emotionally as well as rationally. John Kenneth Galbraith uses an extended metaphor too, in this case to describe the state of the stock market in early 1929:

> A *bubble can easily be punctured*. But *to incise it with a needle* so that it subsides gradually is a task of no small delicacy. —*The Great Crash 1929* (30)

Metaphors, by layering meaning, sometimes reveal the writer's attitude. Keegan's sentence about the war does this, as do the following examples:

> But nothing could keep Paul Jones from Paris. He now *hatched* a trip to France out of the prize-money *egg*. —Samuel Eliot Morison, *John Paul Jones* (338)

Okay, maybe we shouldn't read too much into *fluffernutter* entertainment. But if you think *it's sweet and harmless* and you keep *eating it*, one day you'll wake up and *all your teeth have fallen out.*
—Natalie Angier, *Woman: An Intimate Geography* (284)

Morison could have said, "He now planned a trip to France out of the prize money." And Angier could have said, "Okay, maybe we shouldn't read too much into frivolous entertainment. But if you think it's harmless and you keep watching it, one day you'll wake up and find you don't have a thought in your head." Thankfully, they expressed their ideas metaphorically, conveying attitudes as well as subjects.

Simile.   A close relative of metaphor is the simile. It also compares unlike things for the purpose of describing one of them visually and pointedly. The following examples by John McPhee and Miles Harvey illustrate how both *as* and *like* make the comparison:

She is dour, silent, stolid *as a ceramic cat.* —*Coming into the Country* (109)

Each new map is *like an elusive quarry*, meticulously stalked down, first on the Internet and then in the library itself. —*The Island of Lost Maps* (265–66)

McPhee and Harvey could have written their sentences without the similes; the meaning would have been there, but you wouldn't have had the same visual image. Like metaphors, similes are so common that we hardly notice them when we're reading. (Of course, that doesn't mean that the writer isn't conscious of using them.)

Personification.   When we attribute human qualities to nonhuman objects or abstractions, we're using personification. Like metaphor and simile, it's a useful stylistic tool for expressing our ideas clearly and hinting at our attitude. The following example combines metaphor and personification:

There was no sound to the relentless advance of these cliffs of water except the hiss of their foaming brows when they rose to such a height or charged forward so fast that they lost their balance and their crests tumbled to the force of gravity.
—Alfred Lansing, *Endurance* (226)

Metaphorically, the waves were *cliffs* that had *brows* (as cliffs do metaphorically), but their actions take on human qualities: they "charged forward" and "lost their balance." In the next example, the verbs have metaphoric qualities that tend toward personification:

> The new earth, freshly *torn* from its parent sun, was a ball of whirling gases, intensely hot, *rushing* through the black spaces of the universe on a path and at a speed controlled by immense forces. —Rachel Carson, *The Sea around Us* (4)

Like this vivid personification of the violent parenting of the earth, natural forces are personified also in the following description of a storm:

> One of the worst storms on record had just *drawn a deep breath* off the Carolinas. It *screamed* northward all night and *slammed* into Georges Bank around dawn, *dredging* up seventy-foot waves in the weird shallows of the continental shelf. —Sebastian Junger, *The Perfect Storm* (84)

Here the storm takes on human (or at least animal) qualities of inhalation, voice, and capacity for violence.

Other figures. This chapter barely scratches the surface of figurative language. We won't be going into the 150 or so figures of Euphues, nor even the 36 described by rhetorician Edward P. J. Corbett in *Classical Rhetoric for the Modern Student* (409–11). Several figures are covered elsewhere in *Style and Difference*: asyndeton and polysyndeton in chapter 12, "Omit *and*, Repeat *and*"; anaphora (the repetition of words at the beginning of successive clauses) in chapter 24, "Repeat, Repeat, Repeat"; anastrophe (reversal of normal word order) in chapter 4, "Vary Your Sentences—Again"; and parallelism in chapter 5, "Pack Your Sentences with Parallelism." So let's end this chapter with examples of **allusion**, metonymy, and alliteration.

Allusion is another figure that resembles metaphor. It is a reference to something or someone only indirectly similar to the thing or person at hand. Here are two examples.

> We live in a *philistine* nation filled with *Goliaths*, and we know that science feeds at a public *trough*. —Stephen Jay Gould, *The Lying Stones of Marrakech* (237)

> *Plato* was in the air Augustine breathed, the figure a thoughtful young man must sooner or later test himself against. —Cahill (50)

These references to names in the Bible and to the Greek philosopher Plato help Gould and Cahill make their points. In a not very complimentary sentence, Gould compares Americans to the uncultured ancient enemy of the Israelites, the more powerful of us to their giant warrior defeated by a young David, and government-funded science to—well, you can guess what eats at troughs. Cahill's allusion to Plato might also be seen as an example of the next described figure of speech, metonymy, the representation of something by a related thing. Plato was not really "in the air," but his philosophy was (metaphorically).

Metonymy substitutes a related idea for the one meant. We might, for example, say "Will you give me a hand?" when what we want is the related thing, help. See how Barbara Tuchman describes Lyndon Johnson's attitude toward the Vietnam War:

> Given his *forward-march proposals* as Vice-President in 1961, this attitude could have been expected. —*The March of Folly* (311)

Johnson, of course, was laying out war plans. In another example, this from a book about the Mississippi River, John M. Barry is writing about engineer James Eads:

> He quickly recovered financially, telling his wife, Martha, that they need not join the gold rush to California since they had found *gold* on the river bottom. (26–27)

While Barry's first use of the word *gold* refers to the metal, his second relates to money he could make by retrieving wrecks from the river bottom.

Alliteration is a repetition of consonant sounds:

> And lately that idea has *found* new *fodder* and new *fans*, through the explosive growth of a *field* known as evolutionary psychology.
> —Angier (325)

> They floated in a *soupy sea* of *mush brash* ice composed of ground-up *floes* and *lumps* of *snow*. The *mass* of it closed in around the *ship* like pudding. —Lansing (29)

Angier's *f* sounds seem to lead into the idea of explosion, and Lansing's *s* and *sh* sounds echo the sound of the slushy ice closing in on the ship. Lansing comes close to mixing figures (if not metaphors) when he describes the situation as a "soupy sea" with a mass "like pudding." In another Antarctic example, Daniel J. Boorstin's description of Captain James Cook's voyage relies on metaphor as well as alliteration:

> This was no voyage through any becalmed Sargasso Sea, but one teetering on the edge of Antarctic ice, overshadowed and threatened by *crackling* and *crumbling* iceberg-alps. —*Cleopatra's Nose* (5)

Leading up to his alliterated "crackling and crumbling," Boorstin's metaphoric "teetering on the edge" and "iceberg-alps" give a visual as well as a literal reading.

Though well-crafted alliteration can add a degree of pleasure to a reading, careful writers try to avoid accidental occurrences of this figure.

Summary

Figurative language, like any other stylistic device, is most effective in moderation and in appropriate situations. Too much of it draws attention to itself and away from the idea it's meant to convey. But it can be extremely useful for vividly describing unusual things or circumstances, for expressing the writer's attitude toward the subject, and for surprising the reader with unexpected turns of phrase.

- ❖ *Metaphor* implicitly compares something familiar to something unfamiliar.
- ❖ *Simile* explicitly compares something familiar to something unfamiliar.
- ❖ *Personification* attributes human or animate qualities to things or circumstances that are inanimate or abstract.
- ❖ *Asyndeton* is the absence of conjunctions where you would expect them.
- ❖ *Polysyndeton* is the presence of more conjunctions than you would expect.
- ❖ *Parallelism* is structural repetition of related sentence elements.
- ❖ *Anaphora* is repetition of words at the beginnings of clauses.
- ❖ *Anastrophe* is reversal of normal word order.
- ❖ *Allusion* is reference to something indirectly related to the thing being described.
- ❖ *Metonymy* substitutes a related word for the one meant.
- ❖ *Alliteration* is a repetition of consonant sounds.

❖ Figurative language is most effective if used moderately and appropriately.

❖ Mixed figures can be confusing and sometimes ludicrous.

□ **Practice** □

Using the summary list, identify the figurative language in the following excerpts. Then practice writing figures yourself. Select a photograph from a magazine and describe it with figurative language. Refer to the summary definitions again if necessary.

1.   "In the Kipling world too was the trial of the only traitor that gave the Royal Navy reason to hang its head. He was a young stoker* of faint personality and incurious mind, and the chief charge against him was the betrayal to the Germans of information about radar equipment in the type of motor torpedo boat in which he served, and about the naval and harbour facilities of Portsmouth, neither of which subjects could he have had at his fingertips. But he was up to his neck in dubious goings-on. A slender boy, not unlike the Duke of Windsor, with a long neck, hair pale gold in the light and mousy in the shadow, and pouches under his blue eyes, he made a poor show in the dock, sagging like a plant in need of staking. When he was cross-examined he was pitifully unresentful of injustice and misunderstanding, and borne down by noise."—Rebecca West, *The New Meaning of Treason* (149–50)

* One who supplied a marine steam boiler with fuel.

2.   "By the time they meet, the Yellowstone and the Missouri are both big rivers. When they're low, they expose acres of mud dried to jigsaw cracks. Full, they're both hundreds of yards across, and flow smoothly at the lip of their banks, suddenly boiling up with a sucking sound, then flowing smoothly again. The Great Plains usually give few hints about the uses people should make of them, but the expanse of flat tableland surrounding the confluence of these rivers strongly suggests a city site. It's like the junction of the Schuylkill and the Delaware, minus Philadelphia, or the confluence of the Allegheny and the Monongahela into the Ohio, minus Pittsburgh."—Ian Frazier, *Great Plains* (21)

12

Omit and, Repeat and

*T*he ancient Greeks had a word for it: *asyndeton*. It meant the omission of connectors where you would expect them in a sentence. The opposite was *polysyndeton*, meaning an excess of connectors. Both stylistic devices are options for writers today as variations from the conventional usage of *and* or another coordinating conjunction (*but, or, nor, for, so, yet*) before the last item in a series. Rachel Carson and Daniel J. Boorstin feel comfortable with these options:

ASYNDETON   No species was spared. Among the dead were mullets, snook, mojarras, gambusia.

—Silent Spring (147)

POLYSYNDETON   While there are, of course, traditions *and* styles *and* schools in the arts, every act of creation is a kind of personal declaration of independence.

—Cleopatra's Nose (25)

Carson's omission of *and* in her list of dead fish seems appropriate for leaving the list open-ended. Boorstin seems to imply a complete list with his inclusions of *and*. Both of these sentences are variations of the usual method of treating items in series, a conjunction to connect the last item:

Thirty tons of water flood the crew mess, continue into the officer's mess, explode a steel bulkhead, tear through two more walls,
flood the crew's sleeping quarters, course down a companionway,
and kill the ship's engine. —Sebastian Junger, *The Perfect Storm* (151)

Polysyndeton.   Besides implying a complete list, Boorstin's sentence
also seems to emphasize each of the three items connected with *and.*
That effect seems to be true of the items in the following example too:

Anything you couldn't carry in a pocket you shouldn't be carry-
ing. That's where we carried extra socks and gloves and cigarettes
and matches and K rations and toilet paper and letters from home
and V-mail forms for writing back and a pen to write with.
—Paul Fussell, *Doing Battle* (136)

While the sheer numbers of the list tend to emphasize its size, each
item stands alone as a member of a complete list. We see the same
effect in this example:

Just by placing their big still bodies in the Store at that
precise time, my grandmother and uncle were saying, "Be good.
Be very very good. Somebody is watching you."
We squirmed and grinned and understood. —Maya Angelou,
Gather Together in My Name (66–67)

Asyndeton.   With Rachel Carson's sentence, I suggested that the effect
of omitting a final conjunction is to leave the list open-ended. Let's test
that observation on the following excerpts:

The resentment against Gorbachev never abated. For the men who
led the communist opposition, he was the man who had betrayed
everything: the Party, history, the empire. —David Remnick,
Resurrection (11–12)

In the operations of government, the impotence of reason is serious because it affects everything within reach—citizens, society,
civilization. —Barbara Tuchman, *The March of Folly* (381)

Well, so there goes one theory out the window. Whereas you could add
another fish or two to Carson's sentence, you'd be hard-pressed to expand on Remnick's and Tuchman's sentences. Their lists seem complete.
Incidentally, you'll notice that these sentences illustrate two ways of

introducing explanatory lists—with a colon and with a dash. Generally, colons are said to be more formal than dashes, although the levels of formality here don't seem much different.

So far we've seen *words* in series. Now let's look at two examples of short phrases and independent clauses in asyndeton series:

> His [Mawson's] pulse was pounding, his head spinning with weakness; he had to camp, to fight the wind, to lash the ski shoes to the splinted theodolite legs, to chop out chunks of snow for the skirt, to spread the cover over the frame. —Lennard Bickel, *Mawson's Will* (225)

> I do not mean that we sit silent and judgmental, like doctrinaire Freudian analysts; we speak, we respond, we question.
> —Carolyn G. Heilbrun, *The Last Gift of Time* (163)

Even though Bickel's series of infinitive phrases may be complete (*to camp, to fight, to lash, to chop, to spread*), by omitting the conjunction he emphasizes the sheer enormity of the tasks facing the weary Douglas Mawson and allows the reader to experience each task separately. Heilbrun's sentence, referring to "those who are older" and their acts of communicating with "the young," could possibly go on to include other types of conversation, such as "we listen," "we approve," "we suggest," "we joke."

In addition to series, the connector is sometimes omitted between *paired* grammatical elements, as in these examples:

BETWEEN TWO INDEPENDENT CLAUSES	The roof bristles with lightning rods, the weathercock is proud with new guilt. —Aldo Leopold, *A Sand County Almanac* (119)
BETWEEN TWO ADJECTIVES	Sometimes they [Ghost Dancers] brought back white, grayish earth—a piece of the morning star—as proof. —Ian Frazier, *Great Plains* (42)

Leopold's sentence illustrates what the handbooks call a comma splice (see chapter 17, "Splice with Commas")—two independent clauses joined by a comma. The Frazier example is a common usage: two adjectives (*white, grayish*) separated by a comma rather than joined by a conjunction.

Summary

We've seen only a few examples of the many kinds of lists that can be written in sentences. As established in chapter 1, "Coordinate Balanced Ideas," any grammatical element can be connected to equivalent elements: clauses with clauses (Heilbrun, Leopold), nouns with nouns (e.g. Carson, Tuchman, Boorstin), verbs with verbs (Angelou), and so on. As long as the items are balanced, you have three stylistic choices: connecting the final item with a conjunction (the conventional way), connecting all items with conjunctions (polysyndeton), and omitting all conjunctions (asyndeton).

❖ In a series of three or more grammatical elements, the conventional usage is to connect the final item with a coordinating conjunction.

❖ By connecting all items with conjunctions (polysyndeton), you slow the reading and emphasize each item. The list may seem complete.

❖ By omitting all conjunctions (asyndeton), you speed the reading, emphasize the list as a whole, and (perhaps) imply that other items could be added.

❖ Connectors are also sometimes omitted between two parallel items (Leopold and Frazier).

See also chapter 17, "Splice with Commas," for a discussion of omitting a conjunction between two independent clauses.

□ **Practice** □

Rewrite Carson's and Remnick's sentences with polysyndeton: add *and* between items in the series. Rewrite Boorstin's and Fussell's sentences with asyndeton: omit the conjunction between items. Rewrite Junger's sentence to omit *and* before the final item. What effects do your revisions have on emphasis and implied meanings?

Part Two

Difference

S tyle and usage are always changing, and professionals (including academic and science writers) choose to apply or not to apply rules according to situation. In fact, what you think of as rules of writing may not be rules at all but just artificial constraints that published writers commonly break. Everyone knows that published writers write fragments, splice their sentences with commas, begin their sentences with *and* and end them with prepositions, use passive voice, say *I* and *you*, contract their words, and so on—yet our textbooks of writing reject these elements of style, implying that it's okay for professionals to do it, just don't try it at home.

The fact is that most of the "rules" are made up anyway; many of them are not even real rules. They're more like *lore*, an accumulation of beliefs, pseudofacts, perceptions, biases, and traditions that developed over time for reasons nobody can identify. Real rules are those that describe how the language works, like "Verbs agree with their subjects" and "Prepositions have objects." Made-up rules, or conventions, mostly tell us what things to avoid: "Don't begin your sentences with *and* or *but*," "Avoid repetition," "Don't write sentence fragments." But a study of serious writers, people who write with style, reveals that sentences do begin with *and* or *but*, words are repeated effectively, and sentence fragments often say just the right thing.

These nonrules make your writing more difficult for you than it needs to be. Instead of developing your idea, you're worrying about whether your sentence is going to end with a preposition, or how you can avoid a passive verb, or what you can say to avoid saying *I*. And on top of that, you're writing with a style that you don't like. It sounds stiff. And boring. Not like you at all. Those so-called rules are denying you access to words and phrases and styles of expressing yourself that, were it not for those rules, you'd be using unconsciously as you proceed to composing your ideas. Under some circumstances it's necessary to follow those rules, or some of them anyway, because they've become part of the conventional expectations of that situation. In other words, some of your readers may expect you to observe them. See "Introduction: Style, Situation, and Difference" for suggestions about how to assess situational expectations. But many writing situations allow for bending the rules, sometimes outright breaking them. To do it and not be thought uneducated, you need to know how and when.

In this part of the book, we look at twelve of those traditions and how other writers have disregarded them. You'll find that at times it's a wise stylistic choice to "Use passive verbs," "Begin your sentences with *and*," or "Fragment your sentences." You may want to end a sentence with a preposition or write *which* instead of *that*. Not that you'll want to practice every form of difference every time you sit down to write. Just think about whether you want to do it that way, and put away unnecessary constraints that bind up your writing.

If you don't have to worry any more about repetition, for example, you can experiment with repeating words and phrases for a clearer, more emphatic style. Just as professional writers do, you too can write an occasional sentence fragment if you know how and when to do it. You can use passive verbs if you have stylistic reasons for doing so. You can actually think about comma splices and decide whether a comma between independent clauses would be better than a semicolon or a period.

What it comes down to is there are fewer real restrictions than you may realize. The following chapters show you how flexible they are.

13

Use Passive Verbs

*P*assive voice, it seems to me, has been the recipient of bad press. As a result of what the rule books tell us, we tend to think of it as representing inertia, inactivity, quiescence. It "lacks vigor" and boldness; it's "confusing." We call this style unnecessarily wordy and therefore turgid (meaning the writing flows like glue, and often it does). But look at the following example that has eight instances of passive voice. Does it seem to have no action? Where's the wordiness? I've italicized the passive verbs.

> Houses *are washed* out to sea in Gloucester, Swampscott, and on Cape Cod. Rising waters inundate half of the town of Nantucket. A man *is swept* off the rocks in Point Judith, Rhode Island, and *is never seen* again, and a surfer dies trying to ride twenty-foot shore-break in Massachusetts. Plum Island *is cut* in half by the waves, as *is* Haugh's Neck and Squantum, in Quincy. Over one hundred houses *are destroyed* in the town of Scituate, and the National Guard has *to be called* out to help the inhabitants evacuate. One elderly woman *is taken* from her house by a backhoe while surf breaks down her front door. —Sebastian Junger, *The Perfect Storm* (205)

So does it look as if we can forget about the inactivity description? Actually, the rule books don't tell how "passive" the verb is; they tell us

107

only that when a verb has passive voice its subject receives the verb's action. In other words, the subject doesn't act, it's acted upon—passive.

What passive voice is.   With active voice, then, the subject of a sentence acts, as in "A backhoe takes a woman from her house." The backhoe acts. But in Sebastian Junger's sentence the subject, "One elderly woman," *receives* the action. She gets removed. As you notice, from active to passive there's a reversal of the nouns, and the verb is changed. Like this:

PASSIVE   Subject + *to be* verb and past participle (+ *by* agent)
"One elderly woman + *is taken* from her house + by a backhoe."

ACTIVE   Subject + verb + object
A backhoe + *takes* + one elderly woman from her house.

The passive verb, you see, is a little longer, requiring one of the *be* verbs (*is, are, am, was, were, been, being*) plus the past participle, and a *by* phrase if the writer wants to indicate the agent, or performer, of the action. As a consequence, the sentence is slightly longer. In the shorter active sentence, the subject corresponds to the agent of the action, and the object receives the action. Here's another example:

PASSIVE: "Plum Island is cut in half by the waves."

ACTIVE: The waves cut Plum Island in half.

The passive sentence has an additional verb form (*is*) and a *by* phrase. Sometimes, especially in conversational styles, that extra verb is *get* instead of a form of *be*, as in this sentence from *The Perfect Storm*:

Inevitably, something has broken on the trip—a line *gets wound* around the drive shaft and *must be dove* on, the antennas *get snapped* off, the radios go dead. (209)

And the *by* phrase is often omitted. The verbs in this sentence probably have three different agents: first, the line itself ("a line winds itself around the drive shaft"); second, a member of the crew ("somebody on the crew must dive"); and third, the wind ("the wind snaps off the antennas"). We'll take a look at the reasons for these omissions a little later in the chapter.

Passive voice for coherence and emphasis.   We are advised to avoid writing in passive voice whenever possible. Not like Sebastian Junger in his dynamic description of the storm. Not like William Zinsser in this criticism of some sportswriters:

> What keeps most sportswriters from writing good English is the misapprehension that they shouldn't be trying to. They *have been reared* on so many clichés that they assume they are the required tools of the trade. They *are also obsessed* with synonyms. They have a dread of repeating the word that's easiest for the reader to visualize—batter, runner, golfer, boxer—if a synonym *can be found*. And usually, with exertion, it *can.* —*On Writing Well* (201)

Apparently writers ignore the rule against passive verbs. One reason is that passive voice can sometimes keep their subjects consistent, thus making tighter connections between ideas. Zinsser's passive verbs in sentences two and three allow him to refer back to "sportswriters" and in all three middle sentences to keep a consistent subject. The following example also illustrates this principle of coherence:

> No humanist rose higher in public life than Sir Thomas More, who, until his fall from royal grace, was as distinguished a statesman as he was a scholar. During Henry VIII's early reign More *had been appointed* undersheriff of London, king's councillor, and a judge of the courts of requests. —William Manchester, *A World Lit Only by Fire* (108)

The passive verb of the second sentence allows Manchester to emphasize "More" by putting the name in subject position, tying to the repeated synonymous references in the first sentence (*humanist, Sir Thomas More, who, his, statesman, he, scholar*).

The following examples show again how writers use the construction to establish links to previous sentences and to gain emphasis as well:

> A good description of the standard view of images within cultural studies and related disciplines *may be found* in the *Cultural Glossary of Cultural Theory*. —Steven Pinker, *The Blank Slate* (213)

> The wounds on his hands were due to a beating with barbed wire he *had been given* by a working party of prisoners of war who had discovered that he was an informer. —Rebecca West, *The New Meaning of Treason* (152)

The passive verb enables Pinker to connect his new idea, announcing the title of a book, with the previous discussion of images. West directs attention to the wounds and the beating instead of the perpetrators.

Passive voice allows writers to arrange their sentences so as to take advantage of the emphatic end position. This next sentence by John Keegan not only tells who performed the actions (*sending* and *selecting*) but places those agents at the end for emphasis:

> A particular feature of the legal process was that those *sent* for trial *were selected* by their own officers and NCOs, with the implicit consent of the rank and file. —John Keegan, *The First World War* (331)

Passive voice for missing agents.   Writers frequently use passive voice when the agent (or performer) of the action is not known or doesn't matter. Here's an example:

> It *is often remarked* that the human mind is unique among the thinking systems of the animal kingdom because of its capacity to look ahead and commit its long thoughts to the future. Other animals, *it is said*, cannot do this; they live their lives in the immediate present, making use of memory—which they do possess, *it is conceded*—but only for essentially mindless matters like remembering where to find food or what hurt when last *encountered*, certainly not for creating images from the past to foretell what may happen next year. —Lewis Thomas, *Et Cetera, Et Cetera* (82)

With passive verbs, Thomas distances himself from his statements, attributing them to some unknown source. The next sentence shows how passive voice is effective for expressing generalizations:

> Plans *made* without allowance for the intentions of the enemy are liable to miscarry. —Keegan (277)

A common—and often suspect—use of the passive is to intentionally obscure the agent of the action. It happens often in accounts of government actions:

> It *was emphasized* that only a third of us would survive the course, failures *being dispatched* immediately to fill the enlisted ranks of infantry divisions. —Paul Fussell, *Doing Battle* (87)

> Unfortunately this directive *was not brought* to the attention of the public, or even the Houses of Parliament. Few secrets in this field *have been kept* so well. —West (264)

Sometimes writers adopt the passive voice to reflect a particular style:

> On Sunday there were sermons suggesting that a certain measure of divine retribution *had been visited* on the Republic and that it *had not been entirely unmerited.* —John Kenneth Galbraith, *The Great Crash 1929* (109)

This sentence reporting on the Sunday following the Crash may or may not be intended to match an ecclesiastical style. Passive voice is sometimes effective in narratives, as in this next example of a bit of fishing history:

> Jigging for mackerel worked well, but it was inevitable that the Yankee mind would come up with something more efficient. In 1855 the purse seine *was invented*, a 1,300-foot net of tarred twine with lead weights at the bottom and cork floats at the top. It *was stowed* in a dory that *was towed* behind the schooner, and when the fish *were sighted*, the dory quickly encircled them and cinched the net up tight. It *was hauled* aboard and the fish *were split, gutted, beheaded*, and *thrown* into barrels with salt. —Junger (25)

We have seen that passive voice doesn't really add much wordiness to a piece of writing. Junger's passive verbs tell the tale without even stating who performed the actions. That extra verb, *be*, added to a past participle, extends the sentence a little: *were condemned* rather than *condemned, is swept* instead of *sweeps, are destroyed* instead of *destroy, had been appointed* rather than *had appointed*. Then if the writer wants to name the agent of the action, it has to be done in a prepositional phrase: *by a backhoe, from insecticides, by the nineteenth-century fishermen*. That makes the sentence longer.

Summary

Writers have good reasons for using passive voice:

- ❖ To emphasize a particular word by putting it in subject position.
- ❖ To connect thoughts by keeping subjects consistent.
- ❖ To make generalizations.
- ❖ To make statements when the agent of the action is unknown or unimportant.
- ❖ To conceal the agent of the action.
- ❖ To reflect a distinctive style.

□ **Practice** □

These two paragraphs are written on the same subject, the first using passive verbs, the second using active verbs. Read them both, then rewrite them as a third paragraph using both active and passive verbs as you think best stylistically. Consider matters of coherence, emphasis, and need to identify agents of action. Compare your paragraph with these.

1. Wind power is considered one of the most environmentally friendly means of generating energy. This position has been taken seriously by countries in the European Union, for whom 70 percent of energy is generated by wind. The field has been dominated by nations such as Germany, Spain, and Denmark, although one of the largest wind farms will soon be built by the Netherlands five miles out in the North Sea. In contrast, wind energy has not been taken seriously in the United States despite the fact that many locations are known for their constantly blowing winds.

2. Environmentalists consider wind power one of the most environmentally friendly means of generating energy. Countries of the European Union have taken this position seriously, using wind to generate 70 percent of their energy. Nations such as Germany, Spain, and Denmark have dominated the field, although the Netherlands will soon build one of the largest wind farms five miles out in the North Sea. In contrast, the United States has not taken wind energy seriously despite the fact that we know many locations with constantly blowing winds.

14

Begin Your Sentences with *and* (*but, or, nor, for, yet, so*)

Are you one of those people who learned (in grade school, I suppose) not to begin your sentences with *and* or *but*? For some reason, this bit of lore has come to take precedence over more important aspects of style such as coherence and rhythm. I'm only guessing at its origin, but I suppose it was a second-grade elementary teacher who was getting tired of her pupils starting every sentence with these conjunctions and stringing their words together into a single boxcar-length thought, who finally said "Enough already! *Never* begin your sentences with *and* or *but*." And the admonition stuck. Those little kids may not have remembered anything else about writing, but when they grew up to be teachers themselves they never failed to remind their budding writers, "Never begin your sentences with *and* or *but*."

And so it became an aspect of "lore"—that accumulation of beliefs, pseudofacts, perceptions, biases, and traditions that have no more basis than what we attribute to them. The injunction has simply been passed down from teacher to student until it has assumed the substance of fact. Students in my style classes, I've discovered, are still constrained to avoid beginning their sentences with one of these conjunctions. I don't understand it.

It's obvious to me, after examining a plethora of published examples, that well-respected authors rely on these little tools as the most convenient, the most natural means to connect ideas. Rather than writing the longer and more formal *however*, they use *but*. Rather than more obtrusive terms like *in addition* and *moreover*, they call up *and*. These two, *and* and *but*, are the most common sentence openers of the seven coordinating conjunctions, but the others occur with amazing frequency too.

And to begin sentences and paragraphs.

Notice how the writers of the following examples use *and* to add information to what went before:

> *And* if all these skills and attributes could not turn the tide, Buffon also wrote in an elegant prose that placed him, a "mere" student of nature, among the leading men of letters in his interesting time. —Stephen Jay Gould, *The Lying Stones of Marrakech* (90)

> *And* Paul Jones showed his contempt for the Royal Navy by remaining in its home waters, since he had a score to settle with HMS *Drake*. —Samuel Eliot Morison, *John Paul Jones* (25)

> *And* though a contemporary reader might take all this as metaphor, the Irish believed that gods, druids, poets, and others in touch with the magical world could be literal shape-shifters.
> —Thomas Cahill, *How the Irish Saved Civilization* (129)

Many writers even use the conjunction to connect paragraphs:

> *And yet* business of a kind was being transacted. —Gene Smith, *When the Cheering Stopped* (118)

> ■ At the beginning of a paragraph in a narrative describing the last days of President Woodrow Wilson.

> *And* what are those reasons again? my students ask. —Anne Lamott, *Bird by Bird* (14)

But to begin sentences and paragraphs.

Writers use *but* to begin sentences and paragraphs as often as they use *and*, if not more so. Here are examples:

> The great honeypot was still packed with sustenance, and some of the larvae, protected by waterproof cells, had survived the flood. *But* they would die. —Franklin Russell, *Watchers at the Pond* (182)

But all this existed on and under a film of mud and floodwater on which garbage floated, without a single paved street in sight.
—Robert D. Kaplan, *Balkan Ghosts* (118)

But at the same time, the basic egotism that gave rise to his enormous self-reliance occasionally blinded him [Ernest Shackleton] to realities. —Alfred Lansing, *Endurance* (103)

Notice, please, that the conjunctions are not followed by commas.

Imagine these sentences beginning with the bulkier *however*. It would alter the rhythm as well as the level of formality. In my search, I found only a few occurrences of *however* to connect contrasting ideas. *But* was much more common, even to begin paragraphs, as these examples show:

But complex nature defies the needs of laboratory science for simple and well-controlled situations, where events can be replicated under identical conditions set by few variables.
—Gould (101–02)

▓ In a discussion contrasting natural and laboratory experiments.

But this was not a tenable point of view. —Rebecca West, *The New Meaning of Treason* (41)

▓ After a paragraph examining William Joyce's innocence.

In the following example, the paragraph begins with *but* and later contains a sentence beginning with *and*:

But it turns out that the material being washed into the sea every year has no appreciable effect on the composition of sea water. . . . *And* where salts have accumulated in water from land erosion into lakes without outlets, like the Great Salt Lake and the Dead Sea, the balance of salts in the water is quite different from that in the ocean. —Marston Bates, *The Forest and the Sea* (45)

Respected writer Virginia Woolf even begins her book *A Room of One's Own* with *But*:

But, you may say, we asked you to speak about women and fiction—what has that got to do with a room of one's own? I will try to explain. (3)

About the only restriction I can discover for beginning sentences with conjunctions is generally not to begin two side-by-side sentences with *but.* Since *but* indicates contrast, the reader begins to feel dragged back and forth.

Other conjunctions. The remainder of the coordinating conjunctions begin sentences and paragraphs too, though less frequently than *and* and *but.* What follows are some examples of *so, yet, nor, or,* and *for,* some of them opening their paragraphs. Notice that each conjunction gives you an idea of how the sentence connects to the one before:

> *So* the Greek temple, conceived of as a part of its setting, was simplified, the simplest of all the great buildings of the world.
> —Edith Hamilton, *The Greek Way* (285)

▦ States a result of the previous idea.

> *So,* as a collector, what you do is look for something that you're not supposed to see or possess. *And so,* intrinsically, whatever you discover or obtain by discovery is taboo in one way or another. —Miles Harvey, *The Island of Lost Maps* (260)

> *Yet* Lincoln drew much of his defense of the Union from the speeches of Webster, and few if any have considered Webster a mystic. —Garry Wills, *Lincoln at Gettysburg* (125)

▦ States a truth that refutes the previous statement.

> *Yet* the boom was continuing. —John Kenneth Galbraith, *The Great Crash 1929* (37)

▦ States an occurrence despite previously stated happenings.

> The Gettysburg Address does not mention Gettysburg. *Nor* slavery. *Nor*—more surprising—the Union. —Wills (90)

▦ The fragments state negatives.

> *Nor* do [seaweeds] need the rigid supporting stem or trunk by which a land plant reaches upward into sunlight—they have only to yield themselves to the water. —Carson, *The Edge of the Sea* (72)

▦ States a negative alternative.

If their route was to be over the ice, the sledge drivers would harness their teams with all possible speed while the other men gathered stores and equipment, struck the tents, and then stood by the sledges. *Or* if, as they hoped, they could escape by water, they were to ready the boats. —Lansing (79)

■ States a positive alternative.

For Augustine is the first human being to say "I"—and to mean what we mean today. His *Confessions* are, therefore, the first genuine autobiography in human history. —Cahill (39)

■ States an explanation of the previous statement.

Yet there are no survivors to be offended. *Nor* is the term [Dark Ages] necessarily pejorative. —William Manchester, *A World Lit Only by Fire* (3)

Manchester obviously has no compunction about beginning his sentences with coordinating conjunctions. In the following example, he has two side by side, standing alone as a transitional paragraph:

And yet . . . (11)

■ Ellipsis dots are his.

By now it should be abundantly clear that there is no real rule against beginning sentences with coordinating conjunctions. Each conjunction in these examples implies a connection with what went before and therefore aids the reader in knowing how to read what follows. And they do so without undue formality, being barely noticed in the reading. In consideration of how useful—and how common—they are, it is all the more baffling that such an idea ever could exist. But it did exist—and still does in the minds of some people. So know your reader, and be aware when you open your sentences with conjunctions.

Summary

❖ Sentences beginning with *and* and other coordinating conjunctions are appropriate in all levels of writing, from the most formal to the conversational.
❖ Writers use *and* to connect equivalent ideas in sentences and paragraphs.
❖ To show contrast, writers often prefer *but* to the stiffer *however.*
❖ Generally avoid beginning two side-by-side sentences with the same conjunction.

❖ But writers sometimes use opening conjunctions in more than one sentence in a paragraph.

❖ Writers begin sentences with a variety of conjunctions, not just *and* or *but.*

□ **Practice** □

Examine one of your textbooks for occurrences of *and, but, or, for, nor, so,* and *yet* at the beginning of sentences.

❖ What are the effects of the conjunctions—on the sentences and in context?

❖ Would the sentences be improved if the conjunctions were removed?

❖ What would be the effect of substituting a longer connecting word, such as *moreover, however, therefore,* and *nevertheless*?

15

Begin Your Sentences with because (since, while)

A long with the bit of lore that tells us not to begin our sentences with *and* is the one that says "Don't begin your sentences with *because*." Others closely related are "Don't begin your sentences with *since*" and "Don't begin your sentences with *while*." We'll deal with all three of them here.

Beginning sentences with because. Interestingly, writers don't often begin their sentences with *because*. You can find other **subordinating conjunctions** such as *when* and *after* and *if* and *although*, but very few *because*s. The reason may be that writers are more reluctant to attribute cause than comparison or time relationships—or have less opportunity. But be assured that there is no grammatical reason for avoiding *because*. The following writers had occasion to use it.

> *Because* of the Victrola, waking up to a rainy Saturday became a special treat. —Edgar Allen Imhoff, *Always of Home* (57)

> *Because* of his early experiments, Lincoln's words acquired a flexibility of structure, a rhythmic pacing, a variation in length of words and phrases and clauses and sentences that make his sentences move "naturally," for all their density and scope.
> —Garry Wills, *Lincoln at Gettysburg* (157–58)

> *Because* the Serbs were spread out over wooded and mountainous land that was difficult to subdue, and *because* they were geographically farther removed from Turkey than either Bulgaria or Greece, the Ottoman yoke was never as complete in Serbia as it was in those countries. —Robert D. Kaplan, *Balkan Ghosts* (33)

What proponents of the *because* rule are probably concerned about is that such sentence beginnings could lead to sentence fragments—like the following:

> Language is what preserved us. Not *because* it does real damage to any other species, but *because* we can use it together.
>
> —Lewis Thomas, *Et Cetera, Et Cetera* (106)

▓ Thomas's second statement is a fragment.

> *Because* I don't like the idea that I'll be getting older and lesser; I want to keep becoming more and more and more.
>
> —Elizabeth Wurtzel, *Bitch: In Praise of Difficult Women* (90)

▓ Wurtzel's semicolon makes the first part of her sentence a fragment; an independent clause follows.

But as I say in the following chapter, fragments can sometimes be clearer and less wordy than complete sentences.

Beginning sentences with <u>since</u>.   Often when writers want to show causal relationships they use *since*:

> *Since* the queen had by now settled on Beatrice as the crutch of her old age, she resigned herself to losing Lenchen. —Jerrold M. Packard, *Victoria's Daughters* (111)

> *Since* no historical record mentions a mass slaughter of infants among Herod's crimes, many New Testament scholars regard the story of the "slaughter of the innocents," like the "flight into Egypt," as reflecting Matthew's programmatic conviction that Jesus' life must recapitulate the whole history of Israel.
>
> —Elaine Pagels, *The Origin of Satan* (78)

> *Since* his [Johnson's] opponent was the bellicose Senator Barry Goldwater, he had to appear as the peace candidate.
>
> —Barbara Tuchman, *The March of Folly* (314)

The usual advice about using *since* is that its meaning might be ambiguous since it can mean time as well as cause. But a style-sensitive writer can tell if there is going to be such a problem. There seems to be no ambiguity in the preceding sentences. Here is an example of its use to indicate a time relationship:

> *Since* the failure of the second Austrian offensive in December 1914, the Serbian army had remained deployed on the northern and eastern frontiers. —John Keegan, *The First World War* (250–51)

Beginning sentences with <u>while</u>. Some rule books advise writers not to begin their sentences with *while*. The reason is potential ambiguity, in this case between time and concession, sometimes contrast. Some books recommend using *while* to indicate time, and *although, even if,* or *even though* for concession. But published writers do not heed such advice, often doing just the opposite in sentences like these:

> *While* making his own position clear, Lincoln professes a readiness to alter course if he is proved wrong. —Wills (168)

> ■ Concession; read *even though*

> *While* the Yeltsin supporters and dozens of "undecideds" did not come, he had more than enough for a quorum of the smaller body, the Supreme Soviet—a symbolic victory at least. —David Remnick, *Resurrection* (60)

> ■ Concession; read *even though*

> *While* the royal family's internal relationships were unraveling, Bismarck was laying the ground for the final transformation of Prussia into the Continent's preeminent power. —Packard (139)

> ■ Time; read *while* or *at the same time as*

Clauses of concession acknowledge a truth before stating a difference. They imply *even so, despite,* or *nevertheless.* Take another look at Remnick's sentence: first he concedes that many Russians did not attend the meeting, then he states that Yeltsin got something anyway. Remnick could have written:

> The Yeltsin supporters and dozens of "undecideds" did not come; nevertheless (or even so) he had more than enough for a quorum of the smaller body, the Supreme Soviet—a symbolic victory at least.

Notice how Elaine Pagels uses *while* in the following sentence to ac-knowledge one truth before stating a contrasting one:

> Rereading biblical and extra-biblical accounts of angels, I learned first of all what many scholars have pointed out: that *while* angels often appear in the Hebrew Bible, Satan, along with other fallen angels or demonic beings, is virtually absent. —Pagels (xvi)

Writers, I find, use *while* to indicate concession much more com-monly than time, and I include those writing for scholarly journals, as in these examples from *Philosophy and Rhetoric* and *College English*:

> *While* Smith does not expressly address the resemblance between the respective arguments, she answers the charge of conserva-tism by turning it on its head. —Jeffery L. Geller, "The Stalemate of Reason" (391)

> *While* poststructuralism has usefully pointed out the impossibil-ity of sovereign individuality, it has primarily done so through analyzing matrices of subject positions, through identifying how subject positions are differentially important in a writer's life and writing. —Julie Nelson Christoph, "Reconceiving *Ethos* in Relation to the Personal" (666)

Like *since*, *while* doesn't seem to cause a problem with ambiguity. It's often stylistically effective as a sentence or clause opener, and, in the hands of experienced writers, it usually means concession. But you might continue to bear in mind the alternatives: *although, even though,* and *even if.*

Summary

- ❖ It's okay to begin sentences with *because* when you want to show causal relationships.
- ❖ Consider sometimes showing cause with other words, such as *since* or *as a result.*
- ❖ Be aware of potential time/cause ambiguity when you use *since.*
- ❖ Published writers not only begin sentences with *because*, they also write *because* clause fragments.
- ❖ Writers begin sentences with *while* when they mean time, concession, or sometimes contrast.

❖ All of these words—*because, since, while*—have the potential of being ambiguous, so use them consciously. Also consider using alternatives: *because* instead of *since; when* or *at the same time* for time; *although* or *though* for contrast; and *even though, though, even if,* or *despite* for concession.

□ **Practice** □

1. Sentences sometimes end with a *because* clause instead of beginning with it, and the position may be interchangeable depending on context and style. Although an opening *because* clause is almost always set off with a comma, it may or may not be set off at the end of a sentence. To understand the effect of the comma in a sentence that ends with a *because* clause, first read the following sentence as it was written by William Manchester:

> Because he was an aristocrat, he was spared the garrote.
> —*A World Lit Only by Fire* (259)

Now read these two revised sentences:

a. He was spared the garrote, because he was an aristocrat.

b. He was spared the garrote because he was an aristocrat.

Which sentence, would you say, is closer to the original as you read it—the revision with the comma or the one without?

Manchester's sentence seems to focus on the fact that the person "was spared the garrote" (instead, he was decapitated, drawn, and quartered!). This also seems to be the meaning of revision *a*. But in revision *b*, the focus seems to be on *why* the man was "spared." The effect of the comma, then, is to place greater emphasis on the main clause, treating the *because* clause as a nonrestrictive, unessential, element. Omission of the comma tends to throw meaning forward onto the *because* clause, treating it as essential to the meaning of the sentence. Even so, revision *a* has an awkward sound, which leads one to prefer the sentence the way Manchester wrote it, beginning with the *because* clause.

2. For *while* in each of the following sentences, substitute *at the same time, although,* or *even if*. Then compare your sentences with these and consider possible ambiguities.

a. "But *while* the Turks were still strong enough to crush an open insurgency, they could not prevent new insurgents and propagandists from filtering into the area." —Kaplan (56)

b. "*While* American armed intervention had prevented the insurgents' victory, it had not brought closer their defeat."
—Tuchman, *The March of Folly* (332)

c. "*While* I could never be called fashionable by anyone in her right mind, at least my clothing was within the confines of the acceptable." —Carolyn G. Heilbrun, *The Last Gift of Time* (128)

d. "One elderly woman is taken from her house by a backhoe *while* surf breaks down her front door." —Sebastian Junger, *The Perfect Storm* (205)

16

Fragment Your Sentences

O ne of the most common strictures in handbooks of writing is "Avoid sentence fragments"—or as the famous Strunk and White put it in *The Elements of Style,* "Do not break sentences in two" (7). To be avoided, as they would have it, are statements like the following:

> Language is what preserved us. *Not because it does real damage to any other species, but because we can use it together.* —Lewis Thomas, *Et Cetera, Et Cetera* (106)

We could easily say that the first period of this statement has broken a sentence in two and that Thomas could (should?) have used a comma or a dash to link the second part. But he didn't use a comma or a dash. And because he didn't, he achieved greater emphasis on what he wanted to say about language. Incidentally, this is the type of fragment that is behind the nonrule about not beginning sentences with *because*: they might end up as fragments.

Why not write sentence fragments? An analysis of professional writing reveals that they are quite common. And if Russian psychologist Lev Vygotsky in *Thought in Language* correctly describes how our minds work, we think in fragments anyway (145). If a reader already knows and is thinking about the subject, why is it necessary to state it in writing? In the example above, Thomas has already placed in our minds his first statement about language so that we know exactly what he means in his *because* clauses. His period did not disconnect his ideas.

In the following example from *The New Meaning of Treason*, Rebecca West's idea is clear despite the fact that part of it is not stated in a complete sentence:

> William Joyce owed the Crown allegiance and was capable of committing treason against it. Again he was heading for conviction. *But not for certain.* (15)

West did not need to restate the subject, "heading for conviction," for you to understand what was "not for certain." You already knew it. She did not need a comma instead of the period, and with the period she emphasized her final statement.

Fragments for emphasis.   Fragments draw attention to themselves—exactly because they're fragments. They therefore make a more emphatic statement than if they were attached to a sentence. See what the Thomas and West fragments would look like if their writers had chosen more conventional punctuation:

> Language is what preserved us, not because it does real damage to any other species but because we can use it together.

> Again he was heading for conviction, but not for certain.

These are nice, clear sentences, but they're also pedestrian, unemphatic. Alfred Lansing writes this next sentence and fragment as a paragraph complete in itself:

> It was a chance, a freak. *A hard northerly gale—then quite cold.*
> —Lansing, *Endurance* (30)

Here the information added by the fragment actually clarifies meaning—in addition to gaining emphasis from the preceding period. Compare a connected sentence:

> It was a chance, a freak, a hard northerly gale—then quite cold.

In this revision, the three parallel items (*chance, freak, gale*) receive equal weight—with diminished emphatic effect.

We can find fragments not only in popular nonfiction but in scholarly journals as well. Here's an example from *College English*:

> First, we must believe they can write. *Fiction. Fact. Personal. Scholarly. The Works. And that these aspects of crafting prose are worth discussing and teaching to students.* —Wendy Bishop, "Suddenly Sexy: Creative Nonfiction Rear-ends Composition" 269

Bishop might have separated her five one-word fragments with commas and enclosed them with dashes, then completed the sentence with her *that* fragment, but she would have lost the emphasis that each word gains when followed by a period.

Fragments for transition.   Lansing's fragment serves also as a transition. The short transitional paragraph leads readers into an ensuing discussion of the change in weather. It's common for fragments to serve as transitions into new and related ideas—perhaps because the emphasis helps signal the change in topic. In the next two examples, taken from the beginning of paragraphs, Samuel Eliot Morison and Miles Harvey obviously indicate shifts:

> *Now for* Nina's *rig.* In the Genoa model and in every popular picture generally, she is represented as a three-masted lateener of the Portuguese type, the mainmast with the longest yard being almost amidships, and the other two aft. —Morison, *Admiral of the Ocean Sea* (109)

> *Not that the librarians themselves are likely to talk in such terms.*
> —Harvey, *The Island of Lost Maps* (114)

Both writers could have avoided the fragments, but both are clearly indicating a shift in topic.

<u>Which</u> fragments.   A familiar type of transitional fragment begins with *which*.

> *Which reminds me of the nice expression in the Chinese language meaning too much of a hurry:* Zouma guan-hua. *Zou* is to go or ride, *ma* is a horse, *guan* is looking at, *hua* is flowers. To be trying to observe flowers while galloping on horseback is to be sorry. —Thomas (91)

Because I've taken this fragment out of context, you have to assume that Thomas and his readers know what he means by *which*. In fact, the preceding paragraph ended with a discussion about being in a hurry, so this etymological example adds an interesting aside. David Remnick makes a similar use of the pronoun *this* in his transitional fragment:

> *Not that any of this would help Gorbachev.* He was despised by the communists, who regarded him as no better than the CIA; despised by the "great power" nationalists, who believed he was responsible for the humiliation of a great power and its army; and despised as well by liberal democrats, who felt he had never fully shed his allegiance to the nomenklatura that raised him. —*Resurrection* (7)

Remnick's summary phrase "any of this" refers to his long preceding paragraph, which addresses weaknesses in the opposition to Gorbachev's election campaign. Here's another *which* fragment, appropriate in its context:

> William Randolph Hearst's New York *Journal* sent a train too. It left first but arrived last. *Which peeved Hearst no end.* —Erik Larson, *Isaac's Storm* (273)

Larson's *which* fragment serves to emphasize Hearst's reaction to his train's late arrival in Galveston.

Fragments for response.   Some transitional fragments have an additional function: as rejoinders to what went before. They complete or respond to ideas. Here are two examples from Jay Winik's *April 1865*. In the first, the sentence and fragment occur as separate stand-alone paragraphs. In the second, which refers to the construction of Jefferson's Monticello on an unoccupied hill, I've given the last sentence of the preceding paragraph to show how the fragment completes the idea.

> And it would not be long before the next blush of crisis. *Thirteen years to be exact.* (18)

> But above this barbarous bank, could it be done? Would it be done? *Not easily.* Problems plagued every phase of construction. (4)

As in Winik's second excerpt, replies to questions are often fragments (because the subject is known), and in such cases even handbook restrictions are lifted. In another example, Jay Winik has a short, inverted sentence followed by two fragments, all in rejoinder to a previous paragraph describing visitors to Jefferson's Monticello:

> And come they did. *Even in the Civil War. Even on the eve of April 1865.* (25)

Notice how the emphasis builds with each fragment. Daniel J. Boorstin in *Cleopatra's Nose* uses a *which* fragment to add information to a previous sentence:

> While there are, of course, traditions and styles and schools in the arts, every act of creation is a kind of personal declaration of independence. *Which makes the story of art infinitely more confused and confusing than the story of science.* (25)

Fragments also serve as appositives to add information:

> In a sense, therefore, extraordinary man though he was, Socrates yet holds up the mirror to his own age. *A civilized age, where the really important matters were not those touched, tasted, or handled, an age whose leaders were marked by a devotion to learning and finding out the truth, and an age able to do and dare and endure, still capable of an approach to the heroic deeds of a past only a few years distant.* —Edith Hamilton, *The Greek Way* (106)

With repetition to hold it all together, Hamilton's long fragment expands on her statement about the age of Socrates.

From the foregoing examples of sentence fragments, we can make two assumptions: A fragment is acceptable (1) if it can be attached to a sentence with conventional punctuation to complete an idea or (2) if it expresses a complete idea itself. Fragments for emphasis and response seem to fit the first category; see the West, Lansing, Larson, and Winik examples. Fragments for transition seem to be complete in themselves; see the Morison, Harvey, and Thomas examples. The following fragment would not be acceptable, then, because it meets neither criterion:

> Under current accounting standards, billions of dollars of derivative transactions not reported in financial statements and investors at risk because they lack important information about prospective investments.

This fragment neither makes a complete statement nor could attach to a sentence to make a statement. It leaves a reader confused.

As another example, consider Hamilton's tightly coherent long fragment. Suppose her introductory sentence had read: "In a sense, therefore, extraordinary man though he was, Socrates yet holds up a mirror." Without the inclusion of her reference "to his own age," the repetition of *age* in the fragment would not have anything to tie into.

The fragment would not meet criterion 1, much less criterion 2. Fragments need a contextual connection to a sentence.

Two very long fragments. We often think of sentence fragments ("detached parts") as being short. But that's not necessarily the case; fragments can be very long:

> The First World War was a tragic and unnecessary conflict. *Unnecessary because the train of events that led to its outbreak might have been broken at any point during the five weeks of crisis that preceded the first clash of arms, had prudence or common goodwill found a voice; tragic because the consequences of the first clash ended the lives of ten million human beings, tortured the emotional lives of millions more, destroyed the benevolent and optimistic culture of the European continent and left, when the guns at last fell silent four years later, a legacy of political rancour and racial hatred so intense that no explanation of the causes of the Second World War can stand without reference to those roots.* —John Keegan, *The First World War* (3)

This fragment works because the words "Unnecessary" and "tragic" connect to the sentence.

Sometimes we find a series of fragments, all punctuated with periods, as in this excerpt from Remnick's *Resurrection*:

> In the years after his fall, Mikhail Gorbachev would leave his dacha outside Moscow, fold himself into the backseat of a Volga sedan, and, on the way downtown to his office, survey the contours of the new Russian world. *Billboards and beggars. Strip joints and traffic jams. A small fascist parade. Neon brightness and construction everywhere: a quarter-billion-dollar cathedral rising on the Moscow River embankment, an underground shopping mall burrowing in outside the gates of the Kremlin.* (3)

This descriptive list of items in Gorbachev's line of vision could just as well have followed a colon and been separated by commas, but the stops provided by the periods give each item a glance of its own, so to speak, through the window of the Russian sedan.

Finally, John McPhee uses a collection of fragments and sentences in the midst of a discussion about locating a state capital in Alaska:

> *A simple task. In Indiana.* Corydon was the capital of Indiana until a new-capital-site-selection committee drew a state-size X

on the map and noted where the legs crossed. The spot was in deep forest. Indians owned the land. A treaty took care of them. *Indianapolis, Indiana.* —*Coming into the Country* (102–03)

McPhee engages in a bit of satire regarding the way political decisions are made: draw a big X, move out the Indians, then name the place after them.

Summary

In your reading, you've probably noticed fragments before, even in published writing. Nearly every writer, at one time or another, employs sentence fragments to tell his or her story. As I've said, I limited these examples to published nonfiction because we all know that fiction writers have free access to "poetic license" and can break any rule they want to. But here are writers of books on Greek culture, current Russian history, etymology, medieval European history, adventure and exploration, the American Civil War, and more—all of them relying on sentence fragments as part of their writing style.

The kind of fragment they do *not* use is the incomplete idea. This is the kind of fragment written by inexperienced writers; it is unintentional and requires a reader to work out the meaning. It is the kind of fragment that causes writing teachers and writing handbooks to warn against writing all fragments. Fragments of this type are not just sentences broken in two; they're undeveloped, unexplained, and unconnected ideas. And they should definitely be avoided.

But for mature writers who want to be different and add sentence fragments to their style, what are the guidelines? It takes very few, and all of them imply that you are doing it intentionally:

- ❖ Know what you want to say. Fuzzy ideas become fuzzy fragments.
- ❖ Do it for emphasis. A period following a complete sentence gives the reader a full stop before going forward—headlong into the fragment. This stop plus the fragment attracts reader attention to what you're saying.
- ❖ Do it for transition. For the same reason a fragment works for emphasis, it works for transition. It wakes the reader up.
- ❖ Do it for response. Fragments answer questions and add information.

- ❖ Do it to eliminate unnecessary words. By focusing on the important words, you emphasize what you mean to say. Readers always appreciate brevity.
- ❖ Do it just for fun. To knowingly break a rule, to actually write a sentence fragment is, for an uptight writer, an exhilarating experience.

Enough said.

☐ **Practice** ☐

Lewis Thomas occasionally uses sentence fragments as a way of expressing what he means to say. In the following paragraph from *Et Cetera, Et Cetera*, he comments on a preceding paragraph about the etymological roots of the word *desire* and related words.

> Thus our *desire*, wanting [something special] badly, even being tormented by the wanting, but always at risk of meeting the wrong pattern in the sky, the wrong stars. *Desiring* something is not just sitting around, hoping for it to drop in one's lap; the word implies effort, concentration, hard work, worry. Plus the layout in the sky. Plus fingers crossed. (31)

Identify the three fragments. Do they meet criterion 1, criterion 2, or neither? Revise the paragraph so as to avoid the fragments. Ask yourself—

- ❖ What did you need to do to eliminate the fragments? Was it just a matter of changing the punctuation?
- ❖ Does your revision improve the style? How does it alter the style?
- ❖ Do you think that Thomas was right in using the fragments?

17

Splice with Commas

*I*f there's anything the rule books denounce more than sentence fragments it's comma splices. As Strunk and White state the problem: "Do not join independent clauses with a comma" (5). So the following sentence by Edith Hamilton would be wrong:

> His words must be quoted, they are so characteristically Greek.
> —*The Greek Way* (30)

And this one by Rebecca West:

> Others have faded away, nobody now can remember quite how or when. —The New Meaning of Treason (240)

And this one by Lewis Thomas:

> Dolphins make sounds that seem to be messages beyond our comprehension, whales sing deep mysterious songs to each other across undersea miles. —*Et Cetera, Et Cetera* (93)

Hamilton, West, and Thomas apparently had reasons for deciding on commas rather than a more acceptable choice: semicolons, periods, colons, even dashes.

Comma splices for balance. Each of these more acceptable marks, however, would draw attention to itself in a way that the comma does not. A colon in Hamilton's sentence would say that the next clause explains the first one. A dash in West's sentence would shift more emphasis to the second clause than perhaps she wanted. A semicolon in Thomas's sentence? Could work, but it would effect a greater separation than Thomas gains with the comma. The fact is that any punctuation other than the comma would have upset the fine balance that these writers have established in their two clauses. Even a period between the clauses would have made a very different kind of statement, weakening the balance by separating the parts.

Notice that in each preceding case the second clause begins directly with its subject and verb, so there is no chance of a misreading. The same thing happens in the following examples:

> The roof bristles with lightning rods, the weathercock is proud with new gilt. —Aldo Leopold, *A Sand County Almanac* (119)

> To the Greeks the outside world was real and something more, it was interesting. —Hamilton (26)

> It's too far, they die trying. —Sebastian Junger, *The Perfect Storm* (141)

These writers could have put other punctuation between their clauses, but they didn't. They made the stylistic choice to use commas. They also could have added a conjunction after their commas—perhaps a *so* for Junger, an *and* for Leopold. How conscious their choices were we don't know. At the same time, we *do* know that they "spliced" with commas.

The preceding examples have shown sentences made up of two independent clauses with a splicing that does not really impose difficulty of comprehension on the reader. So let's go a step further: the following sentences have three independent clauses, all spliced with commas.

> Brinksmanship was his contribution, counter-offensive rather than containment was his policy, "a passion to control events" was his motor. —Barbara Tuchman, *The March of Folly* (252)

> It is the essence of having lived long, it is the unstated assurance that most disasters pass, it is the survival of deprivation and death and rejection that renders our sympathy or value. —Carolyn G. Heilbrun, *The Last Gift of Time* (163)

These writers use tight parallel construction to establish balance, rhythm, and emphasis—Tuchman to criticize John Foster Dulles as secretary of state, Heilbrun to answer a question regarding a state of mind the elderly can share with the young.

The right and wrong of comma splices. All the preceding examples have two features in common: the second clause begins with its subject and verb, and that clause has no internal commas. The next two sentences illustrate why this absence of commas has to be so. Like the last two examples, these sentences have three independent clauses, though only two of them are spliced. Notice how the writers use commas and other punctuation:

> The retreat of the wilderness under the barrage of motorized tourists is no local thing; Hudson Bay, Alaska, Mexico, South Africa are giving way, South America and Siberia are next. —Leopold (166)

> But adults are supposed to know better, they are assumed to be able to control their impulses—that is, I suppose, what makes them fit to be called *adults*. —Elizabeth Wurtzel, *Bitch: In Praise of Difficult Women* (122)

In Leopold's sentence, the second clause (beginning "Hudson Bay") has internal punctuation, so it is preceded by a semicolon after *thing*. But his third clause, beginning "South America," has no internal commas and is separated from the previous clause by a comma. Wurtzel's second clause has no internal commas, but her last one does and is set off with a dash.

Having now examined several instances of comma splices that pose no problems for readers, we can make two assumptions: (1) the clause following the comma begins with its subject and verb, and (2) that clause has no internal commas. The following sentence, a rewording of one of Aldo Leopold's comma splices, illustrates a violation of assumption 1:

> The roof bristles with lightning rods, proud with new gilt is the weathercock.

This comma splice lacks clarity because word order is reversed in the second clause. The phrase "proud with new gilt" at first seems to modify "lightning rods."

To illustrate assumption 2, I've rewritten Elizabeth Wurtzel's sentence to replace her dash with a comma. Notice the problem caused by the internal commas of the third clause:

> But adults are supposed to know better, they are assumed to be able to control their impulses, that is, I suppose, what makes them fit to be called adults.

Even though we might be willing to accept the first comma splice (after *better*), we are confused at the second one, not knowing how to read "that is" and "I suppose." Leopold's second sentence, the one that began "The retreat of the wilderness," would have caused the same problem if, instead of the semicolon after *thing*, he had written a comma—as follows:

> The retreat of the wilderness under the barrage of motorized tourists is no local thing, Hudson Bay, Alaska, Mexico, South Africa are giving way, South America and Siberia are next.

Here's another illustration of the problem, this type quite common:

> The ancient Greeks pretended to retreat from Troy, *however,* they left a gift of a wooden horse.

This sentence is ambiguous because a reader doesn't know whether the transitional adverb *however* modifies the first clause or the second. The problem results because *however* is usually followed by a comma. But that problem does not exist in this next sentence, in which Barbara G. Walker introduces her second clause with the transitional *therefore*—without ambiguity:

> They said also that the Goddess rules all cycles, *therefore* the second part of each cycle is no less sacred or important than the first.
>
> —*The Crone* (72)

Unlike *however, therefore* is often not followed by a comma. (I think that *however* is the only transitional adverb for which clarity usually requires a comma, although most of these words, such as *moreover, nevertheless, then, similarly, in fact, in addition,* are at times set off for clarity or rhythm.) A semicolon is needed when any phrase or clause introduces a second independent clause and is set off with a comma:

> At the least, this legislation would seek to contain the lower Mississippi; *at the least,* it would be the most ambitious and expensive

single piece of legislation Congress had ever passed. —John M. Barry, *Rising Tide* (399)

Had Barry omitted the commas after "at the least," he might have separated the clauses with a comma after "Mississippi."

Here's one more example of the ambiguous comma splice:

It's hard to decide how each ad could better catch the reader's attention, *after all*, both ads caught my attention.

With a comma after "attention," the *after all* phrase could be read with either the first statement or the second. Often the problem with comma splices is not the comma but something else in the sentence—the inserted *after all* or *however*, for instance, that causes a reader to stumble. Sometimes it's an ambiguity elsewhere, perhaps with a pronoun, as in this sentence:

Just keep working on the lesson you have already taught your dog, *it* apparently needs more solidifying.

The problem here is not the comma but the unclear pronoun. If the writer had written "the lesson" instead of "it," you might simply have read the sentence and not been aware of the comma splice.

Summary

We can conclude that there can be some problems when we separate independent clauses with commas. But used consciously and intentionally, with a sensitivity to possible ambiguity, comma splices can aid a writer in establishing rhythm and relationships among ideas.

❖ If the second independent clause in your sentence begins with its subject and verb, you may be able to separate it with only a comma.

❖ But do not separate the two clauses with a comma if the second clause has internal commas.

❖ If your second clause includes *however* or another introductory word, phrase, or clause, separate the clauses with a semicolon or a period.

❖ Make sure you don't have any ambiguous words in your comma-spliced sentences.

❖ Omit a coordinating conjunction (*and, but, so, or, nor, for, yet*) after a comma between independent clauses only if the connection is clear without it.

❖ Splice parallel clauses with a comma when other punctuation provides more separation than you want.

□ **Practice** □

Revise these sentences so as to avoid comma splices. Use semicolons, dashes, periods, colons, or the addition of *and*. Try revising in more than one way.

1. "He was not only alarming, he was ugly." —West (3)

2. "Others have faded away, nobody now can remember quite how or when." —West (240)

3. "Dolphins make sounds that seem to be messages beyond our comprehension, whales sing deep mysterious songs to each other across undersea miles." —Thomas (93)

3. "The retreat of the wilderness under the barrage of motorized tourists is no local thing; Hudson Bay, Alaska, Mexico, South Africa are giving way, South America and Siberia are next."
—Leopold (166)

4. "It is the essence of having lived long, it is the unstated assurance that most disasters pass, it is the survival of deprivation and death and rejection that renders our sympathy or value."
—Heilbrun (163)

Review your revisions and answer the following questions:

a. Does your revision improve the clarity of the sentence?

b. Does it have any effect on the balance within the sentence?

c. Does it make any difference to emphasis and rhythm?

d. Which do you prefer—your revision or the original?

18

Refer with a Singular they

The proscription against using the pronoun *they* in a singular sense is not a real rule, but many people believe it is. And many books about writing treat it that way: Use the pronouns *they, them, their,* and *themselves* only in a plural sense, they say.

It's "the law." It's also true that the "rule" is a bit more than lore, given the British Parliament's decree in 1850 that the singular masculine pronoun *he* would serve in all cases where gender is neutral or unknown. So, any time a writer used nouns like *person, writer, driver,* and *supervisor,* indefinite pronouns like *everyone, no one,* and *somebody,* and indefinite adjectives like *every, each,* and *any*—the referring pronouns had to be *he, him, his,* or *himself.*

Why should it be necessary for a legislative body to make rules about grammar? Actually the law had only limited compliance, because *they* in a singular sense has such a long history that uprooting it was not easy. In fact, the scholarly and historical *Oxford English Dictionary,* first published in 1888, includes the following definition under its entry for *they*:

> Often used in reference to a singular noun made universal by *any, every, no,* etc., or applicable to one of either sex (= 'he or she'). (*Compact Edition*)

The *OED* goes on to quote examples:

> He never forsaketh any creature unless *they* before have forsaken themselves.
>
> ■ Year: 1535
>
> If a person is born of a gloomy temper, *they* cannot help it.
>
> ■ Year: 1759
>
> Now, nobody does anything well that *they* cannot help doing.
>
> ■ Year: 1866

It's logic. The rule was simply made up—on the basis of logic rather than usage. The argument goes like this: "The pronoun *they* can't be both singular and plural; it's obviously plural, so it can't be singular." This argument not only overlooks the history of *they* usage, it also overlooks the historical and current acceptability of another pronoun, *you,* that has both singular and plural senses:

> How many of *you* have ever seen a solar eclipse?
>
> ■ Plural
>
> Brenda, have *you* ever seen a solar eclipse?
>
> ■ Singular

The logicians would respond, "Then I suppose we would use singular verbs with *they* (*they is, they has*) when we mean singular? Otherwise how could others tell whether we mean singular or plural?" The reply of course is obvious: We no more use singular verbs with singular *they* than we do with singular *you.* Whether we mean one or many, we say *they are* and *they have* just as we say *you are* and *you have.* And we know the difference by context.

He is not gender-neutral anymore. The singular *they* has experienced a resurgence of interest in recent decades because of efforts moving toward gender-neutral language. In cases where the gender of a singular **antecedent** is unspecified or unknown, the masculine pronouns *he, him,* and *his* are read by more and more readers as being masculine. In fact, legislatures (yes, the law again) and publishing houses have prohibited gender-specific pronouns referring to gender-neutral antecedents in their publications.

On a historical note, I searched two issues of the English professional journal *College Composition and Communication* (a publication of National Council of Teachers of English) for pronoun usage in a generic sense. In the May 1970 issue, nearly every writer used generic nouns in the singular, referenced by masculine pronouns: "The *teacher* in this model has as *his* primary goal . . . ," "The *student* of language, once introduced to Bamboo English, can gain valuable insights as to the contemporary and historical workings of *his* native tongue," "If a *writer* is not intent on using marks to evoke speech associations in *his* reader. . . ." In the December 1978 issue, however, after the journal began requiring compliance with "the NCTE *Guidelines for Non-sexist Use of Language*," writers of articles mostly used the plural: "When *students* begin to learn to write in earnest . . . , *they* may do little more . . . ," "*Students'* reliance on the 'honest face' ethos leads *them*. . . ." One writer used singular "the student" and "he or she." Another wrote about "the writer" and avoided pronouns: "The more *a writer* knows about the subject, the more *the writer* begins to feel about *the* subject."

It's a fact that usage has changed. What was acceptable to general readers forty years ago is no longer read the same way. So what can you do? Handbooks of writing have several suggestions:

1. Use plural. Instead of "The reader of mystery novels knows *their* bookstore well," say "Readers of mystery novels know *their* bookstores well." Instead of "Everyone who reads mystery novels knows *their* bookstore well," say "All the readers of mystery novels know *their* bookstores well." This advice works in cases where the writer is referring to general situations; "the reader" is any reader—actually *"all* readers." But I'm reluctant to advise that we avoid using these indefinite pronouns that convention tells us are singular (such as *everyone* and *anybody*), because by doing so we could risk losing them entirely. That would be an unfortunate loss.

2. Avoid the pronoun altogether. Say "The reader of mystery novels knows *the* bookstore well." Or "The reader of mystery novels knows bookstores well." Notice that meaning has changed with these revisions. With *everyone* you could say "Everyone who reads mystery novels knows a bookstore well."

3. Use *he or she* if you can do so without being too repetitious: "The reader of mystery novels knows *his or her* bookstore well." This option works well when you want to call attention to the

fact that people of both genders are included, not in the general sense that you don't know the gender.

4. Use invented words like *he/she* or even *s/he*. I don't recommend any of these—because, frankly, I don't like them. I don't see any reason to replace a perfectly good word, *they,* with an invented substitute.

We already have a perfectly good word, they. There's still another option, the one we might consider as the first one: Use *they* in a singular sense: "The reader of mystery novels knows *their* bookstore well." We wouldn't even have this problem if singular *they* hadn't been outlawed. As the *OED* examples show, it has had a long history as a generic pronoun, antedating any current restrictions. Among others, the nineteenth-century Scottish philosopher Alexander Bain ignored the English law:

> When both Genders are implied, it is allowable to use the Plural. . . . Grammarians frequently call this construction an error: not reflecting that it is equally an error to apply "his" to feminine subjects. The best writers furnish examples of the plural as a mode of getting out of the difficulty. —*A Higher English Grammar* (310)

Here are some of those "best writers":

> It's enough to drive anyone out of *their* senses. —George Bernard Shaw

> Everyone in the house were in *their* beds. —Henry Fielding

> A person can't help *their* birth. —William Thackeray

Though I must confess difficulty in finding currently published examples, the pronoun does continue to be used, and linguistic evidence shows it to be the generic pronoun of choice—in speech at least. Here's a published example I found recently, and, knowing the writer, I'd guess her use is intentional, not a slip:

> Still, he insisted that anyone claiming total objectivity on this politically charged topic was willfully blind to *their* own bias.
> —Elizabeth Rankin, *The Work of Writing* (70)

The next example is from a textbook I have employed in a graduate course:

> The letter constitutes an appeal from you for the respondent's help. If there are special reasons why *they* should help (for example, the

importance of the study for *their* profession) be sure to mention them. —Bruce W. Tuckman, *Conducting Educational Research* (242–43)

Without a doubt, the singular *they* is common in speech and in informal, uncopyedited publications such as government manuals and, perhaps ironically, academic bulletins:

> Everybody was allowed to express *themselves*. —*Dateline NBC*

> How does a client authorize someone to act on *their* behalf? —Minnesota Department of Human Services, *A New Financial Worker's Guide to the CAF II* (9)

> Petitions must be signed by the student and *their* academic advisor before the graduate office will act upon them. —*St. Cloud State University Graduate Bulletin* (13)

For these last three examples, I'm indebted to a master's thesis entitled "A Linguistic Study of the Third Person Generic Pronoun: Singular *They*," written by Philip Roger Anderson (1995).

The results of Anderson's research showed an overall acceptance of a written singular *they* by 41 percent of the people he surveyed (67). This might be a surprisingly high figure given all the proscriptions, but it also means that any given audience could fall into the other 59 percent.

Another somewhat encouraging sign is that the National Council of Teachers of English in a November 2002 position statement favored the use of this epicene ("neuter") pronoun in cases when the singular indefinite antecedent is clearly plural in meaning, as in sentences like these:

> When <u>everyone</u> contributes *their* own ideas, the discussion will be a success.

> Does <u>everybody</u> have *their* book? —*Guidelines for Gender-Fair Use of Language*

At the same time, the organization attached a caveat: "Be aware that state and/or national assessments may not regard this construction as correct." Neither do the NCTE publications, apparently. My survey of several of the latest NCTE journals turned up no incidence of *they* in a singular sense. Writers preferred plural nouns and pronouns or, when the noun was singular, pronoun avoidance. So you might still want to consider the handbook advice about knowing your readers before you jump in with a historically correct but currently disfavored usage.

Summary

❖ *They* (*them, their*) has long served as a singular pronoun when either or both genders are implied.

❖ Most people consider the singular *they* acceptable informally but not in formal, written usage.

❖ The rule against using *they* in a singular sense is based on logic rather than historical and current usage.

❖ But a singular *they* is no more illogical than a singular *you*.

❖ The masculine pronoun *he* (*him, his*) is no longer acceptable as a gender-neutral pronoun in published writing.

❖ Because of its long history as a singular pronoun, *they* makes sense as a substitute for the masculine pronoun *he* when gender is unknown.

❖ But a writer still needs to consider their audience before using *they* in a singular sense.

You can read more about generic pronouns in chapter 34, "Make Your Pronouns Agree."

□ **Practice** □

Because of decisions by publishing houses on gender-neutral language, readers are becoming accustomed to seeing the singular masculine pronoun used only in a specific, masculine sense. So when they read something published earlier than the last few decades and encounter the masculine pronouns, many readers fail to think as the writer perhaps did, generically. *The American Heritage College Dictionary,* in a long note under *he*, comments that this "linguistically doubtful" generic usage "may be viewed as deliberately calling attention to traditional gender roles or may simply appear to be insensitive" (637). This pattern of thought is still changing and requires publishing writers to avoid using *he* to mean *she*.

Here are three examples from earlier publications, each using masculine pronouns when female members might have been involved in the descriptions. Consider your reactions and think about possible revisions.

1. "It will be granted, I suppose, that there would be no need for certainty about the plan and government of the universe if, as a matter of course, all our desires were regularly fulfilled. In a world where no man desired what he could not have, there would be

no need to regulate human conduct and therefore no need for morality. In a world where each man could have what he desired, there would be no need for consolation and for reassuring guarantees that justice, mercy, and love will ultimately prevail."

—Walter Lippmann, *A Preface to Morals* (135) [Published in 1929.]

2.   "The child who discovers that he loves reading adventure stories will read any and all adventure stories that come to hand. He will coax them from friends, exhaust the shelves that hold them at the public library, badger relatives for more of them as his birthday approaches. In his untamed passion, he will like all of them equally. He may be fond of asking companions who share his enthusiasm 'Which do you think is *best*?' as he rattles off the titles in various series, but he isn't truly trying to arrive at a judgment. He is simply smacking his lips over the full list of his enchantments, recapitulating for the pleasure of remembering."

—Walter Kerr, *The Decline of Pleasure* (279) [Published in 1962.]

3.   "The squirrel could not jump to any nearby branch. The ground lay without obstruction far below. The fox edged along the branch, the near-hypnotic fixity of his eyes inviting the squirrel to run back past him. But the squirrel met this unexpected crisis with a rarely used capability; he launched himself into mid-air, so high he looked like a falling bird, his body flat, his four legs spread out as widely as possible, his fluffy tail bushed to catch the uprushing air. He thumped soggily into grass and mud and bounced away into the forest." —Franklin Russell, *Watchers at the Pond* (93) [Published in 1961.]

19

Say I (we, you)

Pronouns can be described according to whether they refer to the speaker(s) (*I, me, we, us*—first **person**), the person(s) spoken to (*you*—second person), or the person(s) or thing(s) spoken about (*he, him, she, her, it, they, them*—third person). On the chance that they might draw attention away from the subject, first- and second-person pronouns are frowned upon in school writing: "Don't say *I*" and "Don't say *you*." In published writing—both nonfiction and scholarly journals—some writers observe these rules and some don't.

Saying I.   I've gathered examples from a variety of writers who clearly want to include themselves in their writing:

> Reading about this debacle a few weeks before the New York auction, *I* had naturally wondered about the provenance of the Sotheby's *Geographia. I* checked the auction catalog. —Miles Harvey, *The Island of Lost Maps* (74)

> *I* don't want to get sidetracked here into the difference between the philosophical and scientific points of view—a difference perhaps more apparent than real and certainly in itself a product of the modern mind. —Marston Bates, *The Forest and the Sea* (29)

146

It must be recognized, however, that no permanent solution to the problem has been worked out, and *I* doubt very much that it can be. From time to time it is suggested that the Vice-President be converted into the President's top executive assistant—*I* once made such a proposal *myself*, which *I* hereby recant—but the road to this revolution would, *I* feel sure, prove rocky and dangerous.
—Clinton Rossiter, *The American Presidency* (149)

It would require a larger volume than this to follow Vignaud and his successors point by point, and *I* am as eager as *I* hope the reader is to leave this stagnant harbor of idle speculation and get out into blue water. —Samuel Eliot Morison, *Admiral of the Ocean Sea* (51)

Let *me* take one specific example that, it seems to *me*, falls conspicuously under Smith's diagnosis of circular reasoning. —Jeffery L. Geller, "The Stalemate of Reason" (383) [From the scholarly journal *Philosophy and Rhetoric*]

I argue that the books used by Shine and Roser (1999) are not information books per se but a subcategory of information books that may be identified as narrative-informational books. —Cathy Tower, "The Power of Text Characteristics" (57) [From the scholarly journal *Research in the Teaching of English*]

Not only are these writers so in control of their subjects that they permit themselves to comment on them, it seems that the personal comments establish a closer relationship with readers, as in fact Morison openly acknowledges.

In the next examples, the writers become even more involved with their subjects:

Ascending Everest is a long, tedious process, more like a mammoth construction project than climbing as *I'*d previously known it.
—Jon Krakauer, *Into Thin Air* (73)

I am touched by the same emotion in the churches of Vienna where severe stone tablets recall the sacrifice of historic Habsburg regiments now almost forgotten to history. —John Keegan, *The First World War* (5)

As long as *I* can remember, *I've* had an excellent sense of direction. But, though *I* will never fully understand it, *I* suspect *my* boyhood adventures as the Human Compass had a lot more to do with cartography than with clairvoyance. —Harvey (36–37)

> With funding from the Spencer Foundation, *I* have had the opportunity over several years to study the writing assessments of five states (Illinois, Kentucky, New York, Oregon, and Texas) in considerable detail. —George Hillocks Jr., "Fighting Back: Assessing the Assessments" (63)

What you'll notice when reading published writing is that, though writers use the pronoun *I* when they need it, they generally avoid phrases like "I think" and "I believe" to announce their statements. Krakauer and Harvey are here narrating their experiences, so their use of *I* is without question appropriate. Keegan and Harvey could have avoided it if they had so chosen, although their insertion of themselves into their stories does not seem out of place. Hillocks, writing to teacher-readers of *English Journal,* uses the first-person pronoun to establish his authority on the subject of school assessments.

Incidentally, it's not necessary any more to say *shall* to express the future with *I* or *we* unless you want to use it for making a promise or expressing determination.

Saying we. The pronoun *we* (*us, our*) can present problems that *I* doesn't. Whereas *I* refers clearly to the writer, *we* implies the writer and someone else. Unless that someone else is clear to the reader, the singular *I* might actually be better. Here are some examples to illustrate the potential problem:

> *We* are just beginning to understand *our* universe a little, and would hardly wish to abandon the effort, to return to the darkness of simplistic anthropomorphized pseudoexplanations for external phenomena. —Barbara G. Walker, *The Crone* (39)

> What *we* have is an immensely long and superfluously detailed account of virtually every message, meeting, journey, negotiation, and conversation in the fifty months from Kissinger's appointment in November 1968 to the signing of peace with North Vietnam at the end of President Nixon's first term in January 1973.
> —Barbara Tuchman, *Practicing History* (219)

> *We* now all live in a state of suspended nuclear annihilation; *our* destruction can be brought about within a mere 30 minutes after any nuclear-capable adversary decides to make *us* a target. —Jack J. Kraushaar and Robert A. Ristinen, *Energy and Problems of a Technical Society* (454)

In the next sections, *we* shall examine fossil fuel resources other than the conventional resources discussed above. —Kraushaar and Ristinen (59)

In the first example, Walker's *we* seems to refer to all humanity, but Tuchman's may be limited to Americans or even more particularized to American historians. Kraushaar and Ristinen's are more widely differentiated, their first meaning probably all living creatures on earth, the second the writers and their readers. What they avoided was the use of *we* in both the general and the particular senses in close proximity—in other words, not like this:

We now all live in a state of nuclear annihilation, a problem *we* shall examine in the next section.

Here's one more example, this one from an academic paper published in *College English*:

We need to look broadly at many kinds of texts written in many kinds of contexts in order to respond to these questions and better understand the personal. —Julie Nelson Christoph, "Reconceiving *Ethos* in Relation to the Personal" (662)

Like Kraushaar and Ristinen's second example, Christoph's *we* seems to mean writer and reader together, a research community interested in investigating rhetorical contexts. Reports of research and other organizational or technical writing will often use *we* in this inclusive sense.

Saying you.   The variable meaning of *we* is only a *potential* problem, though one writers need to be aware of. The inattentive use of the second-person *you* also has the potential of ambiguity. One might wonder, for example, who is being referred to in this sentence:

The more *you* go out, the more likely *you* are never to come back.
—Sebastian Junger, *The Perfect Storm* (70)

Since I'm not likely ever to go to sea on a swordfishing boat, I seriously doubt if Junger means me personally. But he probably does want me and all his other readers to *imagine* ourselves out there. He is using *you* not in its personal sense but in its indefinite, generalizing sense—as in "*You* [meaning "anyone"] can lead a horse to water but *you* can't make it drink." Given Junger's conversational style, the usage is appropriate.

In the next example, Peter L. Bernstein employs the pronoun in a more directly personal sense:

> Suppose a stranger invites *you* to bet on coin-tossing. She assures *you* that the coin she hands *you* can be trusted. How do *you* know whether she is telling the truth? *You* decide to test the coin by tossing it ten times before *you* agree to play. —*Against the Gods* (207)

Bernstein here, with the imperative verb *suppose* and the direct pronoun *you*, invites the reader to participate in his explanation of risk. In the following example, the *you* and the imperative verb again actively involve the reader:

> But make no mistake: Mr. Atlas is obsessed. If *you* couldn't figure that out from his shirt (which, he complained, was not an accurate reproduction of any specific map but a "cobbled together" representation of "Cook's voyages to the South Pacific—though I've got lots of others"), *you* might have guessed it from the portraits hanging in the front hall. —Harvey (243–44)

Harvey not only puts the reader with him in Mr. Atlas's home but also, with the direct address of the imperative verb *make*, tries to adjust the reader's thinking about what he has been saying about Mr. Atlas. (You can find other examples of the indefinite *you* in chapter 33, "Be Sure Your Pronouns Refer to Something.")

Summary

What these rules regarding *I, we*, and *you* come down to is that the pronouns are acceptable usage as long as a writer uses them attentively.

- ❖ Say *I* when it won't detract from your subject.
- ❖ Say *I* when you are personally involved in your subject, as in a narrative or a report of research you have carried out.
- ❖ Say *I* for personal commentary.
- ❖ Except rarely, avoid phrases like *I think*.
- ❖ The pronoun *I* has gained acceptance in many academic and scientific journals.
- ❖ Say *we* when your reader knows who you mean, especially in a community sense for reports and other professional writing.
- ❖ Say *we* or *you* to include your reader in the development of your subject.

❖ Avoid using *we* in both a general and a particular sense in close proximity.

❖ Avoid using *you* in an indefinite sense unless you've established a conversational tone.

To read more about pronouns, see chapter 35, "Just in Case—Pronouns Again."

□ **Practice** □

First-person pronouns are not restricted to personal narratives, comments, and diaries. They're common in a wide variety of writing. The following three excerpts come from professional journals written and edited by college writing teachers. Read the excerpts for their pronoun usages and consider these questions:

❖ What do you understand these writers to mean by the pronouns *I, we* (*us, our*)?

❖ Are the meanings clear or ambiguous?

❖ Would you want to revise any pronouns to read in some other way?

❖ What is your conclusion about advice to avoid first-person pronouns?

1.   "*We* teach writing for many reasons, but if one goal is to prepare students to write effectively once they leave college, *we* should consider nonacademics' responses to error. *Our* effectiveness, perhaps *our* ethos, can be impeded if *we* stress matters that other professionals see as trivial—or if *we* trivialize points they deem consequential. This is not to say that teachers must always mirror other people's responses to error, but *we* at the very least need to know if the messages *we* send students will be reinforced or negated by how other professionals read errors. . . .

"To study this interpretative process at the level of the individual reader and to explore the variety of elements constituting a person's reaction to error, *I* examined how fourteen business people responded to errors. That is, *I* focused on a few individuals so that *I* might investigate a highly individualistic process."

—Larry Beason, "Ethos and Error" (34, 35)

2.   "Almost universally, current language scholars object that language is fundamentally indirect, imprecise, contingent, and unstable; thus, *we* never transmit a perfect representation of the 'external' world through a secure pipeline leading from giver to receiver. In short, most of *us* have said that the Conduit Metaphor is wrong because language does not work the way the metaphor assumes. *I* want to argue the opposite point: Prevalent objections to the Conduit Metaphor are wrong because metaphors do not work the way the objections assume."
—Philip Eubanks, "Understanding Metaphors for Writing" (93)

3.   "As *we* offer some preliminary definitions of the emerging subdiscipline of *ecocomposition*, *we* also issue a call to English studies to embrace this vital new field of inquiry. In the pages that follow, *we* not only offer some preliminary working definitions for ecocomposition, but *we* also examine the evolution of ecocomposition, distinguish between ecocomposition and ecocriticism, and offer some perspectives on ecocomposition pedagogy. . . .

"Studying environmental rhetoric is a powerful pedagogical approach that serves a number of purposes: it raises student awareness of the ways people use language to construct knowledge and accomplish things in the world; it allows students to see that language is a powerful tool that influences *us* and, in turn, can be used to influence others; it enables them to better recognize ways in which different discourse communities structure the contents, forms, and rhetorical appeals of their language to better communicate with their intended audiences; it gives them powerful discursive tools that they can use in larger public spheres; and last but certainly not least, environmental rhetoric informs students of global issues that are among the most important in the world today. As *we* and *our* students struggle to make sense of the deluge of information surrounding environmental issues, analyzing environmental rhetoric provides a means to organize and clarify much of this information." —Sidney I. Dobrin and Christian R. Weisser, "Breaking Ground in Ecocomposition" (567, 580)

20

Contract Your Words

W riters are sometimes confused about whether contractions are acceptable in writing. The answer is, In most cases yes they are. Contractions, just to be clear, are two words written together with one or more letters omitted, the omission being marked by an apostrophe. The most common contractions are those made with pronouns and verbs (such as *she's, you're, we've, they'll, I'm, he'd, let's*), and those with verbs combined with *not* (such as *can't, won't, couldn't, wouldn't, aren't, isn't*). Less common are contracted nouns and verbs, as in *Wilson's late* for "Wilson is late" and *The committee's decided* for "The committee has decided." In addition, there are those two very common sentence openers *It's* and *There's*.

Contractions for informality. Contractions are generally avoided in the most formal writing. But as we'll see from a variety of examples, contractions are not limited to narrative, personal styles. Let's look first at some less formal examples:

> When I got sick, Charley took over the care of the goats, and, I guess, he just *wasn't* cut out to be a goatmaster—*no one's* perfect. Mom said that if Charley *hadn't* given Linda Lou all that green

fodder, she *wouldn't* have swelled up and died like that. —Edgar Allen Imhoff, *Always of Home* (55)

Ultimately, as flight engineer, *it's* his decision to deploy the swimmer, his job to get everyone safely back into the aircraft. If he has any doubts, Moore *doesn't* jump. —Sebastian Junger, *The Perfect Storm* (160)

Switched off in adulthood, *I'd* guess: *I'll* never in my life learn to speak French convincingly, having tried too late in life.
　　　　　　　　　　　　—Lewis Thomas, *Et Cetera, Et Cetera* (95)

These sentences illustrate contractions of *was not, no one is, had not, would not, it is, does not, I would,* and *I will.* The next examples are from less narrative, more informational sources:

Let's first look at divergencies, at some of the different designs that appear in this web of life. —Marston Bates, *The Forest and the Sea* (33)

Doesn't my little story illustrate a general case? —Stephen Jay Gould, *The Lying Stones of Marrakech* (222)

Problematically, Victoria *wasn't* sure Alice would quite do as the queen of the dour and overenthusiastically democratic Dutch, but discreet inquiries pending future action *couldn't,* in any case, go amiss. —Jerrold M. Packard, *Victoria's Daughters* (63)

I think *it's* safe to say we *don't* often ask ourselves such questions. And in our doctoral programs, where we socialize students into the research culture, we *don't* teach such questioning as a central step in the research process. —Julie E. Wollman-Bonilla, "Does Anybody Really Care?" (320) [In the professional journal *Research in the Teaching of English.*]

These sentences achieve a level of informality with their contractions of *let us, does not, was not, could not, will not, it is,* and *do not.* In contrast, consider the level of formality of this sentence from a physics textbook:

Unfortunately, we *cannot* rely on nature to clean up our air because of the rate at which *we are* fouling it. —Jack J. Kraushaar and Robert A. Ristinen, *Energy and Problems of a Technical Society* (393)

Because my random word search turned up no contractions in their book, I'm guessing that these writers intentionally avoided them. Do you think the formality of the sentence is affected by their choice to not contract *cannot* and *we are?*

Contractions for rhythm and emphasis. Writers make choices to contract and not to contract based not only on the desired level of formality but also on the rhythm and emphasis they want to achieve. Consider the following sentences, in which the writers contract one verb in their sentence and not the other. Read them aloud to see how their choices affect sentence rhythm:

> In short, Neanderthal *could have* spoken at length, if *he'd* known how to speak or what to say. —Thomas (106)

> *Here's* an article from a famed newsmagazine *that is* hard to match for fatigue. —William Zinsser, *On Writing Well* (35)

Emphasis can be affected too, especially with sentence-opening contractions that point to the subject of the sentence:

> *There's* a kind of writing that might be called journalese, and *it's* the death of freshness in anybody's style. —Zinsser (34)

> *It's* a fitting irony that under Richard Nixon "launder" became a dirty word. —Zinsser (47)

The introductory words *There* and *It* (plus *Here* in Zinsser's earlier sentence) are not the subjects of these sentences; rather, they serve as pointers to the delayed subjects ("a kind of writing," "a fitting irony," "an article"), thus altering both emphasis and rhythm. Notice that these introductory contractions work mainly with singular subjects. (*There* might be combined with *have* in the contracted form *There've* as in "There've been several newsmagazines," but it's a bit awkward, and most writers would avoid it. And I can't remember having seen *There're* [*there are*] in writing.)

Note: If you're one of those people who confuse *it's* and *its*, stop using the contracted one—say *it is* instead—and then never use an apostrophe when you write *its*, because you're using the possessive pronoun. You'll always be right.

That odious contraction. There's one more contraction that we should bring up, despite the fact that you won't find it in published writing (except in quoted dialogue). This of course is the abominable *ain't*. It really is a type of contraction—for *am not*—and should be (and once was) acceptable in sentences such as this one:

> I'm right again, *ain't* I?

But this historically acceptable contraction has received such bad press that nobody dares use it. As a result we hear (and use?) the incorrect and illogical *aren't I* (would we ever say "are I not?"). So—use *ain't* with *I* if you dare, but avoid *ain't he, we ain't, you ain't, they ain't, John* (and other nouns) *ain't.*

Summary

Contractions are features of style—both written and spoken—that make our words seem less formal. Whether or not writers choose to use them is just one more stylistic choice. Here's a short summary:

- ❖ Contractions are commonly made with pronouns and verbs, and with verbs and *not*.
- ❖ Omitted letters are marked with an apostrophe.
- ❖ Contractions tend to make writing less formal, more conversational.
- ❖ Using contractions or not can affect sentence rhythm.
- ❖ Using contractions or not can affect sentence emphasis.
- ❖ Don't confuse the contracted *it's* with the possessive *its*.
- ❖ *Ain't* is a word, though much out of favor.

For a further discussion of apostrophes, see chapter 30, "Possess with Apostrophes."

□ **Practice** □

Read these paired sentences in light of formality, rhythm, and emphasis. Then consider the writers' decisions to contract or not to contract.

1.   "It *isn't* enough to say that any invidious comparisons and stereotypes lexicographers perpetuate are already present in the culture."

"Without apologies to Freud, the great majority of women *do not* wish in their hearts that they were men." —Casey Miller and Kate Swift, *Words and Women* (183, 191)

2.   "People who drive around in the pines and see houses like Fred Brown's, with tarpaper peeling from the walls, and automobiles overturned in the front yard, often decide, as they drive on,

that they have just looked destitution in the face. I *wouldn't* call it that."

"If Richard Harris, one of the brothers, happened to see a gate ajar, *he would* look up the resident of the house behind the gate and tell him to try, please not to be so unkempt." —John McPhee, *The Pine Barrens* (55, 39)

3.   "For the false taxonomy, we *don't* restrict adequate knowledge of music to professional players; so why do we limit understanding of science to those who live in laboratories, twirl dials, and publish papers?"

"I *do not*, of course, hold that most people have developed the highly technical skills that lead to professional competence in science." —Gould (223)

21

Split Your Infinitives

Many people don't even know what an infinitive is, much less how to split one. So it's appropriate, I think, for us to begin with definitions. The following sentence has four infinitives, italicized:

> The only way *to learn to write* is *to force* yourself *to produce* a certain number of words on a regular basis. —William Zinsser, *On Writing Well* (49)

An infinitive, as you see, is a verb form introduced by *to*. With four of them in one sentence you could think they're a very common sentence element, and you'd be right. Now, if Zinsser had inserted a *really* or a *somehow* between *to* and *force*, he would have made a *split* infinitive: "to somehow force."

A *dearth of splits.* But he didn't split. The fact is that, contrary to most other rule-breaking advice in this book, most writers don't split their infinitives. Believe me, I've searched, and I've come up with only this one in a search of published nonfiction books:

> Nor did he [Jefferson Davis] successfully subdue the hue and cry of Confederate politicians to go on the offensive, *to aggressively bring* the war to the Yankees, even though it often meant that

such bloody victories would ultimately be Pyrrhic ones. —Jay Winik, *April 1865* (331)

I suppose Winik might be horrified to know that in all my searching the only split infinitive I could find was in his book. On the other hand, he may well have written it intentionally. Even the handbooks allow a little leeway for avoiding awkwardness. Think about it: where else would Winik have placed *aggressively* so it clearly modified *to bring*? Possibly after *Yankees*—but would it have been better there?

Winik, of course, was writing for a general audience, one that would probably never notice his split infinitive (and would more likely notice the awkward phrasing if he *hadn't* split it). What about the academic audience? A further search, this one in academic journals, uncovered examples such as these:

To ask the question this way is *to immediately see* how it is usually deflected into professional and disciplinary terms. —Joseph Harris, "Meet the New Boss, Same as the Old Boss (46) [In *College Composition and Communication*.]

Arguing that the field had yet *to sufficiently explore* its theoretical underpinnings, Faigley (1955) identifies three theoretical per-spectives—the textual, the individual, and the social—that have influenced the ways researchers have examined writing and that can help describe the distinguishing features of writing across settings. —Martin Nystrand, Stuart Green, and Jeffrey Wiemelt, "Where Did Composition Studies Come From?" (268) [In *Written Communication*.]

Harris could have said "to see immediately" without changing his mean-ing much, and the joint authors of the second example could have said "to explore sufficiently," though this would have made their sentence awkward and less clear. These sentences tell you that at least some writ-ing teachers recognize the need to occasionally split infinitives.

To split or not to split.   But some writers seem to make an effort to not split. Maybe the rule is just so ingrained that they can't help them-selves. Here are some more examples of infinitives that are *not* split by their modifiers:

Another function of the movie critic is *to freeze briefly* for our inspection the stars who shoot across the screen in film after film, sometimes arriving from a galaxy previously unknown to stargazers. —Zinsser (220)

To grasp the full horror of the deteriorating climate, it is necessary *only to translate* degrees of southern latitude into northern latitude. —William Manchester, *A World Lit Only by Fire* (256)

The treaty signed between the two countries on 2 March gave Germany rights of free trade with Finland but not Finland with Germany, and bound Finland *not to make* any foreign alliance without German consent. —John Keegan, *The First World War* (380)

The problems *to be faced immediately* were enormous and critical.
—David G. McCullough, *The Johnstown Flood* (188)

Could Zinsser have said "to briefly freeze"? Doing so would have prevented the potential ambiguity of *briefly* modifying "for our inspection." Does Manchester mean "only" to modify *necessary* or *translate*? Wouldn't "to not make" and "to be immediately faced" be more forceful than, or at least an acceptable alternative to, Keegan's "not to make" and McCullough's "to be faced immediately"? Would any or all of these sentences have been better with split infinitives? Are they better without splits? Even the venerable Strunk and White concede that "Some infinitives seem to improve on being split" (78).

And the equally venerable Pence and Emery (writers of my college grammar textbook), after explaining split infinitives and essentially agreeing with Strunk and White, end with this note:

It is a curious fact that some people will remember odd bits of misinformation about English usage—such as, that it is wrong to split an infinitive, it is wrong to end a sentence with a preposition, it is wrong to refer to persons with the relative pronoun *that*, and it is wrong to begin a sentence with *and, but,* or *for*—long after they have forgotten many of the really important matters of English grammar and rhetoric. —*A Grammar of Present-Day English* (321)

What is troublesome for readers is the infinitive that is split with a long modifier—such as this one:

Watson left home at 3:15 *to once and for all time put* an end to the controversy.

Of course, I had to invent this sentence myself, since published writers don't write sentences like this.

Infinitives for action.   My conclusion on splitting or not splitting is, let's not worry about it. Instead, think of what infinitives can do. Have you noticed how much sentence action they carry? Look at the last examples again: *to freeze, to grasp, to translate, to make, to beg.* In some sentences, infinitives (called **verbals** because they're not real verbs) express the action we ordinarily assume is conveyed by verbs. Look at this sentence:

> Carried to its violent extreme, the Enlightenment inspired the citizens of France *to lop off* the head of Louis XVI and *to enthrone* Reason on the altar of Notre Dame. —Peter L. Bernstein, *Against the Gods* (111)

To lop off? *To enthrone*? That's action—expressed in the humble infinitive. Here's another example. See what these infinitives do:

> He attempted *to coerce* Magellan, and when that failed he tried *to intimidate* the Spanish king, first telling him that Portugal would regard continued support of the venture as an unfriendly act, then that Magellan and Faleiro wanted *to return* home but had been denied permission *to leave* Seville—a lie which, when exposed, resulted in the cold dismissal of the bumbling envoy.
> —Manchester (249–50)

Again we see that the main actions are expressed by infinitives. Sometimes the *to* is omitted, especially with a second infinitive:

> The beach in front, where we used *to cavort* in innocence and *toast* our wienies, was now a sinister place, patrolled by soldiers in the new pot helmets and bearing M-1 rifles with fixed bayonets.
> —Paul Fussell, *Doing Battle* (69)

Summary

But back to the subject of splitting. Notice that for most of the infinitives pointed out here, there isn't even the opportunity for a split; in other words, they don't have a modifier that a writer would be tempted to place between the *to* and the verb form. And this is the case with nearly every infinitive. As we've seen, in most cases when we have a single-word modifier, in particular a negative one (such as *not* and *never*), it does no harm to split. I'll still go along with handbook advice about not splitting with a long modifier, because that can definitely lead to awkwardness. But a single-word split? Your ear will tell you if it's okay.

❖ Most infinitives don't have an opportunity to be split.
❖ Single-word splits are usually not awkward, especially negatives.
❖ Splitting infinitives can sometimes prevent ambiguity.
❖ Splitting infinitives can sometimes gain emphasis.
❖ Avoid several-word splits unless you're trying to be funny.
❖ Don't worry about it.

□ **Practice** □

As we've seen, published writers rarely split their infinitives, even with a single modifier, even when doing so might prevent ambiguity or increase emphasis. The writers of the following sentences are no exception. Read the sentences and decide whether the italicized infinitives plus their modifiers read better the way they are or would be better with the modifier placed between the two parts of the infinitive.

1. "There were times in the next thirty years—especially under Grant and Harrison—when the Presidency seemed *to have declined permanently* in relation to Congress." —Clinton Rossiter, *The American Presidency* (103)

2. "Woodrow Wilson was the best prepared President, intellectually and morally, *ever to come* to the White House." —Rossiter (106)

3. "Every decade of the nineteenth century was to produce more and more Matthew Arnolds, who were *to feel furiously* that by all traditional standards they formed the superior class of the community, the sages and the prophets, and that they were wholly disregarded by a rising class of industrial tyrants." —Rebecca West, *The New Meaning of Treason* (157–58)

4. "Under the Geneva arrangements, the French were obligated to supervise the armistice and the eventual elections, and for them it was hard *not to assume* that during the transition period their commercial and administrative and cultural ties could be maintained and developed toward a voluntary inclusion of Indochina in the French Union."—Barbara Tuchman, *The March of Folly* (271)

5. "They hastened to add, with the care of government advisers *never to be* too definitive, that if 'political considerations are overriding' they would 'agree to the assignment of a training mission.'" —Tuchman, *The March of Folly* (273)

22

Use which for that

Someone, somewhere, sometime decided that *which* should be used for particular kinds of clauses and *that* for others. The rule goes like this: Use *which* only for nonrestrictive clauses and *that* only for **restrictive**, defining, clauses. In other words, as in sentences like these:

NONRESTRICTIVE   The exception, *which came to be called the Edison Effect*, occurred quite by accident while he [Edison] was trying to improve his incandescent light bulb. —Daniel J. Boorstin, *Cleopatra's Nose* (152)

RESTRICTIVE   The three faces *that she [Hecate] showed as Hecate Triformis* were said to be the three phases of the moon: the waxing Maiden, the full Mother, the waning Crone. —Barbara G. Walker, *The Crone* (117)

The first sentence has a nonrestrictive *which* clause modifying *exception*, the term *nonrestrictive* meaning that the clause does not define or identify the word it modifies. Because the clause is not essential to the sentence, it is set off with commas. No writer would think of substituting *that* for *which* in a sentence like this. In the second sentence, the *that* clause is restrictive, modifying *faces*; it is essential for defining or identifying *faces* and is not set off with commas. Some writers might consider using *which* in place of *that*, making Walker's sentence read:

> The three faces *which she [Hecate] showed as Hecate Triformis* were said to be the three phases of the moon: the waxing Maiden, the full Mother, the waning Crone.

With this revision, the modifying clause would still be restrictive, and the sentence would have the same meaning.

Restrictive *which* clauses.   Writers just don't seem to pay attention to the "rule." Here's a sampling of sentences with restrictive *which* clauses:

> But there is a form of nonfiction literature *which is not principally journalistic* and *which often does have a place in creative writing programs*. —Robert L. Root Jr., "Naming Nonfiction" (250) [In *College English*.]

> It's a state of mind *which is regenerated throughout the centuries by a body of people who traditionally carry the title of professor*, but even that title is not part of the real University. —Robert M. Pirsig, *Zen and the Art of Motorcycle Maintenance* (143)

> I can vividly recall reading in snatches when my children were young, reading with delicious guilt when I should have been preparing classes or doing research, falling asleep over books *which were nonetheless enthralling*, and these recollections add definite spice and delectability to my reading now, and revive me when I am sad. —Carolyn G. Heilbrun, *The Last Gift of Time* (183)

In these sentences, the rule would say that Root, Pirsig, and Heilbrun should have used *that* instead of *which*. But because the clauses are not set off with commas, we read them for what they are: restrictions on the words they modify. Some critics might say that this usage is just evidence of the contemporary decline in the language, although the following quoted examples show that the usage has been around for a while:

> Edward Gibbon, writing from England in the eighteenth century, depicted Albania as a land "within the sight of Italy *which is less known than the interior of America*." —Robert D. Kaplan, *Balkan Ghosts* (43)

> Alfred Marshall, the pre-eminent economist of the Victorian age, once remarked, "No one should have an occupation *which tends to make him anything less than a gentleman*." —Peter L. Bernstein, *Against the Gods* (190)

Other historical examples can be found in the *Oxford English Dictionary*, which points out that *that* is the ordinary usage in a restrictive sense but that *which* also occurs.

Common uses of the restrictive <u>which</u>.   One common and accepted use of *which* in a restrictive sense is as the object of a preposition:

> Once in motion the American military machine could not readjust to a warfare *in <u>which</u> these elements did not exist.* —Barbara Tuchman, *The March of Folly* (333)

> What might be called political sadness arises, I have found, not from a single affront, or even a multiplicity of them, but as an indirect response to organized and publicly condoned selfishness and revenge *about <u>which</u> it seems one can do little or nothing.*
> —Heilbrun (180)

The clauses beginning *in which* and *about which* are essential to identifying or defining the words they modify, *warfare* in Tuchman's sentence, *selfishness and revenge* in Heilbrun's; as a result they are not set off with commas. Less experienced writers might consider using *that* (or an implied *that*), but such usage would force the sentence to end with a preposition, thus violating another nonrule. Tuchman's sentence might then look like this:

> Once in motion the American military machine could not readjust to a warfare *<u>that</u> these elements did not exist in.*

Or like this, with *that* omitted:

> Once in motion the American military machine could not readjust to a warfare *these elements did not exist in.*

The *which* clause does sound better, don't you think?

Some writers turn to *which* to avoid two *that*'s in a row, as in these sentences:

> We tend to like that <u>*which seems most like us,*</u> because resemblance implies genetic relatedness, and we like our genes; they have given us us. —Natalie Angier, *Woman: An Intimate Geography* (91)

■ But then she intentionally has two *us*'s in a row.

The state of Montana at this time was undergoing an outbreak of ultra-right-wing politics like that *which occurred in Dallas, Texas, just prior to President Kennedy's assassination.* —Pirsig (140)

Instead of *that which,* some writers would use *what* in constructions like these:

We tend to like *what seems most like us* , . . .

. . . ultra-right-wing politics like *what occurred in Dallas, Texas,* . . .

Summary

Whatever the reason, writers clearly use either *that* or *which* to begin restrictive clauses. What they don't do is use *that* for nonrestrictive clauses. In other words, *which* works for either one, *that* only when the clause is not set off with commas.

- ❖ *That* is used in restrictive clauses (and not set off with commas).
- ❖ *Which* is most commonly used in nonrestrictive clauses (and set off with commas).
- ❖ Restrictive uses of *which* occur in clauses where *which* is the object of a preposition or modifies *that.*
- ❖ Writers often use *which* in other kinds of restrictive clauses.
- ❖ Writers do not use *that* for nonrestrictive clauses.

□ **Practice** □

The following quotations have restrictive *that* and *which* clauses. Experiment with replacing *that* with *which* and *which* with *that* to see how the revision affects your reading. Are the two interchangeable? Or is one preferable to the other in each case? How does the revision affect the writer's style?

1. "The event *that shook the balance of forces* was the Communist victory in China in October 1949, a shock as stunning as Pearl Harbor. . . . During these abject years the Rosenbergs were tried for treason, convicted in 1951, and when President Eisenhower refused to commute a death sentence *that would make orphans of two children,* were subsequently executed." —Tuchman, *The March of Folly* (247)

2. "For the first time in her adult life Georgiana questioned the assumptions *which caused men and women to be segregated into different spheres.* She felt that she had the same qualities as a man; it was simply her sex, not her capability, *which barred her from taking part in politics.*" —Amanda Foreman, *Georgiana: Duchess of Devonshire* (314)

   ■ The last clause in this sentence could illustrate the rare case when a restrictive *that* is preceded by a comma—when it follows an interruption. If you substitute *that* for the *which* that refers to *sex*, you see that it is essential for completing the idea and that the purpose of the two commas is to enclose the interrupter "not her capability."

3. "There is, then, no water *that is wholly of the Pacific, or wholly of the Atlantic, or of the Indian or the Antarctic.* The surf *that we find exhilarating at Virginia Beach or at La Jolla today* may have lapped at the base of antarctic icebergs or sparkled in the Mediterranean sun, years ago, before it moved through dark and unseen waterways to the place we find it now. —Rachel Carson, *The Sea around Us* (150)

23

End Your Sentences with Prepositions

Writers don't intentionally set out to end their sentences with prepositions, but if the sentences happen to end that way they often leave them, like these:

> Water fountained from a gap in the river ice, and that is what he lived *on*. —John McPhee, *Coming into the Country* (239)

> Many of them made a sincere effort to be cheerful, but without much success. There was little to be cheerful *about*. —Alfred Lansing, *Endurance* (101)

The rule is really one of the more senseless bits of lore, because there are times when a sentence is better if it *does* end with a preposition. Think how awkward McPhee's sentence would be if he had ended it "and that is *on what* he lived." Lansing's would have been "There was little *about which* to be cheerful." Not quite as awkward, but isn't the rhythm better the way Lansing wrote it?

Clumsy sentences. Some sentences are idiomatic—that is, they just sound like good English—when they *do* end with prepositions. The next two sentences, written by Barbara Walker in her book *The Crone: Woman* *of Age, Wisdom, and Power,* just *sound right,* even though they end with prepositions:

> We no longer know for sure what the symbols stood *for.* Their meanings have been erased from our collective consciousness. (110)

> Six centuries of nominal Christianity failed to eliminate pagan seasonal observances and rituals that the peasants were used *to* and fond *of.* (127)

The rule assumes that because prepositions take objects, the object must follow the preposition. But some sentences sound better with prepositions and their objects separated. How silly would Walker's first sentence sound if she had written "We no longer know for sure *for what* the symbols stood." The second sentence would be even clumsier if it ended ". . . observances and rituals *to and of which* the peasants were used and fond." No writer would write this way of course.

Clauses beginning with *whom, which, what,* and *that* (and understood *that*) are likely candidates for sentence-ending prepositions:

> The mathematical expectation of each man's wealth after the game has been played with this 50–50 set of alternatives is precisely 100 ducats (150 + 50 divided by 2), which is just *what* each player started *with.* —Peter L. Bernstein, *Against the Gods* (112)

Revised, Bernstein's sentence might read ". . . which is just *with what* each player started."

Levels of formality.   The Bernstein and Walker sentences do contain the object of their sentence-ending prepositions (*what* and *that*). In the following sentences, Robert M. Pirsig and David G. McCullough omit the object, *that*:

> He put it up on a kind of mental shelf where he put all kinds of questions ∧ he had no immediate answers *for.* —Pirsig, *Zen and the Art of Motorcycle Maintenance* (232)

> Where they went from there was something ∧ they were not yet ready to think *about.* —McCullough, *The Johnstown Flood* (188)

Revisions of these sentences would require the addition of *which* and would probably raise the level of formality to an unwanted level:

> He put it up on a kind of mental shelf where he put all kinds of questions *for which* he had no immediate answers.

> Where they went from there was something *about which* they were not yet ready to think.

Besides increasing the formality, both sentences would be unnecessarily clumsy.

Lewis Thomas likewise maintains a less than formal level with this sentence:

> For the life of me, I didn't know *what* he was asking *for*. —*Et Cetera, Et Cetera* (167)

To avoid ending with a preposition, Thomas would likely have had a sentence that was not only awkward and stuffy but also unclear:

> For the life of me, I didn't know *for what* he was asking.

Infinitives and questions. Infinitive phrases at the ends of sentences sometimes end with prepositions, and in these cases, as with implied *that*, the objects are not even there. See how the object is implied in this sentence by Lewis Thomas:

> This seems to me, as I write, a cold and excessively orderly way for the collective mind of mankind to be working, too cold to think *about*. (171)

There is an implied *which*: "too cold *about which* to think." This next sentence also has an implied object:

> But the downside to that freedom of expression is that we cannot lift up the facial muscles through strength training; there is nowhere to lift them *to*. —Natalie Angier, *Woman: An Intimate Geography* (286)

Angier's sentence ends with a preposition because she chose an infinitive phrase rather than a *which* clause. A revision would be wordy and awkward: "there is nowhere *to which* to lift them."

As with infinitives, it's not unusual to find questions ending with prepositions:

> Does this eighteen-year-old person have a thought in his head?
> If so, where does it come *from*? —Pirsig (124)

The question could be revised to read "If so, *from where* does it come?" But then, who would want to write that way? Not Pirsig.

Summary

Obviously, this rule is just one more bit of lore that careful writers pay little attention to. It's probably good advice, though, to notice when your sentence ends with a preposition and then ask yourself if the sentence sounds right to you.

Sentences sometimes end with prepositions—

- ❖ When they have a final clause beginning *whom, which, what,* or *that* (or understood *that*).
- ❖ When they have a final infinitive phrase.
- ❖ When the sentence asks a question.
- ❖ When avoiding the ending would increase the formality to an unsuitable level.
- ❖ When avoiding the ending would result in an awkward sentence.

□   **Practice**   □

Rewrite each of the following sentences to avoid ending with a preposition. Then assess the effects:

- ❖ Are the sentences more—or less—awkward?
- ❖ Are the levels of formality more—or less—agreeable?
- ❖ How have you affected the rhythm of the sentences?

1.   "Books or no books, it is a fact, patent both to my dog and myself, that at daybreak I am the sole owner of all the acres I can walk *over*." —Aldo Leopold, *A Sand County Almanac* (41)

2.   "The famous white cliffs of Dover are composed of chalk deposited by the seas of the Cretaceous period, during that

great inundation we have spoken *of*." —Rachel Carson, *The Sea around Us* (102)

3. "But what if you are trying to introduce a topic that others in your field aren't familiar *with*?" —Elizabeth Rankin, *The Work of Writing* (15)

4. "When you have conflicted feelings about the subject you are writing *on*, your ambivalence may, like Walt's, color your writing in ways you are unaware *of*." —Rankin (46)

   ▪ Two end prepositions.

24

Repeat, Repeat, Repeat

Writers sometimes come through school learning that repetition in writing is bad; it's boring and tedious, they've heard, so they try to find synonyms when they need to repeat an idea. As a consequence, they deny themselves access to the clarity, coherence, rhythm, and emphasis they can achieve with an astute use of this tool. If you're one of those people, I invite you to release yourself from that unnecessary constraint. Write sentences, perhaps, like these:

> *Waves* inundate Good Harbor Beach and the parking lot in front of the Stop-n-Shop. *They* rip up entire sections of Ocean Drive. *They* deposit a fifteen-foot-high tangle of lobster traps and sea muck at the end of Grapevine Lane. *They* fill the swimming pool of a Back Shore mansion with ocean-bottom rubble. *They* suck beach cobbles up their huge faces and sling them inland, smashing windows, peppering lawns. *They* overrun the sea wall at Brace Cove, spill into Niles Pond, and continue into the woods beyond. —Sebastian Junger, *The Perfect Storm* (204)

Here we have intentional repetition. Five sentences repeat the pattern begun in the first sentence, the pronoun *they* each time referring to *waves*. Every sentence, then, begins with the subject (*waves* or *they*) followed directly by a verb (*inundate, rip up, deposit, fill, suck, overrun*) with no intervening or preceding modifiers. The effect is to move you the reader along with the destructive waves. To finish off this description, Junger's last sentence sets up another repetitive pattern with parallel verbs (*overrun, spill, continue*).

Repetition for connections and clarity. Writers often rely on repetition to help readers absorb complex ideas. Notice how the repetition of the phrase "to those societies" connects several ideas in the following crowded sentence:

> Unless we destroy ourselves utterly, the future belongs *to those societies* that, while not ignoring the reptilian and mammalian parts of our being, enable the characteristically human components of our nature to flourish; *to those societies* that encourage diversity rather than conformity; *to those societies* willing to invest resources in a variety of social, political, economic and cultural experiments, and prepared to sacrifice short-term advantage for long-term benefit; *to those societies* that treat new ideas as delicate, fragile and immensely valuable pathways to the future. —Carl Sagan, *The Dragons of Eden* (204)

Even with parallel repeated phrases assisting the comprehension of ideas in this long sentence, a reader has to work at it. In the next example, Carolyn G. Heilbrun holds ideas together by repeating the entire beginning of her clauses:

> *If we do not* tiresomely insist that the past was better, that the present is without morals or good habits or healthy living or (heaven help us) family values, whatever they are; *if we do not* insist on recounting ancient anecdotes as original as a tape recording and as easily rendered audible; *if we do not* recount adventures in the past, even if requested to do so, then the young will sometimes actually seek—they will not openly ask—for something we are equipped to give them. What to call it? *It is* the essence of having lived long, *it is* the unstated assurance that most disasters pass, *it is* the survival of deprivation and death and rejection that renders our sympathy of value. —*The Last Gift of Time* (163)

Again, the reader has to work, mainly because the subject and verb of the main statement are delayed by the repeated *if* clauses. Perhaps Heilbrun relies a bit too much on the reader's good will? She uses repetition again to answer her question, tying together three statements with *it is*. The next example also begins with subject-delaying introductory phrases—though, I'm sure you'll agree, without the difficulty of the last two examples.

> In this age *of* negative discovery, *of* the mechanized observer, *of* machine-created data and ever newer kinds of data, we must note a new kind of momentum. —Daniel J. Boorstin, *Cleopatra's Nose* (11)

So far we've seen how ideas can be held together with repeated phrases. The same can be done with repeated single words:

> Not that any of this would help Gorbachev. He was *despised* by the communists, *who* regarded him as no better than the CIA; *despised* by the "great power" nationalists, *who* believed he was responsible for the humiliation of a great power and its army; and *despised* as well by liberal democrats, *who* felt he had never fully shed his allegiance to the nomenklatura that raised him.
> —David Remnick, *Resurrection* (7)

Because of the complexity in this sentence, a reader might get lost without Remnick's repetition of *despised*, as well as of the similar structuring of the *who* clauses.

Repetition for emphasis.   So repetition connects ideas. (For more on making connections see chapter 8, "Connect Your Thoughts Coherently.") Next let's consider repetition's most obvious feature—the way it emphasizes ideas.

> Greek *art* is intellectual *art*, the *art* of men who were clear and lucid thinkers, and it is therefore plain *art*. —Edith Hamilton, *The Greek Way* (49)

Almost too much art? Repetition does draw attention to itself. Here's another example, where words and phrases are repeated:

> While the *problem of the Poles* was diffused by the partition of their ancient kingdom with Germany and Russia, the *problem of the Czechs* by the heavy Germanisation of their cities and the *problem of the Croats* by their Catholicism, nothing, it seemed, could diffuse *that of the Serbs* but the use of force. —John Keegan, *The First World War* (50)

Having twice rejected synonyms for the noun *problem*, Keegan opts for a pronoun in the final phrase. Would the sentence have been any more emphatic if he'd repeated *problem* one more time? Both word and pattern are repeated for emphasis in the next example also:

> The bells rang that day in Washington. *Wherever* there were brick bell towers and whitewashed churches, *wherever* rows of bells hung in ascending niches, *wherever* the common people could crowd belfries to take turns pulling the ropes, the bells sang. —Jay Winik, *April 1865* (29)

Each increment of these *wherever* clauses adds to the universality that Winik emphasizes through repetition and a delayed subject. One can almost sense the rhythm of the bells in the rhythm of the words.

This kind of incremental pattern repetition can emphasize ideas in various ways. The following sentence shows infinitive phrases increasing the gravity of each act mentioned:

> Many of them [women during the Middle Ages] realized that the church sought *to reduce* women's significance, *to mock* their sacred songs and stories as "old wives' tales," *to diabolize* their deities, *to condemn* their magic, even *to blame* them for all the world's sins.
> —Barbara G. Walker, *The Crone* (53)

This pattern of infinitives gives individual emphasis to each item as it leads readers through increasing depths of the subject.

Repetition for rhythm.   One of the really attractive aspects of repetition is that it makes you feel the rhythm of the writer's words, as in Jay Winik's sentence about Washington's bells. In this next sentence, Natalie Angier uses sound to play with your mind:

> Yet there is *blood, blood, blood*, and they must *sop it up* and *sop it up* and cauterize what they can. —*Woman: An Intimate Geography* (88)

On the other hand, maybe that example is *too* sensory. But while we're on unpleasant subjects take a look at how repetition carries you along in this example:

> The Green River was flowing at nearly three thousand cubic feet—about ninety tons—per second. At that rate, *water can wrap* a canoe around a boulder like tinfoil. *Water can uproot* a tree. *Water can squeeze* the air out of a boy's lungs, *undo* knots, *drag off* a life jacket, *lever* a boot so tightly into the riverbed that even if we had had ropes—the ropes that were in the packs that were in

the trucks—we could never have budged him. —Anne Fadiman,
"Under Water" (65)

A rhythmic tension builds from Fadiman's repeated descriptive phrases
as they draw you step by step through the grim facts and then to the
futility of lifesaving efforts in the face of the water's power. Jon Krakauer
takes you in too, here leading you to feel his relief:

Safe now, the crushing strain of the preceding days lifted from
my shoulders, *I cried* for my lost companions, *I cried* because I
was grateful to be alive, *I cried* because I felt terrible for having
survived while others had died. —*Into Thin Air* (267)

The tedium of repetition.   Repetition does tend to draw attention to
itself; that's why it works. It's also why we want to avoid it at times, such
as when it emphasizes unimportant words—too many *that*'s or *which*'s
in a sentence, for example—or when it repeats ideas unnecessarily, as
in this sentence:

Again, please know that the teachers and I appreciate your *support* of the *responsibilities and duties* of the recess aides and your
willingness to *support* our efforts to address the situations which
arise on the playground. —*Quarterly Review of Doublespeak*

Tedium is right. The repetition has the effect of making the request less
direct, less forceful. The sentence could read:

Again, please know that the teachers and I appreciate your support of the recess aides and our efforts to address the situations
on the playground.

An unintentionally repeated rhythmic pattern also can lead to tedium.
Revision is a good time to work on repetition. Look for the unintentional and boring, and delete it; but also find places where intentionally
repeating a word or two will sharpen the expression of your idea.

Summary

Experienced writers do indeed use repetition—for clarity, coherence, emphasis, and rhythm. They also avoid it when they have no need for it.

❖ Repeat for coherence, clarity, emphasis, or rhythm.
❖ Repeat to assist reader comprehension of complex ideas.

❖ Repeat words or phrases or sentence patterns.
❖ Coordinate repeated words and phrases in parallel structure (see chapter 5, "Pack Your Sentences with Parallelism").
❖ Use repetition and parallel structure in long sentences.
❖ Avoid repeating words you don't want to draw attention to.
❖ In general, avoid expressing the same idea twice, especially in the same sentence or in back-to-back sentences.

□ **Practice** □

Author of books on writing William Zinsser advises writers to use a thesaurus for locating synonyms but then later castigates sportswriters for being "obsessed with synonyms." They could write good English, he says, except that "They have a dread of repeating the word that's easiest for the reader to visualize—batter, runner, golfer, boxer—if a synonym can be found" (201).

The sentences that follow have words that the writers repeated for coherence, clarity, emphasis, or rhythm. Experiment with substituting synonyms for the italicized words, using a thesaurus or dictionary if necessary. Then judge the effects:

❖ Do the sentences lose their tight connections?
❖ Are they less clear?
❖ Do your changes increase or decrease the emphasis?
❖ Do the sentences sound better to you now—or not?

1. "Waves inundate Good Harbor Beach and the parking lot in front of the Stop-n-Shop. *They* rip up entire sections of Ocean Drive. *They* deposit a fifteen-foot-high tangle of lobster traps and sea muck at the end of Grapevine Lane. *They* fill the swimming pool of a Back Shore mansion with ocean-bottom rubble. *They* suck beach cobbles up their huge faces and sling them inland, smashing windows, peppering lawns. *They* overrun the sea wall at Brace Cove, spill into Niles Pond, and continue into the woods beyond." —Junger (204)

2. "So then, it hit me: *What if* Delilah was that angry? *What if* she wanted to tear things down? *What if* every time she looked at Samson she just wanted to kill him because his recklessness and fury had an outlet, *he had* his strength, *he could* kill a thousand people with a donkey's jawbone, and *he could* kill a ferocious

lion with his bare hands. But what could Delilah possibly do with all her rage and anger? I mean, it's nearly the twenty-first century and I don't know what to do with mine. So *what if* Delilah just wanted to be able to act out and feel all these things that are so wrong? *What if* she'd walked around day in, day out, her whole life troubled and bothered, so that what she did to Samson *had nothing to do* with spying for the Philistines and *had nothing to do* with betraying Samson—*had nothing to do* with anything at all except a pain and destructiveness that she'd kind of ignored until Samson came along and *reminded her* that it was there, and *reminded her* that she was angry enough to let a whole city come falling down on top of her." —Elizabeth Wurtzel, *Bitch: In Praise of Difficult Women* (86–87)

3.   "While the problem of the Poles was diffused by the partition of their ancient kingdom with Germany and Russia, the *problem* of the Czechs by the heavy Germanisation of their cities and the *problem* of the Croats by their Catholicism, nothing, it seemed, could diffuse *that* of the Serbs but the use of force." —Keegan (50)

Part Three

Punctuation and Style

P unctuation marks, like capitalization and white space, are cues for readers, signals that tell them what to expect in the territory that lies ahead and how to relate what they've just read to what they're about to read. A colon points to words that explain. Commas indicate a variety of relationships that, were the marks not there, would be the reader's task to comprehend. Even though readers do enjoy occasional little surprises as they proceed through a piece, they rely on their expectations for assimilating words and sentences.

We don't realize how much we actually depend on the messages we get from punctuation marks, capitalization, and spaces. Without them, the following passage is nearly unintelligible:

butihadsaidbuttoooftenonecannotgoonsayingbutonemust
finishthesentencesomehowirebukedmyselfshallifinishitbuti
amboredbutwhywasibored

Fortunately Virginia Woolf wrote it this way:

But . . . I had said "but" too often. One cannot go on saying "but." One must finish the sentence somehow, I rebuked myself. Shall I finish it, "But—I am bored!" But why was I bored? —*A Room of One's Own* (104)

Woolf's spaces, capitalization, quotation marks, and other punctuation marks help us make sense of the sentence. All of these mechanics of writing (so called because of their functional capacities) are as essential to communicating an idea in writing as are the words we choose.

Like words and our arrangement of them, punctuation marks are a feature of style. Some people use more commas than other people do, but in general we use fewer commas today than in times past. For example, the King James Version of the Bible, published in 1611, has punctuation that differs from what we'd use today:

> And the Lord God said, Behold, the man is become as one of us, to know good and evil: and now, lest he put forth his hand, and take also of the tree of life, and eat, and live forever: Therefore the Lord God sent him forth from the Garden of Eden, to till the ground from whence he was taken. —Genesis 3.22–23

In addition to commas that we'd omit today (after *us, life, hand, eat,* and *Eden*), this passage uses colons as we more likely would use periods or semicolons, and it omits quotation marks. Yet the style is distinctive, and the punctuation had a practical purpose. When the King James Bible was written, it was more often read aloud than silently, and the commas guided readers by marking breath units, indicating pauses. The colons probably indicated longer pauses than commas, plus a stress and rising voice for the words that followed—"and now" and "Therefore."

Much of what we read today is not read aloud, and that may be why we don't necessarily mark breath units, or pauses, with commas. As our minds and eyes move along the page without vocalization, we prefer to be unhindered by superfluous punctuation. At the same time, we do need signals.

Punctuation necessarily is governed by rules. Like road markers, punctuation applied willy-nilly is worse than useless. A road sign that indicates a curve to the right should not have the possibility of other interpretations. A stop sign, despite the actions of some drivers, means what it says. Stop. In a sentence, a full stop is indicated unambiguously by a period, and when we come to one while reading aloud our voice drops accordingly. Whether reading aloud or silently, we stop, however briefly. We still make that stop even when the period marks the end of a fragment rather than a full sentence, as sometimes happens. We see examples in chapter 16, "Fragment Your Sentences." Commas also sometimes appear in unexpected places and cause us to pause, perhaps unnecessarily. On the other hand, when they are omitted where permitted by a rule, we usually don't notice their absence. In the quoted King James passage, "Therefore" might have been followed by a comma but wasn't.

So even though there are rules, punctuation can bend the rules and be a feature of style. We ordinarily think of a colon as the mark to introduce a list. But observe in the following excerpt from *The Perfect Storm* how Sebastian Junger uses three different marks to introduce ideas in series:

> Inevitably, something has broken on the trip—a line gets wound around the drive shaft and must be dove on, the antennas get snapped off, the radios go dead. Depending on the problem it can take anywhere from an afternoon to several days to fix. Then the engine has to be overhauled: change the belts and filters, check the oil, fill the hydraulics, clean the injectors, clean the plugs, test the generators. Finally there's the endless task of maintaining the deck gear. Blocks have to be greased, ropes have to be spliced, chains and cables have to be replaced, rust spots have to be ground down and painted. One ill-kept piece of gear can kill a man. (14)

The dash, the colon, and the period each effectively precedes the series that follows.

In the next pages, you will find examples of how other writers have used punctuation. You will also see, in these examples and others throughout the book, that writers use punctuation flexibly, applying principles of emphasis and coherence (and personal choice) in their applications of the rules.

25

Control Your Commas

*T*he act of punctuating with commas suffers if not from useless rules then from some well-meaning but wrong advice. Most people use too many commas; and that's because someone once told them to put in a comma whenever they pause. The problem is that people pause frequently when they write—for all kinds of reasons. I've noticed that I sometimes tap on the comma key when I pause to consider how to complete a sentence. Just holding the place maybe? Then I have to go back over my draft and remove useless commas. Notice how comma-stingy John Kenneth Galbraith is in the following sentence:

> Things though bad were still not hopeless. —*The Great Crash 1929* (99)

Most of us would have been tempted to put commas on either side of "though bad."

The comma is the punctuation mark that gives writers the most trouble—and for good reason. It has numerous functions with rules consuming pages and pages in the handbooks. Writers agonize over how to use commas and usually end up with more than they need. Because this is a book on writing style, we have to devote some space to those functions, but my intent is to give you only enough information for you to make your own decisions about when and how to use this ubiquitous mark.

Commas have two basic functions: to separate and to enclose. One comma separates, two enclose. Keeping this principle in mind will help you place commas where you need them and avoid those that may be misleading. To start, let's look at the main separating functions.

Separating independent clauses joined with a conjunction

A reliable witness had seen the crime take place, and fingerprint and handwriting evidence would almost certainly further tie him to the scene. —Miles Harvey, *The Island of Lost Maps* (82)

The gases began to liquefy, and Earth became a molten mass.
—Rachel Carson, *The Sea around Us* (4)

But some writers choose to omit this comma:

Seventy-footers are roaming around the sea state like surly giants   and there's not much Billy can do but take them head-on and try to get over the top before they break. —Junger (138)

They looked at it attentively   and their minds worked upon what they saw. This is essentially the scientific method. The Greeks were the first scientists   and all science goes back to them. —Edith Hamilton, *The Greek Way* (26)

We poison the caddis flies in a stream   and the salmon runs dwindle and die. We poison the gnats in a lake   and the poison travels from link to link of the food chain   and soon the birds of the lake margins become its victims. We spray our elms   and the following springs are silent of robin song, not because we sprayed the robins directly but because the poison traveled, step by step, through the now familiar elm leaf–earthworm–robin cycle. —Rachel Carson, *Silent Spring* (189)

Separating long, participial, or potentially ambiguous introductory sentence elements

By the time Fischer left for Nepal in the spring of 1996, he'd begun to garner more of the recognition that he thought was his due. —Jon Krakauer, *Into Thin Air* (64)

Troubled by his role and the smell of the swamp he was getting into, Kennedy resorted to another fact-finding mission, the now traditional Washington substitute for policy. —Barbara Tuchman, *The March of Folly* (309)

But short introductory phrases are usually not set off:

In a time of change   it is not enough to hang on to the old ways of seeing the universe or society. —Casey Miller and Kate Swift, *Words and Women* (164)

Except when there might be misreading:

In short, Neanderthal could have spoken at length if he'd known how to speak or what to say. —Lewis Thomas, *Et Cetera, Et Cetera* (106)

■ Without the comma following *short,* some readers might read "short Neanderthal."

Separating final nonrestrictive modifiers

In the time-honored fashion of the ancient world, he opens the book at random, intending to receive as a divine message the first sentence his eyes should fall upon. —Thomas Cahill, *How the Irish Saved Civilization* (57)

■ The phrase that begins *intending* modifies the subject, *he;* it is not essential for identification.

The most powerful of modern instruments, invented during the 1980s, are the scanning-tunneling microscope and atomic force microscope, which provide an almost literal view of atoms bonded into molecules. —Edward O. Wilson, *Consilience: The Unity of Knowledge* (50)

■ The *which* clause is not necessary for identifying the two microscopes.

Separating items in a series

The experiment was scheduled to last for eight months, but it was dropped after only three in the face of misinterpretation, misunderstanding, and ridicule. —Miller and Swift (143)

■ I do recommend the last comma even when the *and* is present.

The Greek mind was free to think about the world as it pleased, to reject all traditional explanations, to disregard all the priests taught, to search unhampered by any outside authority for the truth. —Hamilton (28)

▓ Omitting *and* before the final item is the writer's choice.

Separating quotations

The President thanked him for his words and asked, "Well, Colby, what are you going to do?" —Gene Smith, *When the Cheering Stopped* (169)

The preceding examples show commas with separating functions. What follows are examples of the main enclosing functions.

Enclosing nonrestrictive interruptions

A nonrestrictive phrase or clause is one that is not essential for identifying or limiting the word it modifies.

The next morning, like a scared rabbit, I walked a different route to school. —Edgar Allen Imhoff, *Always of Home* (104)

▓ The sentence is readable without "like a scared rabbit."

Aristotle, the model scientist, the man of cool head and detached observation, unbiased and impersonal, does not display any dispassionate aloofness in his consideration of reason. —Hamilton (30)

▓ Hamilton's sentence has three interruptions, none of which is essential for identifying the subject, *Aristotle,* and each is enclosed with commas.

In the Russian imagination, however, Chechnya is an obsession, an image of Islamic defiance, an embodiment of the primitive, the devious, the elusive. —David Remnick, *Resurrection* (266)

▓ In addition to enclosing the transitional adverb *however* with commas, Remnick separates items in series.

"And I am sure," Tumulty went on, "that Dr. Grayson will never certify to his disability. Will you, Grayson?" —Smith (94)

▓ The quotation is interrupted.

Catherine Deneuve, the great beauty whose face has probably sold more bottles of perfume than that of any other woman in history, said to an interviewer that it was hard getting old in any country, but unbearable in the United States. —Natalie Angier, *Woman: An Intimate Geography* (115)

▓ A long modifier, nonrestrictive as are most modifiers of proper, capitalized, nouns.

Enclosing addresses and dates

The new iron dome incorporated some 9 million pounds of cast iron, most of it cast in Brooklyn, New York, at a cost of $1,047,291. —Daniel J. Boorstin, *Cleopatra's Nose* (94)

■ Notice the need for the second comma to enclose *New York*; omitting it would separate parts of the sentence. An argument could be made, on the principle of restriction, that both commas should be omitted since *New York* identifies "Brooklyn." The same argument could be applied to the date in the next example.

On June 28, 1988, the year-long countdown to the sixth centenary of Lazar's martyrdom at Kossovo Polje began. —Robert D. Kaplan, *Balkan Ghosts* (38)

■ Again, notice the need for the second, enclosing, comma. An alternative and perhaps preferable arrangement of the details of the date could be *28 June 1988* with no commas.

Beyond the separating and enclosing functions of commas, we should also take a look at misleading commas. These are commas that careful writers omit, acting on the principle of using no more punctuation than necessary. Like road signs, a faulty signal is worse than no signal at all. The following sentences correctly illustrate the *absence* of misleading commas.

Omitted before restrictive elements

Restrictive phrases and clauses are essential for identifying or limiting the words they modify. They are not set off with commas.

However, he was a man of caution who sought no fame as a martyr to the broken boom.—Galbraith (32)

■ The *who* clause is not set off with a comma because it tells something essential about "man."

She was the widow of an Englishman of whom nothing whatever is known. —Samuel Eliot Morison, *John Paul Jones* (347)

■ The clause beginning *of whom* is necessary for identifying what the writer knows about "an Englishman." Incidentally, if Morison had inserted a comma, the clause would read as a modifier of *She*.

He was sowing the seed   that would reap another four million German corpses. —John Keegan, *The First World War* (6)

■ The *that* clause tells something essential about "seed." *That* clauses are almost never preceded by commas.

They floated in a soupy sea of mush brash ice   composed of ground-up floes and lumps of snow. —Alfred Lansing, *Endurance* (29)

■ Note this absence of a comma. If the phrase beginning *composed* had been set off with a comma, its meaning could have attached itself, misleadingly and illogically, to the subject of the sentence.

Omitted before quotations that are not complete sentences

Plato, never quite certain whether he trusted artists or not, was nevertheless willing to explain that   "we are endowed by the Gods with vision and hearing, and harmony was given by the Muses to him that can use them intellectually" in order to   "assist the soul's interior revolution, to restore it to order and concord with itself." —Walter Kerr, *The Decline of Pleasure* (155)

■ No comma is needed before the quoted phrases.

To Mark Twain a cow was undoubtedly   "she," but the inventor of the German language was a   "he," the average German was a   "he," and so were the reader and the student—a state of affairs as exasperating as the German oddities he lampooned.

—Miller and Swift (48)

■ Whether to italicize or quote words used as words is often the writer's choice. Notice that periods and commas go inside end quotation marks.

Omitted before <u>and</u> and <u>but</u> except when they join independent clauses or items in series

On Sunday there were sermons suggesting that a certain measure of divine retribution had been visited on the Republic   and that it had not been entirely unmerited. —Galbraith (109)

■ Galbraith also, correctly, does not use a comma before the subordinate *that* clauses. But some writers do at times place an ordinarily unnecessary comma before a second subordinate clause joined with *and*. See the following sentence.

Sitting at my new desk, I wrote down all my letters the way I had seen Agnes and Charley do it, and the way Mom and I had practiced. —Imhoff (13)

▉ Imhoff's comma after *it* is not necessary for comprehension because he repeats "the way," but he probably wanted to slow the reading and add weight to this accomplishment of a small boy.

Omitted before parentheses

The tourist office was run by a close friend of Emil Bobu, a close advisor of Ceausescu who came from Suceava   (and was sentenced to life imprisonment after the revolution). —Kaplan (139)

▉ Notice that the period (and a comma if one were needed) *follows* a parenthetical interruption.

It's not possible, of course, to exhaust the possibilities of misleading commas. You probably get some in your writing. But once you have established parsimony in your use of commas, you can achieve emphasis by inserting them in unexpected places, as in this example:

They no longer merely increased [human] capacity to make or improve familiar products—to dig, and cut, and shape, and move, and build, and destroy." —Boorstin (36)

One final point: Many comma functions can be served also by other marks—dashes, semicolons, and perhaps parentheses, colons, or periods. Along with the theme of this book—to stretch the conventions of writing whenever possible—I recommend you experiment with alternative marks of punctuation.

Summary

Use commas to—

- ❖ Separate independent clauses.
- ❖ Separate long, participial, or potentially ambiguous introductory phrases or clauses.
- ❖ Separate final nonrestrictive modifiers.
- ❖ Separate items in series.
- ❖ Separate quotations.
- ❖ Enclose nonrestrictive interruptions.
- ❖ Enclose elements of addresses and dates.

Avoid commas—

- ❖ Before and after restrictive elements.
- ❖ Before quotations that are not complete sentences.
- ❖ Before *and* or *but* except with independent clauses and series.
- ❖ Before parentheses.
- ❖ After short unambiguous introductory phrases.

□ **Practice** □

Read the following paragraph from John M. Barry's *Rising Tide: The Great Mississippi Flood of 1927 and How It Changed America*. Then, referring to the lists above, identify the reason for each numbered comma and omission.

They escaped by angling across to the Arkansas shore. The *Pelican*,[1] a Mississippi River Commission steamboat[2] was not so lucky later that day at a far smaller levee break in Arkansas. In full sight of thousands of workers and refugees[3] the current sucked the *Pelican* toward this crevasse. Desperately trying to stop[4] the captain rammed his bow into the levee. The levee collapsed [5] and the *Pelican* capsized[6] was dragged through the crevasse rolling over and over. In one of the most heroic acts of the flood,[7] a black man [8] named Sam Tucker [9] jumped into a rowboat alone—no one would join him— and headed for the break. The current lifted his boat [10] and rocketed him through the turbulence. Somehow he survived,[11] followed the steamer,[12] and a mile inland picked 2 men out of the water. They were alive; 19 others drowned. The amount of water pouring through this break paled when compared to Mounts Landing. Yet the *Memphis Commercial-Appeal* wrote,[13] "It was as if [the steamer] had been carried over Niagara Falls." (203)

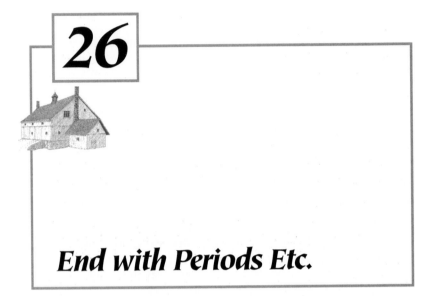

26

End with Periods Etc.

*E*veryone knows where to put periods, right? At the end of sentences. Except—already in this chapter I've used two periods and haven't yet put one at the end of a sentence. My first period marks an abbreviation, and my second one ends a sentence fragment. My first sentence ends with a question mark (this mark, along with the exclamation point, is what I mean by "Etc." in the chapter title). What's more, none of this is surprising. Periods actually have several functions, and only some of them are cut-and-dried.

Ending sentences and fragments.   Let's begin with the cut-and-dried. John Keegan ends the following sentence unsurprisingly with a period:

> Armies make plans. —*The First World War* (24)

Here's a writer using periods to end fragments:

> And come they did. Even in the Civil War. Even on the eve of April 1865. —Jay Winik, *April 1865* (25)

> ■ Winik has two fragments following his sentence.

And question marks, we know, frequently end sentences:

> Where does this leave intellectual life today? —Steven Pinker, *The Blank Slate* (133)

> Why did these advisory voices of the CIA, the Working Group, the Under-Secretary of State, have so little impact? —Barbara Tuchman, *The March of Folly* (320)

> But why Jones? Possibly because Jones is a patronymic, meaning the son of John. —Samuel Eliot Morison, *John Paul Jones* (24)

After ending his question (a fragment), Morison uses a period to end the fragment that answers his question.

As for exclamation points, we're advised to avoid them because it's not nice to shout; however, writers do like to shout now and then:

> Crack! Again the floe had split in two, this time exactly through the spot where Shackleton's tent had stood some minutes before.
> —Alfred Lansing, *Endurance* (137)

Periods with numbers.   While question marks and exclamation points have rather limited, specialized usage, periods range more widely. A common use is to mark decimals in numbers:

> In a separate Public Health Service study, analysis of prison meals disclosed such items as stewed dried fruit containing 69.6 parts per million and bread containing 100.9 parts per million of DDT!
> —Rachel Carson, *Silent Spring* (178–79)

Carson, as we see, ends her sentence emphatically with an exclamation point. Note too that she omits periods in her abbreviation, *DDT*.

Periods in abbreviations.   Abbreviations aren't always marked with periods. The following sentences show some of the range.

> Yet, by June 1917, the commander of an American Expeditionary Force, General John J. Pershing, had arrived in France and on 4 July, American Independence Day, elements of his 1st Division paraded in Paris. —Keegan (372)

■ For initials in names.

At OCS I made no permanent friends, and indeed I made none in the army. —Paul Fussell, *Doing Battle* (90)

▦ Abbreviation for Officer Candidate School; no periods.

A French company needing dollars for a U.S. subsidiary could assume the franc obligations of an American company with a French subsidiary. —Peter L. Bernstein, *Against the Gods* (322)

▦ Note the absence of spaces after periods within abbreviations; periods at the ends of sentences and abbreviations are followed by one space. Usage is moving toward omitting periods in abbreviations made up of all capital letters: *US, USA, UK, NEA, BC*. However, some publishing houses still require them.

The ceremony was performed in St. George's Chapel. —Jerrold M. Packard, *Victoria's Daughters* (148)

▦ In American usage, an abbreviation with both upper- and lowercase letters is followed by a period.

If you're not sure how to write an abbreviation, check your dictionary. Some scientific and technical abbreviations follow other rules.

End punctuation with other marks. In quotations, whether a full sentence or a single word, the period goes inside the end quotation mark. With parentheses, the period goes inside the end parenthesis in stand-alone parenthetical sentences, outside if the parenthesis comes within a sentence. Question marks and exclamation points go inside closing quotation marks and parentheses when the enclosure is a question or an exclamation; otherwise they go outside. A sentence that ends with an abbreviation period does not take a second period to end the sentence.

Periods for ellipsis. In academic and other scholarly writing we frequently need one additional kind of period—the group of three that indicates omissions from something we're quoting. Style manuals are famously inconsistent in their requirements for handling quotations, but with the latest editions of the *MLA Handbook for Writers of Research Papers* (6th edition, by Joseph Gibaldi) and of the *Chicago Manual of Style* (15th edition) and of the *Publication Manual of the American Psychological Association* (5th edition) there is a fair amount of consistency.

The three manuals agree that omissions are shown by three spaced periods with a space before the first and after the last. When a quotation ends in a period, that mark precedes the ellipsis dots. "Placement of other punctuation," according to *Chicago Manual*, "depends on whether the omission precedes or follows the mark" (461), and the other manuals agree. The APA manual and *Chicago Manual* advise against both beginning and ending a quotation with ellipsis dots—on the assumption that something obviously went before and after the words quoted. The *MLA Handbook* seems to avoid ellipsis dots at the beginning though not at the end. All three advise against indicating an ellipsis when quoting only a word or a phrase, since the quotation is obviously not complete.

To illustrate, here's a passage followed by several quotations with omissions.

Original passage

The role a protein molecule plays is determined not just by its primary structure, not just by the sequence of amino acids within it, but also by its shape. The amino acid string of each kind is folded upon itself in a precise manner, coiled about like twine and crumpled together like a piece of wadded paper. The total molecule bears resemblance to forms as variable as clouds in the sky. Looking at these forms, we readily imagine lumpy spheres, donuts, dumbbells, rams' heads, angels with wings spread, and corkscrews. —Edward O. Wilson, *Consilience: The Unity of Knowledge* (91)

Quotations with ellipses

Edward O. Wilson relates shape and function: "The role a protein molecule plays is determined . . . by its shape."

▧ Omission within a sentence.

According to noted biologist Edward O. Wilson, "The role a protein molecule plays is determined not just by its primary structure, not just by the sequence of amino acids within it, but also by its shape. . . . The total molecule bears resemblance to forms as variable as clouds in the sky."

▧ Omission between sentences.

Edward O. Wilson, relating shape and function of protein molecules, says, "The amino acid string of each kind is folded upon itself . . . , coiled about like twine and crumpled together like a piece of wadded paper."

▧ Omission precedes a comma.

Edward O. Wilson relates shape and function of the protein molecule: "The amino acid string of each kind is folded upon itself in a precise manner, . . . crumpled together like a piece of wadded paper."

■ Omission follows a comma.

Edward O. Wilson tells us that a protein molecule is affected "not just by its primary structure, not just by the sequence of amino acids within it, but also by its shape."

■ Omission at beginning of a sentence; no ellipsis marks.

Edward O. Wilson compares protein molecules to "clouds in the sky."

■ Quoted phrase; no ellipsis marks.

The preceding ellipses would be appropriate in a paper that follows any of the three styles—MLA, APA, or Chicago; however, each manual has a different method of documenting the source. Such citations are outside the scope of this book, so I'll say only, regarding periods, that if your source citation is a parenthetical note at the end of your quotation, the period goes at the end of the note, as in:

Edward O. Wilson compares protein molecules to "clouds in the sky" (91).

Differing somewhat on ellipses is the *Associated Press Stylebook,* which calls for three *unspaced* dots with spaces before and after the group (...). AP agrees with the APA and *Chicago Manual* on not indicating ellipses at the beginning or the end of quotations. All four styles caution that any quotation, with or without ellipsis dots, should not distort the meaning of the original.

Summary

❖ Periods end sentences and sentence fragments.
❖ Question marks end questions.
❖ Exclamation points shout.
❖ The rules for periods in abbreviations are fluid; for abbreviations made up of all capital letters, periods tend to be omitted.

❖ Periods that end sentences and abbreviations are followed by one space.
❖ A sentence that ends with an abbreviation period does not take a second period.
❖ Three periods in succession indicate omissions in quotations.
❖ Avoid ellipses unless you need them.

□ **Practice** □

The following excerpts show a variety of period uses. Consider each numbered period (or lack of one) and account for its presence or absence, especially in relation to other punctuation. Then write quotations from the Peter L. Bernstein paragraph, omitting sections and using ellipsis dots like those in the examples in the section "Periods for Ellipses."

1.   "The state-of-the-art Russian-built oxygen system used by Hall consisted of a stiff plastic oxygen mask of the sort worn by MiG [1] fighter pilots during the Vietnam War, connected via a rubber hose and a crude regulator to an orange steel and Kevlar gas canister[2] (Smaller and much lighter than a scuba tank, each one weighed 6.6 [3] pounds when full.) [4] Although we hadn't slept with oxygen during our previous stay at Camp Three, now that we had begun the push to the summit Rob strongly urged us to breathe gas through the night[5] 'Every minute you remain at this altitude and above,' he cautioned, 'your minds and bodies are deteriorating[6]'" —Jon Krakauer, *Into Thin Air* (154)

2.   "To be valid, hypotheses must be subject to falsification— [7] that is, they must be testable in such fashion that the alternative between reject and not-reject is clear and specific and that the probability is measurable[8] The statement 'He is a nice man' [9] is too vague to be testable[10] The statement 'That man does not eat chocolate after every meal' [11] is falsifiable in the sense that we can gather evidence to show whether the man has or has not eaten chocolate after every meal in the past[12] If the evidence covers only a week, the probability that we could reject the hypothesis (we doubt that he does not eat chocolate after every meal) [13] will be higher than if the evidence covers a year[14]" —Peter L[15] Bernstein, *Against the Gods* (207–08)

3.   "Deaths occurred from Kansas, where thirty-two towns and cities were inundated, to West Virginia. Officially, the Red Cross reported 246 people drowned; the U.S.[16] Weather Bureau reported 313.[17] (The Red Cross confidentially warned Hoover its figures on deaths were 'not necessarily reliable.') [18] Official sources attributed an additional 250 deaths indirectly to the flood.[19] But the death toll almost certainly ran far higher.[20]"

—John M. Barry, *Rising Tide* (286)

27

Dash with Dashes

Writers have many uses for the dash. Unlike inexperienced writers who may use it indiscriminately as a substitute for other marks, professional writers employ the dash to mark explanations, interpolations, additions, and long pauses. Whereas handbooks warn against its use, in particular its overuse or faulty use, the writers I've observed use it freely and effectively. (Don't confuse the dash with the hyphen. Dashes come *between* words and, with most keyboards, can be made with two or three taps of the hyphen key. Hyphens—a single tap—are used only *within* words. Neither one has spaces before and after. See also chapter 31, "Connect with Hyphens.")

Explanations.   Notice how the authors of *Words and Women* slip their explanation into this sentence:

> Although *witch* may regain the prestige of one of its former meanings—a woman whose gifts included the power to heal—*bitch* has certain phonetic qualities that make it an unlikely candidate for rehabilitation. —Casey Miller and Kate Swift (131)

Miller and Swift could have set off the phrase with commas, but the dashes direct more attention to the upcoming statement.

Miller and Swift's explanation interrupts their sentence; in the example that follows, it comes at the end and is set off with a single dash:

> Despite extensive diabolization of Crone figures both mortal and divine, there were curious survivals in patriarchy of the wise Crone as a divinity essential to, and perhaps more powerful than, God—like Athene in her role of the Wisdom of Zeus, and her Roman counterpart Minerva as the Wisdom of Jupiter.
> —Barbara G. Walker, *The Crone* (59)

In this sentence, Walker might have set off the explanation with a comma, though the dash is probably the better choice. The dash seems preferable in the following sentence too (which includes a cynical parenthetic interruption):

> What people somehow (inadvertently, I'm sure) forgot to mention when we were children was that we need to make messes in order to find out who we are and why we are here—and, by extension, what we're supposed to be writing. —Anne Lamott, *Bird by Bird* (32)

Dashes are like commas in that it takes two to mark interruptions, only one for a final nonrestrictive addition. In the interests of clarity, writers rarely use dashes to set off more than one interruption in a sentence.

Explanations are often in the form of appositives—they rename something in the main clause:

> The inventor—the Edison on the frontiers of the fourth kingdom—is unconfined by the confident inhibitions of scientific knowledge. In fact it is even misleading to speak of a "frontier"—an outer boundary for the fourth kingdom. —Daniel J. Boorstin, *Cleopatra's Nose* (153)

■ The appositive "Edison" renames and explains *inventor*; "boundary" renames *frontier*.

> Harry S. Truman is a man whom history will delight to remember. Those very lapses from dignity that made him an object of scorn to millions of Republicans—the angry letters, testy press conferences, whistle stops, impossible sport shirts, and early-morning seminars on the streets of dozens of American cities—open his door to immortality. —Clinton Rossiter, *The American Presidency* (170)

■ The appositive series explains *lapses*.

The Kobuk is three hundred miles long and has at least fifty con-
siderable tributaries—fifty branching streams to which salmon
could be returning to spawn—and yet when they have come up
the Kobuk to this point, to the mouth of the Salmon River, thirty
thousand salmon turn left. —John McPhee, *Coming into the Country* (22)

■ The enclosed appositive tells more about *tributaries*.

Boorstin has an appositive in each sentence, the first an interruption
and the second a sentence ending. Rossiter and McPhee interrupt their
sentences, enclosing appositives with two dashes.

Interpolations.   Some interruptions are actually interpolations—
complete statements that are only somewhat related to the main statement, as in this sentence describing a mother's magnified fears:

On nights when I came home far past my promised hour of
return—there were too many of these, I regret to say—I would
often find her sitting by the phone, sobbing, her terror so mani-
fest it seemed to shrivel her six-foot frame. —Miles Harvey, *The Island
of Lost Maps* (320)

Harvey's dashes enclose his admission of failings as a teenager and interrupt his description of his mother's reactions. Stephen Jay Gould
interpolates commentary about proverbial sheep:

We may not attribute much individuality to sheep in general—
they do, after all, establish our icon of blind following and
identical form as they jump over fences in the mental schemes
of insomniacs—but Dolly will grow up to be as unique and as
ornery as any sheep can be. —*The Lying Stones of Marrakech* (294)

Within his interpolated sentence, Gould sets off "after all" with commas.

Pauses for emphasis.   Writers of course know about using the dash
to insert a pause before finishing the sentence:

The lure seems irretrievably snagged—until the river erupts.
                              —McPhee, *Coming into the Country* (22)

This, then, was the Drake Passage, the most dreaded bit of ocean
on the globe—and rightly so. —Alfred Lansing, *Endurance* (225)

> About noon a raw and penetrating mistlike rain began to fall, and the wind slowly started to move around toward the north—dead ahead. —Lansing (226)

> They might invite an unemployed shipmaster, brother to the local tailor, to dine; but to allow a daughter to marry such a person—never! —Samuel Eliot Morison, *John Paul Jones* (27)

In each of these sentences, the dash adds emphasis by delaying the final words. Some writers use it to insert a correction:

> In the ancient Western world, of which I am a historian, many—perhaps most—people assumed that the universe was inhabited by invisible beings whose presence impinged upon the visible world and its human inhabitants. —Elaine Pagels, *The Origin of Satan* (xv)

Summary

We've seen examples of the dash as a reputable punctuation mark that performs a function not served as well by other marks.

- ❖ Dashes look like long hyphens; they go *between* words whereas hyphens go *within* words.
- ❖ Writers use the dash to insert explanations, some of them as appositives renaming the thing they are explaining.
- ❖ Writers use the dash to interpolate complete statements somewhat related to the subject at hand.
- ❖ Writers use the dash to insert a pause to emphasize the sentence end.
- ❖ Writers use the dash to correct previous words or phrases.
- ❖ An interruption in a sentence requires two dashes, one before and one after.
- ❖ To avoid confusing readers, writers rarely use dashes to set off more than one interruption in a sentence.

□ **Practice** □

Read the following sentences and determine the effects of the dashes. Would some other form of punctuation be preferable?

1. "As I mentioned, abilities that seem effortless to us—categorizing events, deducing cause and effect, and pursuing conflicting

goals—are major challenges in designing an intelligent system, ones that robot designers strive, still unsuccessfully, to duplicate."
—Steven Pinker, *The Blank Slate* (52)

2. "From this point forward, the debate over managing risk will converge on the uses of [Bernoulli's] three requisite assumptions—full information, independent trials, and the relevance of quantitative valuation." —Peter L. Bernstein, *Against the Gods* (121)

3. "The only Roman emperors who did not throw Christians to the lions were the Christian emperors: They threw pagans to the lions with the same gusto and for the same crime—having a different religion." —Petr Beckmann, *A History of Pi* (57)

4. "Since the time of Constantine—the time, that is, that the young, fiercely ambitious tetrarch left Trier to impose his unrelenting vision of unity first on his fellow tetrarchs, then on the empire, then on the Church—people who identified themselves as Jews, even when that identification was less than clear, were forced to stand apart." —James Carroll, *Constantine's Sword* (404)

5. "The question of identity—What is a Russian?—touched everyone, including the most committed liberals and former liberals."
—David Remnick, *Resurrection* (113)

6. "What [Karl] Marx derided as otherworldly escapism—those prayer rallies and miracle celebrations and a state-defying medievalism—would, in the Catholic case, prove over the rest of the century to be a spectacularly successful exercise of wily politics, the genius of which involved a steady denial that the movement was at all political." —Carroll (480)

7. "Far stronger than the states as a check on the Presidency is the American system of free enterprise—that fabulous galaxy of corporations, small businesses, partnerships, individual enterprises, trade associations, co-operatives, unions, consumer groups, and foundations through which the power of economic decision is splintered and diffused in the interest of freedom and progress."
—Rossiter (60)

28

Point with Colons

S ome writers avoid colons because of insecurity about how to use them. Interestingly, then, those who do use them acquire a stylistic edge: their writing looks more sophisticated—because it comes from writers who know how to use colons! You too can be a colon user; the rules are easy.

Colons and explanations. First look at the very basic colon usage in the following sentence:

> Instruction was available in three forms: popular education, apprenticeship, and the courses of study at traditional schools and universities. —William Manchester, *A World Lit Only by Fire* (98)

Manchester's colon points to a series that explains and amplifies the first part of the sentence; the three noun phrases identify the three forms of instruction. Worth noting are these points: (1) the items in the series are parallel (all noun phrases), (2) all together they still constitute a sentence fragment, and (3) the sentence part that precedes the colon is an independent clause. These are the primary conventions for using colons in sentences. But as we'll see in the following examples, writers find ways to vary them. In this next example, the list that follows the colon is not a fragment:

> His [Johann Martin Zacharias Dase's] extraordinary calculating powers were timed by renowned mathematicians: He multiplied two 8-digit numbers in his head in 54 seconds; two 20-digit numbers in 6 minutes; two 40-digit numbers in 40 minutes; and two 100-digit numbers (also in his head!) in 8 hours and 45 minutes.
> —Petr Beckmann, *A History of Pi* (105)

Unlike Manchester, Beckmann follows his colon with an independent clause that includes a series of noun phrases (each *numbers* with modifiers) explaining Dase's "extraordinary calculating powers." Beckmann separates the items with semicolons.

The colon is not limited to introducing lists or fragments. Writers employ it to introduce an explanatory independent clause, as in the following sentence about President Eisenhower's televised press conferences:

> The moral is an old one, familiar to all the able Presidents: when you find a bright new tool, don't dull it with too much use.
> —Clinton Rossiter, *The American Presidency* (121)

Following Rossiter's colon is a second complete statement that explains and fills out the first one. Here are two more examples:

> The important difference—the fact on which the existence of coral reefs depends—is this: the coral polyp has the ability to secrete lime, forming a hard cup about itself. —Rachel Carson, *The Edge of the Sea* (174)

> And there are also the dogs: let's not forget the dogs, the dogs in their pen who will surely hurtle and snarl their way out if you ever stop writing, because writing is, for some of us, the latch that keeps the door of the pen closed, keeps those crazy ravenous dogs contained. —Anne Lamott, *Bird by Bird* (26)

The part of the sentence that follows the colon is essential for developing the meaning of the first part.

When an independent clause follows a colon, writers sometimes begin that clause with a capital letter:

> A compelling theory, but it had a significant hole: It could not explain why the prevailing easterlies of the trade belt suddenly

gave way north of the Horse Latitudes to winds blowing in exactly the opposite direction. —Erik Larson, *Isaac's Storm* (54)

But as we've seen, the first word following the colon is usually lowercase. It is more likely to be capitalized when the clause is only the first of several statements, each written as a sentence.

Colons and quotations. A common use of the colon is to introduce a quotation. In the following examples, notice that both quotation and introductory clause are complete statements:

They will be moved by the simple dignity of his [Truman's] confession: "There are probably a million people in this country who could do the presidential job better than I, but I've got the job and I'm doing the very best I can." —Rossiter (171)

Two and a half millennia ago, Plato looked to divine inspiration for an explanation: "A poet is a light and winged thing, and holy, and never able to compose until he has become inspired, . . . for not by art do they utter these, but by power divine." —David Perkins, *Archimedes' Bathtub* (21)

One of the few cautions about colon use is to avoid resuming the opening clause after the explanation or quotation has been stated. Don't do this, for example:

Malaysian women hold several important government offices: attorney general, trade minister, and bank governor, although the law still requires that they cover their heads.

The simplest revision for this sentence would be to change the colon and the last comma to dashes, thus enclosing the list. If Rossiter had wanted to continue his statement about Truman's confession, he could have begun a new sentence after the quotation. The problem with a resumption is that readers may not know whether it goes with the explanation or with the opening clause. One more caution about colons: Use only one colon in a sentence.

Flexibility. Variations in colon use almost always come after the colon, as the preceding examples demonstrate. Writers are quite consistent in leading up to the colon with an independent clause. But writers who are *really* confident about using colons might experiment a little. Look at this example:

> Phylogeny, ontogeny, genetics, endocrinology: all are there to be sampled, and I am a shameless carpetbagger. —Natalie Angier, *Woman: An Intimate Geography* (xiv)

Angier still has an independent clause, but she has put the explanatory series *before* the colon. Most writers would be more likely to use a dash in a case like this. The flexibility of punctuation usage also shows up in the passage by Sebastian Junger on page 183, in which he introduces explanatory lists in three different ways: with a dash, with a colon, and with a period.

Summary

Here are some points to keep in mind about colons:

- ❖ Introduce a colon with an independent clause.
- ❖ Use colons to point to lists and fragments that explain, amplify, and develop what went before.
- ❖ Use colons to point to independent clauses that explain, amplify, and develop what went before.
- ❖ Use colons to point to sentence-length or longer quotations after introducing them with an independent clause.
- ❖ If you need to resume an idea after your explanation, begin a new sentence.
- ❖ Use only one colon in a sentence.

□ **Practice** □

Analyze the excerpt from *The Perfect Storm* on page 183.

- ❖ What is the effect of each punctuation mark: dash, colon, period?
- ❖ Interchange the marks and assess the effects.
- ❖ Do you prefer any mark over the others?
- ❖ Choose one mark (dash, colon, period) to replace the other two and consider the effects.
- ❖ For the sake of consistency, would the same mark be preferable for all three introductions of series?

29

Separate with Semicolons

*T*he main function of the semicolon is to separate and connect related independent clauses without the addition of a coordinating conjunction. The second clause usually adds something to the first that would be too separate with a period and insufficiently separate with a comma. Notice how William Manchester achieves both separation and connection in these sentences describing an aspect of medieval life:

> The everyday dinner of a man of rank ran from fifteen to twenty dishes; England's earl of Warwick, who fed as many as five hundred guests at a sitting, used six oxen a day at the evening meal. The oxen were not as succulent as they sound; by tradition, the meat was kept salted in vats against the possibility of a siege, and boiled in a great copper vat. —*A World Lit Only by Fire* (52)

Manchester's first semicolon might have been a period; his mark, however, implies connection. The second semicolon could perhaps have been a colon, implying an explanation. His choice of both semicolons implies balanced, equivalent ideas.

When novelist and nonfiction writer Virginia Woolf uses the semicolon in the following sentence to balance clauses of unequal length, she implies equal weight:

> But it is obvious that the values of women differ very often from the values which have been made by the other sex; naturally, this is so. —*A Room of One's Own* (76–77)

Shifts from the usual.   Semicolons are sometimes seen as boring marks—the kind that staid old professors use in their stuffy monographs. But if you look closely, you'll see that writers of all types use them for all kinds of reasons. Occasionally the information added by the second clause is unexpected:

> [Karl] Marx had ancestors; so did his genius. —James Carroll, *Constantine's Sword* (403)

Rarely, the unexpected addition might even be a fragment:

> But now the sixteenth [century] was more than half gone and it had produced no woman to match [Joan of Arc]; indeed, no heroines at all. —Manchester (218)

Fragments after semicolons, such as the preceding one, are ordinarily frowned upon. The ideas and sentence elements on either side of the mark are supposed to be balanced, we say, equivalent. True, semicolons usually separate independent clauses. But then so do periods. And just as periods sometimes separate fragments from sentences, so do semicolons. Not usually, but it does happen. And when it does, the writer achieves a certain emphasis along with the connection. Manchester might have gained that emphasis with a dash before the final phrase, but he didn't make that choice. He opted for balance.

Another shift from the usual is the semicolon followed by a grammatically unnecessary coordinating conjunction, such as *and, but,* or *so.*

> Careful observers can distinguish among tens or even hundreds of thousands of different faces; and the "Identikit," widely used by Interpol and by police forces in the West generally, is capable of reconstructing more than ten billion different faces. —Carl Sagan, *The Dragons of Eden* (165)

What published writers seem not to do is begin the second clause with a transitional adverb such as *however*—as in this sentence:

> Clouds can be harbingers of the coming weather; however, the observer needs to know how to read them.

I'm sure some do, but I didn't find examples. When writers do use these transitional words, it seems to be at or near the beginning of sentences, making connections to foregoing sentences, or inserted after several words of the second clause.

Separations in series. A common use for the semicolon is to separate series items that have internal punctuation:

> On the following Monday, the inauguration rush would include a grand ball for 4,000: they would waltz and polka to the beat of a military band; feast on an elegant medley of beef, veal, poultry, game, smoked meats, terrapin oysters, and salads; finish with an astounding wartime array of ices, tarts, cakes, fruits, and nuts; and then retire for the evening with steaming coffee and good rich chocolate. —Jay Winik, *April 1865* (30)

> Inside the thick black border lines of this ideal Macedonian state were one-third of mainland Greece; the Greek island of Thasos, called "Aegean Macedonia"; a chunk of southwestern Bulgaria, called "Pirin Macedonia" after the Pirin Mountains there; a slice of "Macedonian" land in Albania; and the former-Yugoslav Macedonia, the only "liberated" part of the country, called "Vardar Macedonia" after the Vardar River, which runs through Skopje. —Robert D. Kaplan, *Balkan Ghosts* (67)

The items in the series might be connected to one another with conjunctions following the semicolons. The inclusion of *or* several times in the next well-crafted sentence has the effect of adding the idea of alternatives.

> Others [fables] derived from romantic yarns told by wanderers; or the legends of Alexander the Great and Saint Thomas the Apostle; or the imaginative figments of Ctesias, a Greek who lived in the Persian court four centuries before Christ; or the Roman concoctions of Pliny and Gaius Julius Solinus; or in the extraordinarily popular fourteenth-century hoax *Voyage of Sir John Mandeville, Knight.* —Manchester (232)

You too can use the semicolon.   Most writers, it seems, use semi-colons, but some writers rely on them more than others do. Even though this mark tends to be a little more formal than the dash or the period, it does make its appearance in the sentences of writers who assume a less formal stance. Here are two examples:

> [Books] show us what community and friendship mean; they show us how to live and die. —Anne Lamott, *Bird by Bird* (15)

> Stuart Hutchison—the young Canadian cardiologist—and I were assigned to one tent; Rob, Frank, Mike Groom, John Taske, and Yasuko Namba were in another; Lou, Beck Weathers, Andy Harris, and Doug Hansen occupied a third. —Jon Krakauer, *Into Thin Air* (162)

We might conclude that the semicolon is an appropriate mark of punctuation at any level of formality.

Summary

- ❖ Semicolons separate and connect closely related independent clauses.
- ❖ Semicolons separate items in series that have internal punctuation.
- ❖ Writers sometimes use coordinating conjunctions (such as *and, but,* and *or*) along with the semicolons.
- ❖ Apparently, writers rarely use transitional adverbs (such as *however*) immediately following semicolons.
- ❖ Some writers use semicolons more frequently than others.

□ **Practice** □

Read the following sentences and consider whether each semicolon might be replaced by some other mark of punctuation—say a dash, a period, or a colon. Then compare what you think is the effect of each new mark with how you read the effect of the semicolon.

1.   "Every morning before dawn our Base Camp sirdar—an avun-cular, highly respected, forty-something Sherpa named Ang Tshering—would light sprigs of juniper incense and chant prayers at the chorten; before heading into the Icefall, West-erners and Sherpas alike would walk past the altar—keeping it

always on the right—and through the sweet clouds of smoke to receive a blessing from Ang Tshering." —Krakauer (128–29)

2. "On top of all the miseries inflicted by predators and parasites, the members of a species show no pity to their own kind. Infanticide, siblicide, and rape can be observed in many kinds of animals; infidelity is common even in so-called pair-bonded species; cannibalism can be expected in all species that are not strict vegetarians; death from fighting is more common in most animal species than it is in the most violent American cities."
—Steven Pinker, *The Blank Slate* (163)

3. "In any closed system, including the universe, entropy will increase with time; to effect a local decrease of entropy, work must be brought in from the outside. This is, of course, impossible for the universe. Just after you have cleaned and arranged your room, it is in a state of low entropy. As time passes, it will tend toward a state of randomness; restoring it will require work, or the expenditure of energy obtained through your food and electricity for the vacuum cleaner. Entropy increases as things decay, as organisms age, as rich deposits of ores are washed downstream. Localized iron deposits are of low entropy; as time passes, the iron becomes distributed randomly through the junk yards of the nation. To reclaim it into a neat, orderly pile requires work." —Jack J. Kraushaar and Robert A. Ristinen, *Energy and Problems of a Technical Society* (82)

30

Possess with Apostrophes

Despite numerous misuses, the rules for showing possession with apostrophes are really quite simple. In English, we indicate possession or connection by affixing an apostrophe to the end of nouns; in some cases we also add an -*s*.

Singular nouns. To make singular nouns possessive, we add an apostrophe plus an -*s*: *person* + *-'s* = *person's, bus* + *-'s* = *bus's.* As I said, simple. Look at these examples:

> Sitting under the *king's* shadow, Diogenes made only one request: that Alexander should stand out of his light. —Barbara G. Walker, *The Crone* (150)

> A box of penguin eggs was brought to the *cook's* table, a small block of blubber was thrown on the dull fire to spark it to life, and an apron was tied on Mertz with orders to produce breakfast. —Lennard Bickel, *Mawson's Will* (86)

> Just north of the shop is Como Bluff, a low ridge about six miles long which was the site of one of the *world's* classic discoveries of dinosaur and early-mammal fossils. —Ian Frazier, *Great Plains* (82)

New Year's came and January went. —Gene Smith, *When the Cheering Stopped* (166)

You see from the last two examples that the simple rule applies also to place and time connections. The rule isn't any more complicated for capitalized names:

Grey's marriage increased *Georgiana's* sense of isolation.
—Amanda Foreman, *Georgiana: Duchess of Devonshire* (286)

Nor for names that end in *s* sounds:

Lewis *Thomas's* first two books, *Lives of a Cell* and *The Medusa and the Snail,* were first written as essays for the *New England Journal of Medicine.* —William Zinsser, *On Writing Well* (61)

Rumor blamed a palace conspiracy involving *Commodus's* athletic trainer and Marcia, his concubine. —Elaine Pagels, *The Origin of Satan* (135)

Georgiana judged *Fox's* decision less harshly than the others.
—Foreman (299)

Plural nouns.   The rule is even simpler for plural nouns—just add an apostrophe: *persons* + ' = *persons'.*

Not for another eight years would the excessive substances now attacking Mawson and Mertz through the *dogs'* livers be isolated in Britain and named "vitamin A." —Bickel (149)

It [a computer program] can also learn from other *players'* experience, and it will "study" other people's games and moves recommended by champions. —Petr Beckmann, *A History of Pi* (187)

Beckmann's sentence illustrates both a regular plural possessive (*players'*) and one formed with a plural noun that doesn't end in -*s* (*people's*). For those few plural nouns that don't end in -*s*, add an apostrophe plus an -*s*: *children* + -'*s* = *children's.* Here's another example:

An advertisement for the NBC news department listed *women's* liberation along with crime in the streets and the Vietnam War as "bad news." —Casey Miller and Kate Swift, *Words and Women* (186)

Names and other proper nouns are made possessive in the same way as common nouns are:

Singular Possessive	*Plural Possessive*
Petr Beckmann**'s** book	the Beckmann**s'** house
John M. Barry**'s** book	the Barry**s'** house
Lewis Thomas**'s** book	the Thomas**es'** house

Other uses.   Besides marking possession and connection, the apostrophe can indicate omissions:

As for Pozzuoli, I *can't* claim any more adventure than a trip to South Ferry or Ozone Park would provide. Pozzuoli is the last stop on the Neapolitan subway. —Stephen Jay Gould, *The Lying Stones of Marrakech* (152)

■ Contraction of *cannot.*

Francis Parkman was Harvard *'44*, of an old Boston family.

—Frazier (162)

■ Omission of century number.

I understand why this style is so attractive to my students: *it's* like primitive art. *It's* simple and decorative, with rich colors, satisfying old forms, and a lot of sophistication underneath that you feel but *don't* really see. —Anne Lamott, *Bird by Bird* (196)

■ Contractions of *it is* and *do not.*

People are sometimes confused about using apostrophes with pronouns (*its* or *it's*?), even though this rule is another simple one: With pronouns, use apostrophes *only in contractions* (such as *we'll, let's, who's*). (See also chapter 20, "Contract Your Words," and chapter 35, "Just in Case—Pronouns Again.")

One additional function of apostrophes is sometimes (but not necessarily) to mark plural numbers, letters, and words: *7'*s, *A's, and's*. (But *7*s and *and*s, without the apostrophe, are also common. Notice that both styles italicize or underline the word, number, or letter but not the -*s* or apostrophe, if used.) Apostrophes are not used for plural years in decades, however:

In the late *1700***s,** the phlogiston theory ran into trouble.

—David Perkins, *Archimedes' Bathtub* (175)

In a sense, Transylvania in 1990 was like Vienna or Berlin in the *1930s.* —Robert D. Kaplan, *Balkan Ghosts* (153)

Caution: If you're following the guidelines of the Associated Press or the American Psychological Association, check the AP or APA style manual for possible differences from these recommendations.

Summary

- ❖ To indicate possession or connection on singular nouns, add apostrophe-plus-*s*.
- ❖ To indicate possession or connection on singular capitalized names, whether or not they end in -*s*, add apostrophe-plus-*s*.
- ❖ To indicate possession or connection on most plural nouns, add an apostrophe.
- ❖ Make names and other proper nouns possessive in the same way as common nouns.
- ❖ To indicate possession or connection on plural nouns that do not end in -*s*, add apostrophe-plus-*s*.
- ❖ Use the apostrophe with pronouns only in contractions.
- ❖ Use the apostrophe to indicate number or letter omissions.
- ❖ Some writers use the apostrophe to indicate plural numbers, letters, or words. Use only an -*s* to indicate years in a decade.

☐ **Practice** ☐

Read these sentences and decide which items in the summary describe the apostrophe usages.

1. "To fans of the British television program 'Upstairs, Downstairs' it came as a surprise that Mrs. Bridges, the Bellamys' cook, had never been married." —Miller and Swift (109)

2. "Randall Blake Michael, a member of Professor Cox's class, also sensed the deep currents of pain his fellow students were expressing." —Miller and Swift (83)

3. "Again, Levoisier's insights are subtle and detailed—and several specific predictions can be derived from his model." —Gould (106)

4. "Leo wasn't a great sinner, but religion ranked rather low in his priorities, below learning, living well, serving as head of the

Medici family, and making war." —William Manchester, *A World Lit Only by Fire* (193)

5. "I had heard about the bizarre case of Stephen Carrie Blumberg, who, during the 1970s and 1980s, removed as many as 23,600 books and manuscripts from 268 libraries in forty-five states, two Canadian provinces, and the District of Columbia." —Miles Harvey, *The Island of Lost Maps* (xviii)

6. "A three hours' drive north of Dodge City is the town of Oberlin, Kansas." —Frazier (152)

7. "Maybe thirty-five years ago this woman had to perform for her parents' friends. Maybe she was their little Charlie McCarthy."
    —Lamott (49)

8. "At court, the women's days were spent mostly 'gazing into space' in an agony of leisure ('suffering from leisure' is a recurrent phrase) something akin to the European melancholy."
    —Alberto Manguel, *A History of Reading* (230)

31

Connect with Hyphens

*D*espite its placement at the end of handbooks—usually in the company of spelling rules—the hyphen is an essential mark of punctuation. It does for words what most other marks do for sentences: it assists reading. One reason for the inattention may be that, unlike some other marks, say commas or periods, its misapplication doesn't often result in a gross misreading. If you were to unnecessarily hyphenate *nonfiction* ("non-fiction," as certain bookstores do), there'd be no confusion or loss of meaning. All the same, if you omit a hyphen in a phrase such as *rare book review* your reader might wonder what is rare, the book or the review. So there are good reasons for understanding hyphens. At the very least, your application of the rules could demonstrate that you know what's up in the world of punctuation.

There are only a few uses for the hyphen: in some compound words, in prefixed words, in separated words, and for omissions in words. Notice that all of these uses occur *within* words. Dashes, on the other hand, though similar in form, are used *outside* of words and look like long hyphens (two or three taps of the hyphen key). (See chapter 27, "Dash with Dashes.")

Compound words.   Words are compounded in three ways: as separate words, with hyphens, and as single words.

SEPARATE WORDS	African Americans, flip chart, lock step, stage fright
HYPHENATED WORDS	cross-cultural, good-sized, rose-colored, son-in-law
SINGLE WORDS	campfire, locksmith, officeholder, roommate

To know which is correct with given words, the safest approach is to refer to a dictionary, where hyphenated words are shown with hyphens, single words have syllable markers, and words written separately, if listed, are spaced. But knowing a few guidelines can save you trips to the dictionary.

Lewis Thomas uses a compound word in the following sentence.

> It is a rather nice surprise to find this idea so threaded through what has become our quite ordinary *day-to-day* discourse.
>
> —*Et Cetera, Et Cetera* (59)

In case you're wondering, his compound word does indeed appear in the dictionary. As a group of three words connected to make a single modifier of *discourse*, it is hyphenated. The main reason these made-up words are hyphenated is to show that it's the combination of words, not the separate words, that modifies the noun. If you decide to coin a modifier, connect the parts with hyphens, as in "a worst-case-scenario decision."

Incidentally, Lewis Thomas might have written "our quite ordinary *everyday* discourse" because it's something that happens *every day*. These two related terms (*everyday* and *every day*) are often confused. The first one—an unhyphenated compound adjective—comes before a noun. The separated words—an adjective and a noun—stand alone.

In the next sentence, we see examples of hyphenated compound words and a nonhyphenated compound.

> The sciences say nothing, of course, about differences in values that are associated with particular *right-wing* and *left-wing* positions (such as in the *tradeoffs* between unemployment and

> environmental protection, diversity and economic efficiency,
> or individual freedom and community cohesion). —Steven Pinker,
> *The Blank Slate* (293–94)

If you were to check your dictionary, you'd see that *right-wing* and *left-wing* are not hyphenated; however, that designation is for nouns. Because Pinker uses them as adjectives preceding their nouns, they are hyphenated.

Adjectives following the words they modify are written as separate words, not hyphenated. We would write "a *well-known* author" but "an author who is *well known*." Adverbs such as *well, better, less,* and *best* are usually hyphenated to the adjectives they modify when they come before the noun but not when they follow the noun. Adverbs that end in *-ly* are not hyphenated with the adjective (for example, "a carefully manicured lawn"). Your dictionary check of Pinker's compound words could also reveal that his choice of *tradeoff* without the hyphen is the preferred spelling but that a hyphenated word is also acceptable.

Here's another example of compound words hyphenated as adjectives preceding a noun:

> The *state-of-the-art Russian-built* oxygen system used by Hall
> consisted of a stiff plastic oxygen mask of the sort worn by MiG
> fighter pilots during the Vietnam War, connected via a rubber
> hose and a crude regulator to an orange steel and Kevlar gas
> canister. —Jon Krakauer, *Into Thin Air* (154)

Both "state-of-the-art" and "Russian-built" would not be hyphenated if they followed the noun: "an oxygen system that was *state of the art* and *Russian built*."

Hyphenate numbers that you combine and use as adjectives: *thirteen-year-old boy, nineteenth-century novel, twenty-five pennies, thirty-first call, three-fourths cup*; but, *a boy who is thirteen years old, a novel of the nineteenth century, three fourths of an apple*. Hyphenate numbers from twenty-one to ninety-nine when using them as either adjectives or nouns.

Prefixed words.   Most prefixes are not hyphenated; they include *anti, co, de, multi, non, over, post, pre, pro, re, semi, sub, un,* and *under*. So we have words like *antioxidant, multinational, nonliteral, postdate, semiliterate, submerge,* and *undernourish*. These prefixes are hyphenated only when there might be a misreading, as in *re-creation*; or when they're attached to a proper noun, as in *anti-American*; or when doubled vowels are awkward, as in *semi-itinerant*. A few prefixes are almost always hyphenated: *all-, ex-* meaning "former," *half-, quasi-*, and *self-*. They appear in words like *all-important, ex-president, half-hour*, and *self-taught*. But we also have *half dollar, halfhearted*, and *selfless*. Again, check the dictionary if you're not sure.

This sentence by Rachel Carson illustrates not only a hyphenated compound word but also an unhyphenated prefixed one:

> The *ice-covered* Antarctic continent, bathed by seas of uniform coldness, is in the grip of the polar *anticyclone*. —*The Sea around Us* (176)

The sentence aptly illustrates the reason for hyphenating compound modifiers. If Carson had written *ice-covered* as two words, an unwary reader might have first read *ice* as the subject of the sentence and *covered* as the verb.

Divided words.   With the advent of word-wrap in word-processing programs, writers seldom need be concerned with breaking words at the ends of lines. But we do still encounter these divisions in our reading because they are common in printed works, as in this example:

> . . . unimaginable, down to the last atomic particle. Probability now governs. Randomness is the controlling urgency in nature. So, it is of interest to take a look at . . .
>
> —Thomas (85)

Division occurs between syllables but avoids separating capitalized names and leaving one- or two-letter remainders. (Also notice my hyphen in *one-* indicating a compound with *letter*. Notice the space before *or*.)

Omissions in words.   Another disappearing hyphen is the one that substitutes for letters in words the writer doesn't want to spell out: names and taboo words usually. Here's an example:

> Whenever newspapers feel obliged to allude to the word, in verbatim news accounts, the convention is to print f - - - . —Thomas (85)

Sometimes an underline is used instead. You probably won't have any use for this dying convention, although you may encounter it in your reading. You can see another example on page 76, where I'm reluctant to name names.

Caution: If you're following the guidelines of the Associated Press or the American Psychological Association, check the AP or APA style manual for possible differences from these recommendations.

Summary

❖ Compound words are written as single words, hyphenated words, or separate words.

❖ Dictionaries are the best source of information on whether to hyphenate particular words.

❖ Adverb modifiers ending in *-ly* are usually not hyphenated with their adjectives.

❖ Two-word modifiers that precede their nouns are often hyphenated.

❖ The prefixes *anti, co, de, multi, non, over, post, pre, pro, re, semi, sub, un,* and *under* are usually not hyphenated.

❖ The prefixes *all-, ex-* meaning "former," *half-, quasi-,* and *self-* are usually hyphenated.

❖ Words separated at the ends of lines are hyphenated at syllable breaks.

❖ An older custom (now often with humorous intent) uses hyphens to indicate omitted letters of words to be avoided.

☐ **Practice** ☐

Writers use hyphens in various situations for the ultimate purpose of clarity. Consider and discuss the hyphens (or lack of them) in the following sentences.

1.   "Where proud antebellum homes and mansions once stood, there is rotting wood and cracked paint and weed-choked grass; where Southerners once took evening promenade walks down hundred-foot-wide boulevards and through acres of rich green parks, there is the stench of urine and feces and decaying animal carcasses; and where there was once the clamor of commerce and exchange, there are now ghost towns and equally ghostly urban pockets." —Jay Winik, *April 1865* (301)

2.   "In mathematics, which is but a mirror of the society in which it thrives or suffers, the pre-Athenian period is one of colorful men and important discoveries." —Petr Beckmann, *A History of Pi* (36)

3.   "Probably the ones best adapted for travel by raft are the wood-boring insects, which, of all the insect tribe, are most commonly found on oceanic islands. The poorest raft travelers must be the mammals. But even a mammal might cover short interisland distances." — Carson, *The Sea around Us* (90)

4.   "The trails would go along, well cut and stamped out through moss campion, reindeer moss, sedge tussocks, crowberries, prostrate willows, dwarf birch, bog blueberries, white mountain avens, low-bush cranberries, lichens, Labrador tea; then, abruptly, and for no apparent reason, the trails would disappear. Their well-worn ruts suggested hundreds of animals, heavy traffic. So where did they go when the trail vanished?" —John McPhee, *Coming into the Country* (52)

Part Four

A Few Good Rules

R ules describe how parts of a language fit together. They say that verbs agree with their subjects, that pronouns have antecedents and must agree with their antecedents, that prepositions have objects. They tell us that verbs can have tense, **number**, **mood**, and voice, and that pronouns can have **case**, number, and gender. And more. The main purpose of the rules is to help writers to write clearly and readers to understand what a writer has written. Rules prevent ambiguity. They aid clarity.

If English is your first language, you learned most of its rules before you ever started kindergarten, and you learned most of the rest of them too without referring to a textbook. The most beautiful part about the rules is that you can know them without even knowing their names. You don't need to run off a list of prepositions in order to use them in sentences. You don't need to know what an antecedent is in order to have one. Real rules come so naturally, in fact, that most of the time we use them without thinking about them.

Most of the rules of language that you know are the ones you use in speech, and you learned them by listening to other people speak, by speaking yourself, and, sometimes, by being corrected when you used a wrong form. (Your mom said, "Don't say 'Me want,' say 'I want.'") If

English is not your first language, you may have learned it in much the same way as native speakers—by listening, speaking, and trying out new words and forms—maybe in an English class but, if you're fluent in the language, in social situations as well. The difference is that you probably needed to learn more of the grammar rules in class than native speakers do.

Most of the rules for speaking apply to written English as well—with some exceptions. The most notable exceptions are the addition of punctuation marks and the requirement that words be spelled in conventional ways, so these are things we all learn from books and teachers. Another is that we write types of sentences that we don't often speak: for instance, those with long interruptions between subjects and verbs or between pronouns and their antecedents, or with introductory participial modifiers. We write a wide variety of sentences that we have little use for in everyday speech.

Most of these rules for writing we learn in the same way we learn rules for speaking—from observation, in this case from books. Through reading, we observe how other writers write, how they begin their sentences, how they use their subjects and verbs, their modifiers, their pronouns. And we learn by trying out new sentences, maybe getting them wrong and being corrected, but not giving up on writing—just as we never gave up on talking.

There are times when as writers we may need to remind ourselves of what the rules for writing are. We write ourselves into situations where we are forced to think about grammatical matters such as antecedents of pronouns or tense of verbs. We may be trying for a particularly tricky type of sentence, for variety or emphasis, and we are suddenly faced with making a decision about whether our verb should be singular or plural when we've lost track of our subject.

Although this book is mainly about stretching the rules, expanding them, and exploring usage as a way of removing some of the constraints on our writing style, this section deals with some of those sticky situations. I've selected some of the stickier ones, those that seem to confound even experienced writers at one time or another:

- ❖ "Make Your Verbs Agree with Your Subjects" (chapter 32)
- ❖ "Be Sure Your Pronouns Refer to Something" (chapter 33)
- ❖ "Make Your Pronouns Agree" (chapter 34)
- ❖ "Just in Case—Pronouns Again" (chapter 35)
- ❖ "Don't Dangle Your Modifiers" (chapter 36)

32

Make Your Verbs Agree with Your Subjects

*T*he simple version of this rule is that verbs agree with their subjects in number (singular, plural) and person (first person—the writer, *I, we*; second person—the reader, *you*; third person—the subject, *he, she, it, they*, and all nouns). It's not difficult keeping track of person; the only complication is that the third-person-singular verb takes an *-s* ending in the present tense: "She *walks* to work every day" and "Karen *walks* to work every day" as compared to "I *walk* to work every day" and "We *walk* to work every day."

More difficult to keep an eye on is number; singular subjects need singular verbs, and plural subjects need plural verbs. We say "Writers *are* odd people," but "This writer *is* the oddest one yet." Granted, that's not so difficult either—under most circumstances. We complicate our work, though, with some of our perfectly normal sentence constructions—when we separate our verbs from our subjects, invert our sentence order, compound our subjects in various ways, and use collective subjects in both singular and plural ways.

Verbs separated from their subjects. Verbs are frequently separated from their subjects. Notice in the following sentence how Rachel Carson separates her verb, *has become*, from her subject, *position*.

> The position of the prey animals—the mussels, barnacles, and periwinkles—on sheltered shores *has become* difficult. —*The Edge of the Sea* (97)

A less attentive writer might have written *have become* to agree with the closer noun, *shores* (or even *animals*). Here's another example, this one by John McPhee:

> The journey itself—two thousand miles, a large part of it on scarcely charted Arctic rivers—*was* an accomplishment in exploration, but to Harper that was incidental. —*Coming into the Country* (212)

McPhee's verb, *was*, agrees with its singular subject, *journey*, despite the intervening plural nouns. We may sometimes have trouble because our subjects *feel* plural next to those intervening words, as in this example:

> A variety of recovery methods *has been analyzed*.

Variety is singular despite the plural modifier; the verb agrees.

How about something a little trickier, where you might not be sure whether the subject is singular or plural?

> All that is missing [*are? is?*] copies of the manuscript.

Keep in mind that verbs agree with subjects, not necessarily with any complements (which ordinarily follow their verbs). The subject of the sentence, of course, is *All*, with an intervening *that* clause, but is *All* singular or plural? Well, we can assume that the writer intended it as singular because of the first *is*, which agrees with *that*, which refers to *All*. So the second *is* agrees with a singular *All*. The plural complement, *copies*, has nothing to do with it. Try again on this sentence:

> All that matters now [*are? is?*] your help and support in finding those copies.

The correct verb is again *is*; we know because the first verb, *matters*, is singular, so *All* is singular. Mainly this rule tells writers to agree with themselves: if you write *matters* to indicate a singular *All*, then you can't change your mind when you get closer to a plural complement.

The next sentence illustrates a similar, though usually easier, problem:

> What is missing here *is* the manuscript and all its copies.

Actually, most *what* clauses of this type are singular, as is this one. The subject of the second *is* is the entire clause (*What is missing here*). It's a single thing, one clause, therefore a singular subject. In Robert M. Pirsig's hands the construction looks like this:

> What's left now *is* just fragments: debris, scattered notes, which can be pieced together but which leave huge areas unexplained.
> —*Zen and the Art of Motorcycle Maintenance* (183)

Pirsig's verb *is* agrees with the singular *what* clause, not with the plural complement, *fragments*. As a side note, his sentence has two clauses beginning *which*, both of them plural referring to the plural noun *notes*. Here's one more *what* example from Pirsig, a rather cynical one, again singular:

> What you're supposed to do in most freshman-rhetoric courses *is* to read a little essay or short story, discuss how the writer has done certain little things to achieve certain little effects, and then have the students write an imitative little essay or short story to see if they can do the same little things. (170)

Though tricky to use, it's a good type of sentence to keep in mind when you're looking for a variation that will emphasize your point. (There's another example, by Garry Wills, on p. 42.)

Verbs in inverted order.   The following sentence from Carson's *The Edge of the Sea* illustrates two difficulties, not only the separated subject and verb but also an inverted order:

> Off some of the Keys, in shallow water, *lives* the so-called slate-pencil <u>urchin</u>, named for its short stout spines. (193)

Carson's verb, *lives*, follows two introductory phrases and comes before its subject, *urchin*. In another example, David G. McCullough begins a sentence with two inverted clauses:

> And nowhere *was* there more <u>talk</u>, or *were* <u>things</u> in such turmoil, than at the Pennsylvania depot and yards, where tons of food and supplies were piling up, and the crowds were so thick, any hour of the day, that you could barely make your way through.
> —*The Johnstown Flood* (239)

Probably the most common kind of inverted order is that begun with *there*, as in the following sentence from *Georgiana: Duchess of Devonshire* where the plural subject, *periods*, follows the verb:

> There *were* often long <u>periods</u> of calm. —Amanda Foreman (311)

Because *there* has a singular feeling, we're sometimes tempted to follow it with a singular verb. Another example, on page 38, is accompanied by a caution about overusing this form.

Verbs after <u>one</u> . . . <u>who</u> (or <u>that</u>).   If you have trouble with this next agreement situation, you have lots of company. Rather than avoiding sentences like these, observe how they work so they can be part of your stylistic repertoire. See what you can do with these two sentences:

> She is one of those writers <u>who</u> still [*compose*? *composes*?] on yellow legal tablets.

> One of the problems <u>that</u> [*have*? *has*?] resisted a solution is everyday violence.

Like all verbs, those following *who* and *that* agree with their subjects; the problem is that *who* and *that*, being pronouns, can be either singular or plural depending on the words they refer to. So the questions to ask are, What does *who* mean? What does *that* mean? In the first sentence, the *who* clause identifies "those writers," so the verb is the plural *compose*. (But compare "She is the only one of those writers who still *composes* on yellow legal tablets.") In the second example, the *that* clause identifies "the problems," so the verb is the plural *have*.

Try one more, this one with two verb choices.

> One of the things <u>that</u> [*were*? *was*?] criticized about my paper [*were*? *was*?] its length.

Here, *that* means "things," so the first verb is *were*, and, in the second case, *was* agrees with the subject of the sentence, *One*. (This kind of agreement is not as much a problem as it may seem, because writers almost always know what their pronouns refer to.)

Verbs with compound subjects.   Compound subjects joined by *and* are plural—one plus one equals two!—so they take plural verbs:

> Quantum <u>electrodynamics</u> and <u>evolution</u> by natural selection *are* examples of successful big theories, addressing important phenomena. —Edward O. Wilson, *Consilience: The Unity of Knowledge* (52)

It's only when the two subjects are joined by *or* or *nor* that agreement gets tricky. That's because the rule says that the verb agrees with the nearer subject, whatever its number. We would write "Neither Smith nor

Chapman *is* right," "Either Smith or his board <u>members</u> *are* wrong," and "Either the board members or <u>Jones</u> *is* right." Because of the potential awkwardness of this construction, most writers avoid it. Here's one example that I managed to find:

> The person or <u>persons</u> who sent the tape *were* never found."
> —Judith Miller, Stephen Engelberg, and William Broad,
> *Germs: Biological Weapons and America's Secret War* (159)

The verb *were* agrees with the nearer subject, *persons*. This is probably the sensible way to go with such constructions, since our ear tells us that "the person or persons were" sounds better than "the persons or person was."

Verbs after collective nouns.   Words like *team*, *family*, and *troop* are collective nouns, meaning that they refer to a group of people. So do they take singular or plural verbs? The short answer is that they are usually singular:

> The <u>team</u> *has* won its first game of the season.

> The <u>family</u> *is* going on a two-week vacation to Hawaii.

> The <u>troop</u> of soldiers *was* surrounded.

When the meaning is plural, the writer probably has to make a conscious effort to use a plural verb:

> The <u>team</u> *do* not agree on who should be the new coach.

> The <u>family</u> *differ* on the choice of Hawaii.

> The <u>troop</u> of soldiers *were* separated by the insurgents.

Writers more often avoid the awkward-sounding plural, as Barbara G. Walker does in this sentence:

> <u>Members</u> of this tribe *were* hereditary guardians of the sacred Black Stone. —*The Crone* (55)

So we might say "Members of the team do not agree," "Members of the family differ," and "The soldiers in the troop were separated." (Note that collective nouns can also have plural forms—*teams, families, troops*—indicating more than one of the collective group, but they're so clearly plural that there is no problem with verb agreement.)

Verbs after indefinite pronouns and adjectives.   Indefinite pronouns and adjectives like *each, every, everyone, somebody*, and *either* are singular, so the verbs in the following sentences are correct:

Each member of the team *has stated* a preference.

Neither of the top picks *has accepted* the job.

Everyone in both schools *wants* the selection process to be over.

Getting these verbs to agree often requires some thought because the subjects feel plural and, in fact, we often use them with plural pronouns when speaking.

Summary

This chapter does not deal with all possible trouble spots for subject-verb agreement, only some of the stickier ones, the ones that writers may have to stop and consider even when they've been writing for many years. By observing these rules, you relieve your readers of potential confusion.

- ❖ Singular subjects take singular verbs; plural subjects take plural verbs.
- ❖ Watch for verbs widely separated from their subjects.
- ❖ Carefully check verbs in sentences that begin *All that, What*, or *One of*.
- ❖ Watch for verbs that precede their subjects (inverted order).
- ❖ Collective nouns (like *team, family,* and *troop*) are usually singular and so usually take singular verbs.
- ❖ When collective nouns refer to actions of individuals within the collective, the verbs are plural.
- ❖ Singular indefinite pronouns and adjectives (such as *anyone* and *each*) are followed by singular verbs.

□ **Practice** □

Decide whether the verbs in the following tricky sentences should be singular or plural.

1. The couple (*are, is*) celebrating their twenty-fifth wedding anniversary.
2. As a finale to the graduation ceremony, the class (*throw, throws*) their hats into the air.

3. The board of commissioners (*differ, differs*) from one another on where to build the bridge.

4. What appears to be tact and courtesy (*are, is*) really ambition and desire to acquire a promotion.

5. All I ever seem to write (*is, are*) essays.

6. She is one of twenty people who (*is, are*) trying out for the part.

7. Either the board members or the chairperson (*is, are*) going to nullify the contract.

33

Be Sure Your Pronouns Refer to Something

Pronouns can mean nothing and everything. The pronoun *he* can mean any male person, *she* can mean any female person, and *it* can mean any *thing* in the universe. The plural *they* can mean more than one of any persons or things. The pronoun *I* naturally has its limitations, as does *you*, and *we* can lend itself to ambiguity. The flexibility of pronouns, this ability to mean almost anything, is both an advantage and a liability for writers. On the side of advantage, pronouns make it possible to avoid tiresome repetition of a noun:

> But there is another way to think about <u>Cupid</u> and *his* name. *He* surely was, despite the attested fact that *he* held high rank among the gods, being well-born and early in *his* appearance in the pantheon, a rather trivial sort of deity. —Lewis Thomas, *Et Cetera, Et Cetera* (71)
>
> ■ The antecedent is underlined; pronouns are italicized.

The *he* and *his* pronouns in these sentences clearly refer to *Cupid*, making it unnecessary for Thomas to repeat the noun four times. Try reading the sentence by replacing all the italicized words with *Cupid*. Too many *Cupid*'s? Here's another example:

Artificialized management has, in effect, bought fishing at the expense of another and perhaps higher recreation; *it* has paid dividends to one citizen out of capital stock belonging to all.
—Aldo Leopold, *A Sand County Almanac* (170)

The pronoun *it* saved Leopold and his readers from a repetition of *artificialized management*. Though repetition can be an effective stylistic device (see chapter 24, "Repeat, Repeat, Repeat"), it can also be cumbersome and tedious.

Antecedents.   Pronouns can be a problem for writers. A pronoun needs something to refer to, an *antecedent*. But writers, absorbed in getting their ideas down, may not notice that that something is not readily and clearly available to their readers. If Lewis Thomas had also included in his first sentence a reference to Cupid's mythical father Mars, the pronouns that followed would have been less clear. So there are two principles at work here:

❖ A pronoun needs a noun (or another pronoun) to refer to (its antecedent).
❖ A pronoun needs to refer unambiguously to its antecedent.

The following example shows two pronouns with two antecedents.

Throughout the night the wind continued to shriek down from the mountains. *It* got hold of the *Docker*, the heaviest of the boats, and swung *her* completely around. —Alfred Lansing, *Endurance* (185)

It refers clearly to *wind*; *her*, in typical old-salt fashion (and, we hope, a tenuous hold on usage of the feminine form), refers to the boat *Docker*. Here's another example with *it*.

The mouse is a sober citizen *who* knows that grass grows in order that mice may store *it* as underground haystacks, and that snow falls in order that mice may build subways from stack to stack: supply, demand, and transport all neatly organized. —Leopold (4)

In addition to the *it* referring to *grass*, the pronoun *who* refers to *citizen*. (For a matrix of pronoun forms and a discussion of whether to use *who* or *whom*, see chapter 35, "Just in Case—Pronouns Again.") In the clause describing snow, Leopold repeats *mice* rather than substituting the pronoun *they*, so there is no confusion with *haystacks*.

Just to complicate things for writers, *it* isn't always a pronoun. In the following sentence, the word functions as a place holder for the real subject:

> *It* is a rather sad footnote in linguistic history that another Englishman, James Parsons, just missed his chance at the scholarly immortality now attributed to Sir William Jones. —Thomas (12)

In this case, *It* stands in place of the long *that* clause. Thomas might have begun his sentence with the clause in subject position:

> That another Englishman, James Parsons, just missed his chance at the scholarly immortality now attributed to Sir William Jones is a rather sad footnote in linguistic history.

This rewriting of the sentence aptly illustrates why writers use the place holder. Emphasis has been altered here, and the style is more formal.

Another common use of *it* without an antecedent is to express conditions of weather and time, as in "What time is *it*?" and

> *It* was terribly cold. —Paul Fussell, *Doing Battle* (130)

Experienced writers bear in mind the multiple functions of *it* and avoid its overuse.

Ambiguities.   There are several circumstances in which pronouns may be unclear:

- ❖ The pronoun can refer to more than one word.
- ❖ The intended antecedent is a modifier, not a noun.
- ❖ The pronoun has no antecedent.
- ❖ The antecedent is too distant from the pronoun.

The first circumstance was illustrated near the beginning of this chapter when I brought up the problem Lewis Thomas would have had with his pronouns if he had mentioned a second male person in his sentence about Cupid. His pronouns *he* and *his* might have been taken to mean either Cupid or Mars. But Carolyn G. Heilbrun doesn't seem to have a problem with *them* in this sentence despite the two plural nouns:

> I am sharply aware that people do, more and more often these days, live past eighty, and many of *them* are reported to live productive, satisfying lives. —*The Last Gift of Time* (206)

Them clearly refers to *people,* not *days.* Sometimes, though, nouns need to be repeated for clarity, or to be replaced by synonyms. Notice how Amanda Foreman furthers her idea by writing *waverers* as a synonym for "defecting supporters," rather than using a potentially ambiguous *them*:

> Although the core membership of the party was stable, there were at least a hundred more supporters who had to be prevented from defecting. Georgiana used lavish entertainments and her own popularity to entice *waverers* back to meetings at Devonshire House. —*Georgiana: Duchess of Devonshire* (152)

The second type of vague pronoun can occur in sentences like this one:

> In Lewis Thomas's book *Et Cetera, Et Cetera, he* tells stories about words.

The pronoun *he* means "Lewis Thomas," but in this sentence *Lewis Thomas's* is a possessive modifier of *book* and doesn't function as a noun. Antecedents, you remember, are nouns or pronouns. While most readers would not be confused by the reference in this particular example, a writer can avoid potential misreading:

> In *his* book *Et Cetera, Et Cetera,* <u>Lewis Thomas</u> tells stories about words.

The third problematic circumstance happens sometimes with the pronoun *this,* which, like other pronouns, has no meaning except in reference to a noun. Here are two examples of *unambiguous* usage:

> Members of *this* tribe were hereditary guardians of the sacred Black Stone. —Barbara G. Walker, *The Crone* (55)

> Certainly a man well qualified to speak on *this* issue is the leader of the Wildlife Research Unit of Auburn, Alabama, Dr. Maurice F. Baker, who has had many years' experience in the area.
> —Rachel Carson, *Silent Spring* (149)

Walker avoids ambiguity by making *this* an adjective modifying *tribe*; Carson, *this* modifying *issue.* The noun that follows a *this* is usually a reference to a previous statement, so by including it the writer makes a connection, gaining coherence as well as clarity. Summary nouns avoid leaving the reader to attach meaning to the pronoun.

Yet skilled writers do at times leave interpretation to readers. David Remnick begins a paragraph with the following statement:

> Not that any of *this* would help Gorbachev. —*Resurrection* (7)

Remnick's pronoun seems meant to summarize the entire preceding paragraph, which details the problems of the opposing Russian presidential candidates. What saves it is the inclusion of *any*. If Remnick had said "Not that this would help Gorbachev," a reader would rightly be confused, given the variety of ideas mentioned, but *any* includes all those ideas.

To illustrate the fourth problem, the distant antecedent, notice how Garry Wills uses a synonym for "Lincoln" for the sake of clarity and reading ease:

> Lincoln sat his horse gracefully (to the surprise of some), and looked meditative during the long wait while marshals tried to coax into line important people more concerned with their dignity than the President was with his. —*Lincoln at Gettysburg* (32)

Had Wills written *he* instead of "the President," a reader might have searched back in the sentence for an antecedent.

I, You, We.   Finally, let me refer to three pronouns mentioned at the beginning of this chapter: *I, you*, and *we*. While a few writing situations do not allow the first-person pronoun *I*, most usage has become relaxed enough to permit it. For examples and a discussion, see chapter 19, "Say *I (we, you)*." The pronoun *you* presents a little different problem. When used to refer to the reader, its reference is clear and, though verging on informality, appropriate, as in this sentence from *The Perfect Storm*:

> The dangers are numerous and random: the rogue wave that wipes *you* off the deck; the hook and leader that catches *your* palm; the tanker that plots a course through the center of *your* boat.
> —Sebastian Junger (70)

Puts you right there, doesn't he? But the pronoun is also sometimes used in a general sense. Robert M. Pirsig uses it that way frequently in *Zen and the Art of Motorcycle Maintenance*:

> I suppose *you* could call that a personality. Each machine has its own, unique personality which probably could be defined as the intuitive sum total of everything *you* know and feel about it. (42)

Even though most readers are not involved in swordfishing or in maintaining a motorcycle, the writers' intentions seem to be to put them in the midst of the action. David G. McCullough also uses *you* to invite the reader's participation:

> And nowhere was there more talk, or were things in such turmoil, than at the Pennsylvania depot and yards, where tons of food and supplies were still piling up, and the crowds were so thick, any hour of the day, that *you* could barely make *your* way through.
>
> —*The Johnstown Flood* (239)

Neither McCullough nor his readers were in Johnstown in 1889, but they can visualize being there.

The problem with using *you* in an indefinite sense is that some people insist that it creates a lack of clarity, as in the following sentence:

> The wind was so strong that *you* could see leaves, plastic bags, and other debris being tossed about in the air.

The reader clearly is not part of this story, though perhaps is being invited in. The writer might mean *I* or perhaps *anyone*. The sentence could read:

> The wind was so strong that *I* could see leaves, plastic bags, and other debris being tossed about in the air.

■ If the writer were there.

> The wind was so strong that *one* could see leaves, plastic bags, and other debris being tossed about in the air.

■ Too formal?

> The wind was so strong that leaves, plastic bags, and other debris were being tossed about in the air.

■ Good choice?

You can find other examples in chapter 19, "Say *I* (*we, you*)." Also discussed and illustrated in that chapter are the potential problems with clarity in using *we*. Briefly, they stem from the fact that *we* means the writer and someone else—the writer and the reader, the writer and all humanity, or the writer and a particularized someone. It's up to the writer in context to establish the meaning.

Summary

❖ Be sure your pronoun has an antecedent noun (or another pronoun, such as *everyone* or *all*).

❖ Make your pronoun refer clearly to its antecedent.

❖ Avoid having pronouns refer to modifiers instead of to nouns.

❖ Keep your pronouns and their antecedents close together.

❖ Use *you* and *we* when the reference is clear.

❖ Use *I* when suitable for your style and situation.

For more on pronouns, see chapter 34, "Make Your Pronouns Agree," and chapter 35, "Just in Case—Pronouns Again."

☐ **Practice** ☐

Account for the pronouns and antecedents in the following passages. What makes the meaning of the pronouns clear?

1. "On July 30, 1935, the first ten Penguins were launched at sixpence a volume. [Allen] Lane had calculated that he would break even after seventeen thousand copies of each title were sold, but the first sales brought the number only to about seven thousand. He went to see the buyer for the vast Woolworth general store chain, a Mr. Clifford Prescott, who demurred; the idea of selling books like any other merchandise, together with sets of socks and tins of tea, seemed to him somehow ludicrous. By chance, at that very moment Mrs. Prescott entered her husband's office. Asked what she thought, she responded enthusiastically. Why not, she asked. Why should books not be treated as everyday objects, as necessary and as available as socks and tea? Thanks to Mrs. Prescott, the sale was made." —Alberto Manguel, *A History of Reading* (143–44)

2. "Before the great political and economic changes of the late eighties and early nineties, the most remarkable feature of Moscow was its astonishing drabness: its lack of color; its lack of restaurants; its lack of foreign goods and foreign culture; the absence of billboards, neon, and commercialism of any kind." —Remnick (162–63)

34

Make Your Pronouns Agree

*B*ecause the meaning of pronouns depends on the nouns they substitute for, the connections need to be clear and accurate. In addition to referring unambiguously to an antecedent noun or pronoun (such as *everyone*), a pronoun must also *agree* with that noun or pronoun. If the antecedent is singular, the pronoun is singular; if it is plural, the pronoun is plural. This basic principle is illustrated in the following sentences (pronouns are italicized and antecedents are underlined).

> But there is another way to think about Cupid and *his* name.
> —Lewis Thomas, *Et Cetera, Et Cetera* (71)

> When Georgiana had a secret *she* would often "confess" *it* by issuing a denial to a question no one had asked. —Amanda Foreman, *Georgiana: Duchesse of Devonshire* (126)

■ Two pronouns, two antecedents.

> The philosophical postmodernists, a rebel crew milling beneath the black flag of anarchy, challenge the very foundations of science and traditional philosophy. Reality, *they* propose, is a state constructed by the mind, not perceived by *it*. —Edward O. Wilson, *Consilience: The Unity of Knowledge* (40)

241

I put my pale-moon <u>animal</u> back in *its* hole, but to be held and thrust against *its* own volition apparently immobilized *it*, so I let *it* go free down the sands. —John Hay, *The Great Beach* (91)

Everyone had heard the stories about ancient eruptions, true; and there were <u>those</u> who looked at maps and thought *they* had heard tell of when Java and Sumatra were one island that had broken apart during some terrific volcanic ages. —Simon Winchester, *Krakatoa* (153)

■ Pronoun as antecedent.

Agreement in these examples is quite straightforward. The following sentence is uncomplicated also except that, like the Foreman and Wilson examples, it has two pronoun references:

All sorts of witnesses have testified to this effect, and it would be virtually impossible for a non-Communist to write of these <u>years</u> without alluding to this party <u>policy</u>, or for a Communist to write of *them* without defending *it* or denying that *it* existed.
—Rebecca West, *The New Meaning of Treason* (203)

Because one pronoun is plural, referring to *years*, and the second (and third) are singular, referring to *policy*, there is no problem with clarity. Actually, agreement problems arise in only a few situations:

❖ With compound antecedents.
❖ With distant antecedents.
❖ With collective antecedents.
❖ With generic nouns.
❖ With indefinite pronouns and adjectives.

Compound antecedents. Getting pronouns to agree with compound antecedents joined by *and* is uncomplicated; a simple one-plus-one-equals-two tells you that the pronoun is plural, as in this example:

One year earlier, after a weekend spent with <u>Agatha Christie and her second husband</u> in *their* house in Devon, the English publisher Allen Lane, waiting for his train back to London, looked through the bookstalls at the station for something to read.
—Alberto Manguel, *A History of Reading* (143)

■ A second pronoun, *his,* refers to *Allen Lane.*

The agreement gets more complicated when the two antecedents are joined by *or*. Here the simple math doesn't work. In fact, the rule can get rather messy. The short version is that the pronoun agrees with the nearer antecedent. If both antecedents are singular or both plural, there's no problem. But when one is singular and the other plural, agreement can be awkward. As I said, a bit messy, and you might decide to rephrase; the good news is that this situation is uncommon. So uncommon that I had a difficult time finding any examples in my reading. Here's what I finally came up with, just a straightforward singular:

> These headquarters were in a house on the water's edge, and Potemkin had an irritating habit of spotting a Turkish <u>ship or small craft</u> with his telescope and sending Jones an order to "Go get *it*!" —Samuel Eliot Morison, *John Paul Jones* (384)

■ A second pronoun, *his,* refers to *Potemkin.*

Though Morison's *it* is singular without question, it technically refers to the singular *craft.* Because of the awkwardness of antecedents that are both singular and plural, writers apparently avoid them whenever possible.

Distant antecedents.   With distant antecedents, agreement is mostly a matter of keeping track of what you're saying. Sometimes in the process of drafting we use pronouns that agree with the closest noun when we mean them to refer to a more distant one. But if we're on our toes while editing, we'll catch this type of agreement problem. Here we have an example of a pronoun near the end of a sentence referring to a noun at the beginning:

> By breeding <u>mosquitoes</u> of known egg type in the laboratory, it was possible to make comparative studies of different aspects of *their* behavior. —Marston Bates, *The Forest and the Sea* (130)

Some distant pronouns are better replaced with a repetition of the antecedent or with a synonym (see the Garry Wills sentence on p. 238).

Collective antecedents.   Getting pronouns to agree with collective antecedents also requires generally no more than an alert writer. These are nouns such as *committee, team, class, troop, audience,* and *family.* They usually function in a singular sense—as in "The committee records *its* minutes," "The family enjoys *its* new home," "The troop carries out its orders." We report one collective action. On the other hand, we occasionally refer to individual actions within a collective group: "The class expressed *their* opinions," "The team retreated to *their* lockers." Here's an example from Rebecca West and another from Samuel Eliot Morison; antecedents in both cases are considered singular.

> He [Klaus Fuchs] was reunited with his scattered children, and though he was now over seventy he embarked on an active life as a Quaker preacher and teacher, traveling all over Germany to find and reassemble the remnants of the <u>Society of Friends</u> and to welcome those who wished to join *it*. —West (197)

> ▪ Other pronouns refer to *Klaus Fuchs*, named in an earlier sentence.

> In this attack, which opened at daylight, the <u>Flotilla</u> again distinguished *itself* by inflicting severe punishment on the Turkish fleet anchored under the walls of the fortress, and Nassau's stock accordingly rose. —Morison, *John Paul Jones* (382)

Generic antecedents and indefinite pronouns and adjectives. We use generic nouns when we make statements such as "A person never knows what tomorrow will bring." Generic nouns like *person* are singular; the problem is that we often think of them as *plural—a person* is "all of us." Unfortunately, in English we don't have a generic singular pronoun that refers to people. *They* can work generically for plural, and *it* can serve as a neutral singular, as in "A cat can get a dizzy high by chasing *its* tail." For other singulars, the rule says to use *he or she*, as in "A person never knows what *he or she* will meet tomorrow." Here's another example:

> The <u>child</u> learning to read is admitted into the communal memory by way of books, and thereby becomes acquainted with a common past which *he or she* renews, to a greater or lesser degree, in every reading. —Manguel (71)

Indefinite pronouns and adjectives have the same problem. Many of them are singular grammatically but feel plural. Here are some examples; the first two illustrate indefinite adjectives, the second two indefinite pronouns:

> <u>Each branch</u> of the animal kingdom had needs that could be satisfied only by the conditions of *its* appropriate environment.
> —Daniel J. Boorstin, *Cleopatra's Nose* (133)

But order results when <u>every individual</u> knows *his or her* place.

—Bates (197)

In Pittsburgh the papers urged <u>everyone</u> to boil *his* water.

—David G. McCullough, *The Johnstown Flood* (209)

The Anglo-American poet W. H. Auden once observed that the most remarkable feature of an American presidential election is that on election night <u>none</u> of the candidates—win or lose— would be packing *his* baggage to leave the country. —Boorstin (79)

The advantage of the reciprocal pronouns *he or she* (*him or her, his or her*) is their clear assertion that the antecedent can be either male or female. (Nice to know about children learning to read and creatures knowing their place. I suppose Boorstin can be forgiven his *he,* considering our presidential record, but McCullough's *his,* written back in 1968, just sounds outmoded.)

The disadvantage of the reciprocals is that they can become tedious if they have to be repeated. So the rule says you can do other things: use *s/he* (in my opinion a cure worse than the disease), or avoid the singular generic, using plural instead (say "Children learning to read . . ." and "All persons"), or use no pronoun (say ". . . urged everyone to boil water for drinking"). I have no hesitation about avoiding unnecessary pronouns, or even switching to plural when I want to be inclusive; what I object to is that we overlook another choice, the singular *they.* Like the singular *you,* it's been around for centuries. In speech we have no compunctions about saying "Everyone had polished *their* shoes." We just worry about it when we write. You can read more on this subject in chapter 18, "Refer with a Singular *they.*"

Special cases.   A few indefinite pronouns have a long history of taking either singular or plural pronouns; *none* and *no one* are two. Compare these examples with Boorstin's preceding sentence:

Three men determined what went into newspapers in the city. <u>None</u> of them cared about the news per se; *they* used their papers like artillery, to pound *their* enemies and advance *their* own goals.

—John M. Barry, *Rising Tide* (225)

<u>No one</u> really knew for sure the extent of what had happened, but *they* knew it had been terrible beyond belief, and if the

whereabouts of someone was not known, then only the worst could be imagined. —McCullough (173)

All, any, and *some* are three more indefinites that are singular or plural depending on context.

Summary

❖ A pronoun agrees with the noun or pronoun it refers to (its antecedent).

❖ Compound antecedents joined by *and* take plural pronouns.

❖ When compound antecedents are joined by *or*, the pronoun agrees with the nearer antecedent.

❖ Collective antecedents (like *family* and *team*) are usually singular and take the singular pronoun *it*; when individual members of the collective are meant, the pronoun is plural (*they*).

❖ Singular generic nouns (like *a child* and *the writer*) take singular pronouns.

❖ Most singular indefinite pronouns and adjectives (like *anyone* and *every*) take singular pronouns.

You can read more about pronouns in chapter 33, "Be Sure Your Pronouns Refer to Something," and chapter 35, "Just in Case—Pronouns Again."

□ Practice □

The following sentences, written by established writers, have pronoun usages that may be controversial. Analyze them for pronoun-antecedent agreement. Have these writers made the right stylistic choices?

1. "Since then I have lived to see state after state extirpate *its* wolves." —Aldo Leopold, *A Sand County Almanac* (130)

2. "The banks, the foreign businesses, the political actors, the cultural and intellectual institutions, the information and communications centers, the trends in fashion, language, and popular culture—all of *it* is centered in the capital." —David Remnick, *Resurrection* (164)

3. "Three men determined what went into newspapers in the city. None of *them* cared about the news per se; *they* used their

papers like artillery, to pound *their* enemies and advance *their* own goals." —Barry (225)

4. "No one really knew for sure the extent of what had happened, but *they* knew it had been terrible beyond belief, and if the whereabouts of someone was not known, then only the worst could be imagined." —McCullough (173)

5. "In Pittsburgh the papers urged everyone to boil *his* water."

—McCullough (209)

6. "Everybody, it seemed, had *his* own latest story from Johnstown."

—McCullough (239)

35

Just in Case— Pronouns Again

Should it be *I* or *me, we* or *us, they* or *them, who* or *whom*? Next to verbs, perhaps, pronouns present the most frequently asked questions on usage. And many of those questions relate to the feature of pronouns called *case*, or the way they change forms according to function. A pronoun that functions as, or renames, a subject is said to be in *nominative* case; one that serves as an object of another word in the sentence, in *objective* case; one that modifies in a possessive sense, in *possessive* case. And a particular kind of repeating pronoun is the *reflexive*. Here's the pronoun matrix:

	Nominative	*Objective*	*Possessive*	*Reflexive*
Personal	I	me	my, mine	myself
	you	you	your, yours	yourself
	he	him	his	himself
	she	her	her, hers	herself
	it	it	its	itself
	we	us	our, ours	ourselves
	you	you	your, yours	yourselves
	they	them	their, theirs	themselves
Relative	who	whom	whose	
	whoever	whomever	whosever	

Before we go on to seeing how pronoun case works in sentences, let's just pause a second to notice that none—that is, absolutely *none*—of these pronouns has an apostrophe. Apostrophes in pronouns are used only for contractions (as in "It's a long way to Tipperary"). (For more on apostrophes, see chapter 30, "Possess with Apostrophes"; for more on contractions, see chapter 20, "Contract Your Words.")

Here's a sentence using a nominative pronoun and an objective one:

> *He* was succeeded by Heliogabalus, Caracalla's cousin, a reclusive, fanatical young worshiper of the sun god, a man *whom* many people regarded as insane. —Elaine Pagels, *The Origin of Satan* (137)

He is subject of the sentence, and *whom*, meaning "man," is object of *regarded* (read: "many people regarded *him* as insane"). This next sentence has similar usages, plus two pronouns in possessive case:

> Of *my* father's family *I* knew nothing, not even that *he* had three older sisters, all of *whom* were merely prologue to the birth, finally, of a son, *my* father. —Carolyn G. Heilbrun, *The Last Gift of Time* (192)

I and *he* are subjects of their verbs; *whom*, meaning "sisters," is object of the preposition *of*; and the two occurrences of *my* function as possessive modifiers.

Who, whom.   Some people find the usage of *who* and *whom* troublesome, probably because we seldom use the objective form in speech, so let's look at some examples of these relative pronouns.

> None of the great mathematicians and philosophers of the past *whom* we have met so far doubted that they had the tools they needed to determine what the future held. —Peter L. Bernstein, *Against the Gods* (215)

> The disquieting thing in the modern picture is the trophy-hunter *who* never grows up, in *whom* the capacity for isolation, perception, and husbandry is undeveloped, or perhaps lost.
> —Aldo Leopold, *A Sand County Almanac* (176)

> Only later did Kafka discover in his own notions of reading a common ground with the ancient Talmudists, for *whom* the Bible encoded a multiplicity of meanings *whose* continuous pursuit was the purpose of our voyage on earth. —Alberto Manguel, *A History of Reading* (89)

The choice of *who* or *whom* depends on the pronoun's function within its own clause. In Bernstein's sentence, *whom*, meaning "mathematicians and philosophers," is the object of the verb *have met*. In Leopold's sentence, *who* means "trophy-hunter" and is the subject of the verb *grows up*; *whom*, also meaning "trophy-hunter," is the object of the preposition *in*. In Manguel's sentence, *whom*, meaning "Talmudists," is the object of the preposition *for*, and *whose*, representing "meanings," is the possessive modifier of *pursuit*. If you don't want to bother with the grammar, try rephrasing each sentence to use personal pronouns: "we have met *them* (not *they*)," "in *them* (not *they*) the capacity for isolation . . . ," "for *them* (not *they*) the Bible encoded. . . ." In less formal usage, Bernstein might have substituted *that* for *whom* ("that we have met").

The following sentences have *who* usages that are a little more complicated:

> I had agreed with her that I should start collecting the Dial records featuring Bird, Max Roach, Al Haig, Bud Powell, Dizzy Gillespie and others *who* she said were going to be the "masters."
> —Maya Angelou, *Gather Together in My Name* (80)

> In his own time, only the Irish appreciated him [St. Patrick] for *who* he was; beyond their borders he was as little known as Augustine was in Ireland. —Thomas Cahill, *How the Irish Saved Civilization* (114)

Knowing that the case of a pronoun is determined by its function in its own clause, we see that Angelou says "who were going to be the 'masters'"—that is, *who* (like *they*) is subject of *were going*. The words "she said" are just an interruption. In Cahill's sentence, the clause would read "he was who"—that is, *who* is a nominative linked to the subject *he*.

The -*self* words.   Another group of problem pronouns is the -*self* words. Some people use unconventional forms such as *hisself* and *themself*; other people may use *myself* in place of *I* or *me* when they're unsure which of those two is correct (as in "Jake and *myself* have a question" instead of "Jake and *I*" and "Send the bill to myself" instead of "Send the bill to *me*"). To see how these pronouns are meant to work, observe the way two writers have used them:

> Speaking as a man trying to tame the passions of anger and grief, Marcus [Aurelius] continually reminds *himself* that "death, like

birth, is a mystery of nature," each necessarily complementing the other. —Pagels (127)

Sometime later Justin *himself* was accused, arrested, and interrogated. —Pagels (125)

The woman who needs to create works of art is born with a kind of psychic tension in her which drives her unmercifully to find a way to balance, to make *herself* whole. —Heilbrun (145)

Notice that in each case the *-self* pronoun refers to a noun elsewhere in the sentence, either immediately preceding the *-self* pronoun (called "intensive") or earlier in the sentence (called "reflexive"). In Pagels's first sentence, *himself* refers to *Marcus*; in her next sentence, it means *Justin*; and in Heilbrun's sentence *herself* refers to *woman*. The *-self* pronouns can also connect to another pronoun, as in "I *myself* have no opinion" and "I try to think for *myself.*" What they don't do is stand alone in a sentence.

Appositive pronouns.   Another pronoun usage that writers are sometimes unsure about is the appositive, a pronoun used along with a noun, as in the following sentences:

We Americans are tempted to take a displacive view of technology and social change. —Daniel J. Boorstin, *Cleopatra's Nose* (159)

It is more than ever difficult for *us* laymen to grasp the quantitative meaning of scientific phenomena and social problems.
—Boorstin (155)

The easiest way to know whether to say *we* or *us* is to think which you would use if the noun weren't there: "*We* (not *us*) are tempted," "difficult for *us* (not *we*) to grasp."

Compounds.   A similar question arises when pronouns are joined to nouns or other pronouns by *and* or *or*, as in these sentences: "*She* and her employer wanted to restructure the company" and "*He* and *I* walked home again." In sentences like these, you can know which pronoun to use by omitting the noun or pronoun it is linked to: "*She* (not *her*) wanted . . . " and "*He* (not *him*) walked. . . ." This problem turns up at times after *between* and *for*. As prepositions, these words are followed by nouns or pronouns in the objective case (*between you and me, for him and her*). Another situation occurs in a passage by Aldo Leopold:

> *He who* hopes for spring with upturned eye never sees so small a thing as Draba. *He who* despairs of spring with downcast eye steps on it, unknowing. *He who* searches for spring with his knees in the mud finds it, in abundance. (26)

Leopold's italicized pronouns take nominative case, being subjects of their clauses ("He sees," "who hopes for spring . . ."; "He steps," "who despairs of spring . . ."; "He finds," "who searches for spring . . .").

After *than*.   Okay, just one more pronoun situation: the case of the pronoun that follows *than*.

> We met in graduate school, although he is five years younger *than I*; we were at different stages. —Heilbrun (64)

> Some adults sincerely believe that children will project themselves into everything they read and that they will be deeply disturbed to read that someone else is taller than *they*, or that other children had a birthday party or live in a big house when perhaps they are not similarly privileged. —Diane Ravitch, *The Language Police* (23)

Because *than* actually introduces a new, elliptical, clause, the pronoun has nominative case as the subject of the new clause. It helps to think of the verb that follows the pronoun: "younger than I was," "taller than they are."

Summary

- ❖ Pronouns have case according to their function.
- ❖ Subject pronouns and those renaming the subject have nominative case (*I, you, he, she, it, we, they, who*).
- ❖ Object pronouns have objective case (*me, you, him, her, it, us, them, whom*).
- ❖ Possessive pronouns have possessive case (*my, mine, your, yours, his, her, hers, its, our, ours, their, theirs, whose*).
- ❖ The *-self* pronouns (*myself, ourselves, yourself, yourselves, himself, herself, itself, themselves*) are used only to refer to nouns or other pronouns in the sentence.

❖ The use of *who* or *whom* depends on the pronoun's function within its own clause.

❖ The case of a pronoun appositive (such as *"we* Americans") is the same as it would be without the noun it refers to.

❖ The case of a pronoun linked to a noun or another pronoun by *and* (such as "*she* and her employer") is the same as it would be without the other element.

❖ A pronoun following a comparative *than* (such as "younger than *I*") functions as the subject of a new, elliptical clause and is in nominative case.

❖ Pronouns take apostrophes only to show contractions.

□ **Practice** □

The case of the relative pronouns *who, whom, whose* is often more troublesome than that of personal pronouns—perhaps because we use them less often, especially the objective form *whom*. The writers of the following sentences have used these pronouns correctly. Study the sentences and consider how each pronoun relates to other words within its own clause and in the sentence.

1. "A foreign visitor *who* returned to England after the civil wars found that the people, *whom* he remembered as friendly and good-humoured, had become 'melancholy, spiteful, as if bewitched.'"—C. V. Wedgwood, *A Coffin for King Charles* (41)

2. "It was he *who* took the lead in 1927 in easing money rates to help the hard-pressed Europeans." —John Kenneth Galbraith, *The Great Crash 1929* (32)

3. "Twenty-three centuries ago, just beyond the walls of Athens, in the shade of a tall plane tree by the edge of the river, a young man of *whom* we know little more than his name, Phaedrus, read out to Socrates a speech by a certain Lysias, *whom* Phaedrus passionately admired." —Manguel (58)

4. "She was the widow of an Englishman of *whom* nothing whatever is known." —Samuel Eliot Morison, *John Paul Jones* (347)

5. "In his own time, only the Irish appreciated [St. Patrick] for *who* he was; beyond their borders he was as little known as Augustine was in Ireland." —Cahill (114)

6. "The salesman *whose* trip line I had happened onto one summer evening was named John Leifer." —John McPhee, *Coming into the Country* (160)

7. "Then he told me that his father, murdered in Sachsenhausen, had been a famous scholar *who* knew many of the classics by heart and *who*, during his time in the concentration camp, had offered himself as a library to be read to his fellow inmates."
    —Manguel (64)

8. "Whatever his personal faults, Pecke was a newsman of ability *whose* paper was always full, informative and fairly free of deliberate inaccuracy." —Wedgwood (41)

36

Don't Dangle Your Modifiers

*E*ven the most careful writers sometimes dangle their modifiers. They begin a sentence with a nicely stated participial phrase and end it with a well-stated independent clause, but something happens at the break between the two. The parts don't fit together. Here's an example:

> Walking to the public library, trash and broken tree limbs were strewn everywhere.

This sentence illustrates what is known as a *dangling modifier*. Obviously the writer (or someone described by the writer) was the one walking to the library, not the trash and broken tree limbs, but the reader of this sentence may well pause a moment to consider the ludicrous situation—at the expense of concentrating on what the writer meant to say. Here's another example:

> Standing by a sparkling stream in the woods on a clear fall day in Vermont, it was tempting to forget about the problems that I needed to solve.

Again, the writer (or narrator) surely is meant as the performer of the action, but because the independent clause begins with *it* the meaning is fuzzy. The person "standing" should begin the main clause:

Standing by a sparkling stream in the woods on a clear fall day in Vermont, I was tempted to forget about the problems that I needed to solve.

The first sentence could read:

Walking to the public library, she saw trash and broken tree limbs strewn everywhere.

In each of the revised sentences, the subjects, *I* and *she*, perform the action of the *-ing* phrases.

No danglers here. Now read the following sentences in which the meaning of each modifying phrase is clear; the action of each one is performed by the (underlined) subject of the sentence.

Abandoning the past's preoccupation with eternity, <u>humanists</u> preached enrichment of life in the here and now.
—William Manchester, *A World Lit Only by Fire* (113)

Sitting at my new desk, <u>I</u> wrote down all my letters the way I had seen Agnes and Charley do it, and the way Mom and I had practiced. —Edgar Allen Imhoff, *Always of Home* (13)

Finding a means to be alone for a few moments, <u>he</u> [General Alexander Samsonov] shot himself. —John Keegan, *The First World War* (150)

Humanists were abandoning, *I* (the narrator) was sitting, *he* (the general) was finding. Participles, both the present form (*-ing*) and the past (*-ed*), always have someone or something performing the action. In that feature, they are like verbs. Unlike verbs, however, the persons or things doing the actions are only implied. In most cases, especially with phrases that come at the beginning of sentences, the doer is the same as the subject of the sentence, as in the preceding three examples.

Past participles. The following sentences show that *past* participles work in the same way as the present participles we've seen:

Tried by a jury which included Anne's father, the <u>musician</u> pleaded guilty and, as a commoner, was merely hanged.
—Manchester (216)

■ The musician was tried.

Armed with his credentials and contracts, full of energy and eager to be off and away, <u>Columbus</u> arrived on May 22, 1492, at Palos de la Frontera. —Samuel Eliot Morison, *Admiral of the Ocean Sea* (101)

■ Columbus was armed.

Motivated by a misguided desire to help his fellow man, <u>Wilson</u> had concluded that climbing Everest would be the perfect way to publicize his belief that the myriad ills of humankind could be cured through a combination of fasting and faith in the powers of God. —Jon Krakauer, *Into Thin Air* (89)

■ Wilson was motivated.

The implied subject of each participial phrase is the subject of the sentence, and the phrase modifies the sentence subject. Notice too that each phrase is set off by a comma.

Gerund and infinitive phrases.   Participles sometimes follow prepositions such as *in* or *by,* in which case these verbals function as nouns and are called **gerunds.** Unless the writer is careful, the sentence might turn out like this one:

By *examining* these theories, it is possible to arrive at only one conclusion.

Whoever is doing the examining is absent from this sentence. Worse is the following example:

By *teaching* a process for writing, students will have a method for getting started.

The sentence implies that the students are doing the teaching. In contrast, the **gerund phrases** do not go wrong in these sentences:

By *taking* on the farmer's contract, the <u>processor</u> lets the farmer assume the risk that agricultural prices might rise. —Peter L. Bernstein, *Against the Gods* (306)

■ The processor is taking.

Instead of *aging* normally through their full life cycle, <u>women</u> are constrained to create an illusion that their growth process stops in the first decade or two of adulthood. —Barbara G. Walker, *The Crone* (31)

■ Women are aging.

Another kind of verbal phrase, the infinitive, also can function as an opening modifier. As in participial and gerund phrases, the performer of the action is usually implied in the phrase but completed in the subject of the sentence:

> *To begin* this short essay about learning in science, <u>I</u> vowed to explicate the Pierian spring so I could dare to quote this couplet that I have never cited for fear that someone would ask.
> —Stephen Jay Gould, *The Lying Stones of Marrakech* (222)

> *To liquidate* inventories, wholesale <u>suppliers</u> were cutting prices in half and begging customers around the country to buy.
> —John M. Barry, *Rising Tide* (231)

Passive voice.   As we've seen, opening **verbal phrases** are more likely to be clear when they modify the subjects of their sentences. For that reason, and because it shifts the subject further to the end of the sentence, passive voice can often be the culprit in the making of dangling modifiers. Here I've rewritten William Manchester's sentence, changing his active verb *preached* to passive:

> *Abandoning* the past's preoccupation with eternity, the enrichment of life in the here and now was preached by humanists.

The revision shifts the subject, *humanists*, to the end of the sentence, leaving the *abandoning* phrase to illogically modify the new subject, *enrichment*. (Read more about passive voice in chapter 13, "Use Passive Verbs.")

Phrases elsewhere in the sentence.   Verbal phrases also occur at the end or middle of sentences, although they're less likely to dangle there:

> On 13 September <u>he</u> [General Pavel Rennenkampf] crossed back into Russian territory, *having extricated* his whole army, *drawing* the Germans behind him. —Keegan (150)

The two participial phrases modify the subject of the sentence, *he*. In the following sentences, the final participial phrases modify not the subjects but the closest nouns. Notice the difference in punctuation:

> The journey took just a little over an hour. He [Professor James Murray] was pleasantly surprised, on arriving at Crowthorne, to find a brougham and a liveried coachman *waiting* for him.
> —Simon Winchester, *The Professor and the Madman* (169)

> The magic hypothesis of animal art is reinforced by other forms
> of behavior *displayed* by extant stone-age people. —Edward O. Wilson,
> *Consilience: The Unity of Knowledge* (228)

The *waiting* phrase of Winchester's second sentence modifies *brougham*
and *coachman,* and Wilson's *displayed* phrase modifies the immediately
preceding "forms of behavior." Modifying phrases that occur at the end
of sentences and modify the *subjects* are usually set off with commas,
like Keegan's "having extricated his whole army" in the earlier sentence; if they modify the closer nouns, they are usually not set off with
commas. The following sentence shows how ambiguity can result from
questionable punctuation:

> I left Johnson not quite knowing where I was going.

As it stands, the sentence implies that Johnson is the one in the dark;
a comma after *Johnson* would have the *knowing* phrase modifying the
narrator, "I."

Many ambiguous sentence-ending modifiers are not participial,
such as this one:

> I read the article I'd isolated one more time.

The reader can wonder whether the final phrase, "one more time,"
modifies *isolated* or *read*. In many such cases, the modifier can be
moved to another part of the sentence, often to the beginning if it
modifies the main verb.

Confusing phrases can turn up in odd places. The following infinitive phrase was on a yogurt container: "Avoid stirring to maintain
light texture." I know I can be accused of being too literal-minded, but
I really couldn't decide whether stirring *would* "maintain the light texture" or whether it *wouldn't*. After trying the new light yogurt, I decided
that the modifying phrase should be placed at the beginning of the
sentence: "To maintain the light texture, avoid stirring the product."
Thankfully, I hadn't stirred it.

Dangling modifiers, unfortunately, are problems in writing that
never seem to go away. No matter how experienced the writer, modifiers can dangle or be misplaced. Yet participial and gerund phrases are
extremely useful stylistic options and shouldn't be avoided just because
they give us trouble. But we need to watch for them, checking the
potential ambiguity of all modifiers at the beginning and at the end of
our sentences.

Summary

- ❖ Participles (*-ing* and *-ed* words), gerunds (*-ing* words), and most infinitives have implied subjects.
- ❖ The implied subject is the word the phrase modifies.
- ❖ Participial and gerund phrases that occur at the beginning of sentences usually modify the subjects of the sentences.
- ❖ A dangling participial modifier is one that appears to modify something other than the participle's implied subject.
- ❖ Check for dangling modifiers in sentences with passive voice.
- ❖ Check punctuation for modifiers at the end of sentences.
- ❖ Consider moving sentence-ending modifiers to the beginning of their sentences.

For additional discussions of modifiers, see chapter 7, "Modify with Style."

□ **Practice** □

The following sentences have verbal modifying phrases that do not dangle. Some occur at the beginning of sentences, some elsewhere. Read the sentences, locate the modifiers and their implied subjects, and consider how the writers phrased their sentences to assure that the meanings are clear.

1. "To control the reactor at this low power level, the operators had to withdraw the control rods and turn off the generator which powered the pumps providing cooling water. At this point the reactor went out of control; the thermal power surged, the fuel started to disintegrate, the cooling channels ruptured, and an explosion ripped open the reactor, exposing the core and starting many fires. The graphite moderator began to burn."

    —Jack J. Kraushaar and Robert A. Ristinen, *Energy and Problems of a Technical Society* (138)

2. "In searching for the answers to such questions, Galton makes little mention of early mathematicians and ignores social statisticians like Graunt. He does, however, cite at great length a set of empirical studies carried out in the 1820s and 1830s by a Belgian scientist named Lambert Adolphe Jacques Quetelet.

Quetelet was twenty years older than Galton, a dogged investigator into social conditions, and as obsessed with measurement as Galton himself." —Bernstein (157)

3.   "Indeed, virtually everything about Forrest was self-made, making him a telling counterpoint to the charge that the South was simply fighting an aristocrat's war. The keystone of his life was his beginnings. Born in the backcountry of Bedford County, Tennessee, Forrest was the son of an illiterate blacksmith, who scraped out a fragile existence before dying when Forrest was sixteen." —Jay Winik, *April 1865* (275)

Part Five

Writers on Style

*T*his book has asked you to think about style in all its variability and flexibility. We've tried to define it, analyze it, and see how it works in the hands of published writers. We've considered it as situational, personal, adjustable, malleable, liberated. By now you know my thoughts on the subject. What a few other writers have said about style will finish off the book to get you thinking about their ideas.

We begin with Richard A. Lanham, who reminds us that writing ought to be fun. And why shouldn't it be? If we're not constricted by baseless conventions, the hard work of shaping our ideas can truly be a pleasure. "[T]he delight in form for its own sake," he says. We usually think of form as the hard part, the requirements, the rules—as in con-*form*. But if we put ourselves in charge of the rules instead of letting them dictate to us, if we understand which ones we need to observe in given situations and which ones we can disregard, we can enjoy the process of making our ideas develop and take shape in words.

Those very rules, or conventions, are the subject of Frank Smith's first paragraph. Smith balances freedom of choice with the need for conventions, for "Without convention, how could one ever be unconventional?" Think of it: if the rules weren't there—say, the one about sentence fragments—what fun would there be in writing a fragment? And as Smith goes on to say, the conventions will even fade away as more and more writers defy them. Take the rule of not using the pronoun *I* in a scholarly paper. *I* is being used so much now, in so many fields of study, that there's not much of a convention anymore.

Smith also tells us how we can learn to incorporate new features of style into our writing—not by learning more rules but by reading other writers. These "collaborators," as Smith calls them, show us how to pack our sentences with parallelism, connect our thoughts coherently, use passive verbs effectively, and lots more. How to begin our sentences, how to end them emphatically, how to use colons and semicolons, when not to use commas. Whatever you want to know, he says, those collaborators are ready to show you. All you need to do is read like a writer.

Which is a good thing since, as William Zinsser says, "There is no style store." Like Smith, Zinsser tells us that the way to learn writing is to read. We acquire new features of style by reading the writing that we would like to do, "trying to figure out how they did it." You may notice a particularly apt sentence opener, an effective use of repetition, a nicely balanced sentence. And you pause to reread it, to think beyond the subject to how it's been expressed. "But cultivate the best models," he says.

Winston Weathers and Otis Winchester pick up the same theme. Writing, they say, "draws upon the experience and practices of the masters." Serious writers do not "ignore what others have produced and are producing." This is not to say that writers do not strive for distinctive styles, just that they all start with the same basic materials: "words, patterns, constructions, and procedures." We can learn from other writers without any concern that we'll become them. Think of it: you decide to emulate Hemingway's style. Does that make you another Hemingway? Of course not, not even close. But you may have moved some distance along developing a new style of your own.

Annie Dillard tells us what authors were in Hemingway's reading— and in Ralph Ellison's and William Faulkner's and Isaac Bashevis Singer's. The twenty-one-year-old, she says, might also choose models. But in another part of her book *The Writing Life* she asks the question "Who will teach me to write?" and responds with a different answer.

That eighteenth-century French naturalist Georges Louis Leclerc, comte de Buffon, in his book on style said something, most famously, that was more like Dillard's second piece of advice: "Le style, c'est l'homme même." Which is to say in English that style is identity. Your style is indivisible from you. Then is it possible to develop a new style? Well, that's something for you to think about. Scholarly discussions about style are full of dichotomies. Is it this, or is it that? Is style integral to the person, or is it something to be manipulated?

Louis T. Milic takes on another of those dichotomies: is style conscious artistry or unconscious habit? Some scholars say it's one, some say it's the other. Milic says it's both. He refers to "conscious rhetorical choices" and unconscious "stylistic options." Most of our writing is done unconsciously, relying on our established language-generating systems, but all writers do occasionally pause to consider choices in words or construction of phrases. This thinking is related to another dichotomy: to pause while writing so you can change whatever doesn't seem right, or to move inexorably to the end so you don't interrupt your flow of thought. Keith Hjortshoj takes up this case of either/or.

Many books on writing, Hjortshoj says, advise writers to avoid editing until they have completed a draft because an interruption might make them forget what they were going to say. He taught this advice to his writing classes until he realized that he didn't follow it himself. Seeing problems in a sentence he'd written, he'd pause to work with it, then continue. Like all writers, he'd sometimes pause to think about what he'd said and where he was going next; while pausing he'd read back over what he'd written and maybe do some revising. Hjortshoj seems to support Milic's position that writers write both unconsciously and consciously.

But (and there's always a *but* when working with dichotomies) then there's Monroe C. Beardsley's single-sentence quotation: "To change style is always to change meaning." If Hjortshoj revises a sentence or two before going on, can he still continue as he intended if the meaning has changed? Well, whether he can or not, it's better that he revise the sentence now rather than later, when he might have whole chunks of writing that need to be revised to follow the sentence. But does Beardsley really mean *always*? That covers a lot of territory. What do you think? Does every change you make in style—say, from passive voice to active— change your meaning?

Walker Gibson gives you something else to worry about: your reader can walk out on you at any time, shut the book, tear up the page, take a break and never come back. You have to *please* your reader, *interest* your reader. And all you've got to work with is words. Your words, Gibson says, reveal you; your style is your identity.

Aristotle, the ancient Greek philosopher, suggests one way of keeping the interest of your audience: metaphors, and by extension other colorful language. Used appropriately, they give "clearness, charm, and distinction" to a person's style. But they have pitfalls. To learn how to avoid the traps and use them effectively, go to those "unwitting collaborators" that Frank Smith tells us about—other writers.

It's been said that "what goes around comes around" and "there's nothing new under the sun." Well, the Roman educator Quintilian might be given credit for originating some of the ideas we've been discussing here. He says: Write slowly—in other words edit and revise as you go along, making sure you've used the right words and structures to convey your thoughts in the clearest way. That's what Hjortshoj says. Quintilian tells us that our words "must be carefully estimated"—implying, as Milic says, conscious choices. In the quotation here, the ancient Roman goes on to say that writers can gain both coherence and emphasis by means of repetition, as suggested in earlier chapters of this book.

Finally comes the old guard, William Strunk Jr. and E. B. White, reminding us once more that we are our style; our style is our identity. To articulate our identity we may need to make choices in style that are outside the rules and conventions. By observing published writing, by reading like a writer, we can hope to learn when and how to step outside those conventions.

Richard A. Lanham

At the base of prose style, then, we find not only the need to communicate but the spirit of play, the delight in form for its own sake. A zeal to inform has in our time bleached out this delight, but we should not therefore confuse the two. . . . Clarity is simple, not plain.

If clarity indicates a successful relationship between reader and writer, pleasure makes part of the success. —*Style: An Anti-Textbook* (34–35, 38)

Frank Smith

It may also be objected that if everything in language is conventional, if there is a convention for everything and no freedom of choice, then how can anything original ever be said? How can we find language to express something new? But paradoxically, it is because conventions exist that new things can be said. Without convention, how could one ever be unconventional? Creative writers deliberately contravene convention to make a point. . . . Of course, the innovator runs risks. If unconventionality is attributed to ignorance or intransigence or if its purpose remains opaque, the creativity will fail. Unconventionality only works when its purpose is understood. And when a contravention of convention is particularly successful, when its utility becomes evident to a number of people, then it may well become conventional itself. Thus new conventions arise and old conventions die.

—*Writing and the Writer* (63)

Frank Smith

To read like a writer we engage vicariously with what the author is writing. We anticipate what the author will say, so that the author is in effect writing on our behalf, not simply showing how something is done but doing it with us. The situation is identical to that in spoken language when adults help children to say what they want to say or would like and expect to be able to say. The author becomes an unwitting collaborator. Everything the learner would want to spell the author spells. Everything the learner would want to punctuate the author punctuates. Every nuance of expression, every relevant syntactic device, every turn of phrase, the author and learner write together. Bit by bit, one thing at a time but incalculably often over the passage of time, the learner learns through *reading* like a writer to *write* like a writer. —"Reading like a Writer" (25)

William Zinsser

There is no style store; style is organic to the person doing the writing, as much a part of him as his hair, or, if he is bald, his lack of it. Trying to add style is like adding a toupee. At first glance the formerly bald man looks young and even handsome. But at second glance—and with a toupee there's always a second glance—he doesn't look quite right. The problem is not that he doesn't look well groomed; he does, and we can only admire the wigmaker's skill. The point is that he doesn't look like himself. . . .

Make a habit of reading what is being written today and what has been written before. Writing is learned by imitation. If anyone asked me how I learned to write, I'd say I learned by reading the men and women who were doing the kind of writing *I* wanted to do and trying to figure out how they did it. But cultivate the best models. —*On Writing Well* (20, 36)

Winston Weathers and Otis Winchester

Surely, only the rankest amateurs subscribe to the fallacious philosophy of writing that counsels us simply to "look into our hearts and write." Writing, after all, is a civilized art that is rooted in tradition. It draws upon the experience and practices of the masters, and all successful experimentation and novelty in writing is ultimately based upon techniques that have already been successfully demonstrated. Certainly, no serious writer can be so smug as to ignore what others have produced and are producing; nor can he be so dull as to be unaware of past achievements and present ventures in the realm of style and techniques.

Every writer strives, of course, for his own distinctive style, his own particular way of handling words; but originality and individuality in composition (or in any other art for that matter) do not spring entirely from one's own mysterious depths. Originality and individuality are outgrowths of a familiarity with originality in the work of others, and they emerge from a knowledge of words, patterns, constructions, and procedures that all writers use. Even the most original and exceptional styles are ultimately but variations on common locutions, structures, and designs.

—*Copy and Compose* (2)

Annie Dillard

Hemingway studied, as models, the novels of Knut Hamsun and Ivan Turgenev. Isaac Bashevis Singer, as it happened, also chose Hamsun and Turgenev as models. Ralph Ellison studied Hemingway and Gertrude Stein. Thoreau loved Homer; Eudora Welty loved Chekhov. Faulkner described his debt to Sherwood Anderson and Joyce; E. M. Forster, his debt to Jane Austen and Proust. By contrast, if you ask a twenty-one-year-old poet whose poetry he likes, he might say, unblushing, "Nobody's." In his youth, he has not yet understood that poets like poetry, and novelists like novels; he himself likes only the role, the thought of himself in a hat. —*The Writing Life* (70)

Annie Dillard

Who will teach me to write? A reader wanted to know.

The page, the page, that eternal blankness, the blankness of eternity which you cover slowly, affirming time's scrawl as a right and your daring as necessity; the page, which you cover woodenly, ruining it, but asserting your freedom and power to act, acknowledging that you ruin everything you touch but touching it nevertheless, because acting is better than being here in mere opacity; the page, which you cover slowly with the crabbed thread of your gut; the page in the purity of its possibilities; the page of your death, against which you pit such flawed excellences as you can muster with all your life's strength: that page will teach you to write. —*The Writing Life* (58–59)

Georges Louis Leclerc, comte de Buffon

Le style, c'est l'homme même. (Style is identity.) —*Discours sur le style*

Louis T. Milic

By suggesting that the analysis of style be more concerned with the writer's unconscious machinery, I am not suggesting anything really new, for the studies of individual style that are most commonly admired are in fact, for the most part, investigations of stylistic options. Where I differ from most investigators is in the conviction that they have erroneously treated all decisions constituting style as conscious rhetoric choices, representing the realization of artistic intentions, or that they have mingled together habitual and artistic characteristics. Without for a moment denying the possibility that some part of a writer's style is conscious artistry or craftsmanship, I am convinced that most writers, even some of the greatest, knew very little about what they were doing when they wrote and had much less conscious control over the final product than is commonly supposed.

—"Rhetorical Choice and Stylistic Option" (87)

Keith Hjortshoj

Several years ago, I often told my students "Avoid editing while you compose." This seemed like reasonable advice, and you will find it in many books on writing. Editorial attention interrupts composing and breaks the connection with speech that allows new, fluent sentences to unfold. As a consequence, excessive editing can entangle writers in corrections to the extent that they become immobilized.

When I paid close attention to my own methods, however, I realized that I frequently pause to edit sentences while I compose. Sometimes I hear problems in a sentence while I'm writing it and immediately make changes before I continue. When I stop to read back over a draft, to restore my train of thought, I also notice things I want to change and make those alterations before I go on. I suspect that most writers do this to some extent, and editing does not necessarily interfere with their progress. Clarifying and polishing previous sentences can also clarify our sense of direction and smooth out the path on which we move ahead, much as a ski trail becomes faster when the rough spots are worn down. I don't feel that I can continue very far if I leave rough, murky writing behind me.

—*Understanding Writing Blocks* (39)

Monroe C. Beardsley

To change style is always to change meaning. —"Style and Good Style" (14)

Walker Gibson

The distinction I am working toward should be obvious enough. *The writer is not physically present to his reader.* He is all words. The writer has no resources at all for dramatizing himself and his message to his reader except those scratches on paper— he has no bulk, no audible voice on the airwaves, no way of introducing himself beyond what he can make his reader "see" by means of abstract written words in various arrangements. To these words the reader responds in a social situation—that is, he infers a personality—but he has only words to go on. Therefore the writer's particular choices of words as he makes his introduction in prose have an absolute kind of importance and finality. His reader is by no means so ready to reserve judgment, to wait and see, as a new social acquaintance. A reader can shut the book at any moment, at the slightest displeasure.

—*Tough, Sweet and Stuffy* (8)

Aristotle

Metaphor . . . gives style clearness, charm, and distinction as nothing else can: and it is not a thing whose use can be taught by one man to another. Metaphors, like epithets, must be fitting, which means that they must fairly correspond to the thing signified: failing this, their inappropriateness will be conspicuous: the want of harmony between two things is emphasized by their being placed side by side. It is like having to ask ourselves what dress will suit an old man; certainly not the crimson cloak that suits a young man. And if you wish to pay a compliment, you must take your metaphor from something better in the same line; if to disparage, from something worse. To illustrate my meaning: since opposites are in the same class, you do what I have suggested if you say that a man who begs "prays," and a man who prays "begs"; for praying and begging are both varieties of asking. —*The Rhetoric and the Poetics of Aristotle* (168–69)

Quintilian

But as two questions arise from this subject, *how* and *what* we ought principally to write, I shall consider them both in this order. Let our pen be at first slow, provided that it be accurate. Let us search for what is best, and not allow ourselves to be readily pleased with whatever presents itself; let judgment be applied to our thoughts, and skill in arrangement to such of them as the judgment sanctions; for we must make a selection from our thoughts and words, and the weight of each must be carefully estimated; and then must follow the art of collocation, and the rhythm of our phrases must be tried in every possible way since any word must not take its position just as it offers itself. That we may acquire this accomplishment with the more precision, we must frequently repeat the last words of what we have just written; for besides that by this means what follows is better connected with what precedes, the ardor of thought, which has cooled by the delay of writing, recovers its strength anew, and by going again over the ground, acquires new force.

—*Institutes of Oratory* III.5–6

William Strunk Jr. and E. B. White

Style takes its final shape more from attitudes of mind than from principles of composition, for, as an elderly practitioner once remarked, "Writing is an act of faith, not a trick of grammar." This moral observation would have no place in a rule book were it not that style *is* the writer, and therefore what you are, rather than what you know, will at last determine your style. —*The Elements of Style* (84)

□ **Think about Style** □

1. Do you know what Lanham means by the "spirit of play" in writing? What do you enjoy most about writing?

2. Smith says, "Creative writers [meaning, I think, writers who are creative] deliberately contravene convention to make a point." How does an innovator convince an audience (such as a teacher) that the unconventionalities in a piece of writing are intentional and not a result of "ignorance or intransigence"?

3. Usage changes with time, and so does style. As Smith says, "[N]ew conventions arise and old conventions die." What changes have you seen in the acceptability of features of writing style? Would you say that the unconventionalities illustrated in part two, "Difference," are acquiring acceptability? Which ones do you think are the most acceptable? The least?

4. Do you agree with Smith, Zinsser, and Dillard that writing is learned through exposure to the writing of other writers? How can you imitate the style of other writers and still develop an individual style yourself?

5. Which writers quoted throughout this book would you consider emulating?

6. Zinsser, like Buffon, says that style is integral to the writer (like hair on the head, says Zinsser). Does that mean you can't alter your style according to the situation? Does a person have A (capital letter) style?

7. Compare Zinsser's and Buffon's statements with what Weathers and Winchester have to say about writers "striving" to develop a "distinctive style." If it's integral with the self, why would you need to work at it? What can you change?

8. How can "the page" teach a person to write, as Dillard advises?

9. Milic wrestles with a perennial question about style: Are style choices conscious or unconscious? He ends up saying that they're both. What do you think? How much of your writing is unconscious? How much conscious?

10. How does the writer/reader relationship described by Gibson compare with that described by Smith?

11. What can a writer do to keep a reader reading?

12. Gibson seems to be concerned that writers choose their words to fit an audience. Do you agree? Or is one's individual style so ingrained that it can't be altered according to situation?

13. If the use of metaphors can't be taught, according to Aristotle, how can a writer learn to use them appropriately?

14. The first-century rhetorician Quintilian, in his elegant way, tells us why repetition of key words brings about coherence and emphasis. Consider yourself as a reader: why does it help your reading when a sentence begins by repeating (with key words, synonyms, pronouns) the last stated idea?

15. Hjortshoj compares two kinds of advice about writing: (a) Don't pause to edit until you've completed a draft. (b) Clarify and polish sentences as you go along. Proponents of the first kind say that pausing to edit may cause the writer to lose track of the idea, and those of the second kind, like Hjortshoj, say that clarifying sentences clarifies ideas and enables the writer to move on. Where do you stand on this issue?

16. How does Hjortshoj's advice compare with Quintilian's: "Let our pen be at first slow, provided that it be accurate"? Are they saying the same thing?

17. Do you think Beardsley is advising against revision when he says that a change in how we express an idea is a change in the idea?

18. Do you believe that style is so tightly connected to substance that altering style changes meaning? What is the relationship of style to substance, or content?

19. How can we reconcile Strunk and White's statement that "what you are, rather than what you know, will at last determine your style" with Smith's and Zinsser's ideas that style is acquired from reading other writers? Can we change our style?

20. What have been the major influences on your writing style?

Glossary of Terms

absolute phrase a **participle** plus the **noun** it modifies plus any other modifiers (*The paper written,* she went home).

adjective a **part of speech** that describes, identifies, qualifies, or otherwise modifies a **noun** or **pronoun**.

adverb a **part of speech** that describes, qualifies, intensifies, or otherwise modifies a **verb**, an **adjective**, or another **adverb**.

alliteration **figurative language** that repeats consonant sounds.

allusion a reference to something or someone only indirectly similar to the thing or person at hand.

anaphora the repetition of words at the beginning of successive clauses.

anastrophe reversal of normal word order.

antecedent a **noun** or **pronoun** to which a pronoun refers (The *book* lost its cover).

appositive a **noun** plus any of its **modifiers** that renames and follows another noun or a **pronoun** (The dog, *a Border collie,* is barking).

asyndeton a coordinate series of words, **phrases**, or **clauses** with no connecting **conjunction**.

case   **pronoun** forms indicating function: nominative for **subjects** and nouns renaming subjects; objective for **objects** and words renaming objects; possessive to show ownership.

clarity   an aspect of style that enables readers to grasp a writer's meaning.

clause   a group of words made up of a **subject** and a **verb** plus any **modifiers** and **complements**; **independent** (or main) **clauses** can stand alone as sentences, **subordinate** (or dependent) **clauses** connect to independent clauses.

coherence   an aspect of style that allows readers to make connections between words and ideas.

colon   a punctuation mark that introduces a series, a quotation, or some other explanation for the **independent clause** it follows (The dog is barking: it's a Border collie).

comma   a punctuation mark with a variety of functions that can be classified as either separating parts of a sentence or enclosing parts of a sentence (The dog, a Border collie, is barking).

comma splice   two **independent clauses** in a sentence, separated only by a **comma**.

complement   a word or group of words that completes a sentence; subject complements rename or describe the **subject**, **direct objects** receive the action of the **verb**, object complements rename or describe the direct object.

conjunction   a part of speech that connects words, **phrases**, and **clauses**; **coordinating conjunctions** connect equal elements, **subordinating conjunctions** connect subordinate elements.

coordinating conjunction   a word that connects equivalent ideas and sentence elements: *and, but, or, nor, for, yet, so.*

coordination   two or more equivalent sentence elements connected with or without a **coordinating conjunction: parts of speech** with the same parts of speech, **phrases** with similar phrases, **clauses** with similar clauses.

cumulative sentence   a sentence style in which an accumulation of **modifiers** follows the statement of the main idea.

dangling modifier   an **adjective phrase**, usually a **verbal phrase**, that does not clearly refer to the word it is meant to modify.

dash   a punctuation mark used to separate or enclose an explanation, an interpolation, or a pause in a sentence (The dog—a Border collie—is barking).

declarative   a sentence that makes a statement, ending with a period.

direct object   a **noun**, noun **phrase**, or noun **clause** that receives the action of a **verb** (The dog chased the *truck*).

discourse   speaking or writing; verbal expression.

emphasis   an aspect of style that draws attention to particular parts of a sentence.

expletive   a word that begins a sentence and delays the **subject**: *it, there* (*There* was a truck in the alley).

figurative language   nonliteral words that add color and emotion to writing, sometimes called figures of speech: **metaphor, simile, personification, alliteration, metonymy, asyndeton, polysyndeton, parallelism, allusion, anaphora, anastrophe.**

fragment   a period-ended group of words that does not include a **subject**, a **verb**, or both; sometimes called an incomplete sentence.

gerund   an *-ing* verbal that functions as a **noun** (The dog's *barking* disturbed the neighborhood).

gerund phrase   a **phrase** consisting of a **gerund** and any **modifiers** and **complements** (After *delivering the package*, the truck driver left).

imperative   a type of sentence that expresses a mild command (*Open the package*).

independent clause   a **clause** that can stand alone as a sentence; sometimes called main clause.

infinitive   a verbal that does not have an ending but often is preceded by *to*; it can function as a **noun**, an **adjective**, and an **adverb** (We wanted *to open* the package).

infinitive phrase   a **phrase** consisting of an **infinitive** and its **modifiers** and **complements** (They wanted *to open the package*).

metadiscourse   discourse about discourse, words that tell readers how to read the words (*incidentally, as a matter of fact, however, in my opinion,* etc.).

metaphor   an implied comparison between a literal meaning and an implied meaning (Clouds *skated* over the city).

metonymy   substitution of a related idea for the one meant (Give me a *hand* [for *help*]).

modifier   a word, **phrase**, or **clause** that describes, limits, broadens, identifies, explains, or intensifies another part of a sentence; **adjective** and **adverb**.

mood   an aspect of **verbs** that shows attitudes; indicative makes **declarative** statements, **imperative** expresses mild commands, and subjunctive shows conditions contrary to fact.

nominalization   a **noun** formed from a **verb** and sometimes an **adjective** (*transformations* from *transform*).

nonrestrictive   applies to a **modifier**, usually a **phrase** or **clause**, that does not define or identify the word it modifies; because it is not essential to the sentence, it is set off with **commas** or other punctuation.

noun   a **part of speech** that names persons, places, things, concepts, actions, qualities, and so on; it has singular and plural forms (*idea, ideas*).

noun phrase   a **noun** plus its **modifiers** (*the unusual idea*).

number   a property of **nouns, pronouns,** and **verbs** that shows singular or plural, one or more than one (*idea, ideas; I, we; goes, go*).

object   a **noun** or **pronoun** that completes a sentence by receiving the action of the **verb** or by following a **preposition**.

parallelism   words, **phrases,** or **clauses** that are structurally similar and coordinate.

part of speech   the function of words in a sentence: **noun, pronoun, verb, adjective, adverb, preposition, conjunction,** interjection.

participial phrase   a **phrase** consisting of a **participle** and any **modifiers** and **complements**; it functions as an **adjective** (*Barking at the truck*, the dog ran in circles).

participle   a **verb** form ending in *-ing*, functioning as adjective (a *barking* dog).

periodic sentence   a sentence style in which an accumulation of **modifiers** precedes the statement of the main idea.

person   a feature of **verbs, nouns,** and **pronouns**; first person represents the writer, *I, we;* second person represents the reader, *you;* third person refers to the subject, *he, she, it, they,* and all **nouns**.

phrase   a group of related words; unlike a **clause**, a phrase does not have a **subject** and a **verb**.

polysyndeton   the use of more **conjunctions** than usual, such as connecting all items in a series.

preposition   a **part of speech** that connects its **object** to another part of a sentence; *at, by, in, of, on, to* are examples.

prepositional phrase   a **preposition** and its **object**, functioning as an **adjective** or an **adverb**.

pronoun   a **part of speech** that substitutes for a **noun**; *you, he, they, we, this, everyone* are examples.

redundancies   words that say the obvious, either something already stated or something an intelligent reader could assume.

relative pronoun   a **pronoun** that introduces a relative **clause**; *who, which, that* are examples.

restrictive   applies to a modifier, usually a **phrase** or a **clause**, that identifies or otherwise limits the meaning of the word it modifies; it is not set off with commas or other punctuation.

rhythm   stressed and unstressed elements of a sentence that together create alternating patterns of sound and thought.

semicolon   a punctuation mark that separates and connects related **independent clauses** without the addition of a **coordinating conjunction** (The dog is a Border collie; it's barking).

simile   a comparison of two unlike things, usually with *like* or *as*.

subject   the word, **phrase**, or **clause** that, with a **verb**, forms the base of a sentence (*Dogs* bark).

subordinate clause   a **clause** that is dependent on an **independent clause**, functioning as an **adjective**, an **adverb**, or a **noun**; sometimes called dependent clause.

subordinating conjunction   a **conjunction** that introduces a **subordinate clause** (*after, because, before, since, while*, etc.).

subordination   sentence elements dependent on other sentence elements; words, **phrases**, and **clauses** may function as **adjectives**, adverbs, or nouns.

tense   a function of **verbs** to indicate time of an action: present (*bark[s]*), past (*barked*), future (*will bark*), present perfect (*has barked*), past perfect (*had barked*), future perfect (*will have barked*).

transition   the connection between two parts of a piece of writing, contributing to **coherence**; it may be achieved with a single word (**transitional adverb**), a **phrase**, a **clause**, a sentence, or an entire paragraph.

transitional adverb   an adverb whose function is to relate ideas within a sentence or between sentences (*finally, however, moreover, then, therefore*, etc.).

verb   with a **subject** it forms the base of a sentence (Dogs *bark*); it can show **tense**, **voice**, and **mood**.

verb phrase   the base form of a **verb** plus auxiliary verbs (*has been gone, is going, was being seen*, etc.).

verbal   a verb form that functions as an adjective, an adverb, or a noun. See **gerund**, **infinitive**, and **participle**.

verbal phrase   a **phrase** made up of a **verbal** (**participle**, **gerund**, or **infinitive**) and its **modifiers** and **complements**, functioning as an **adjective**, an **adverb**, or a **noun**.

voice (1)   an aspect of **verbs** that shows whether the subject is acting (active voice: We *made* a mistake) or being acted upon (passive voice: A mistake *was made*).

voice (2)   the sound of a writer's words conveyed by stylistic features such as word choice and sentence structure, tone or attitude, and timbre.

Works Cited and Quoted

Adams, Henry. *The Education of Henry Adams: An Autobiography.* Vol. 1. Boston: Houghton, 1918. New York: Time, 1964. [Privately published by Adams in 1907]

The American Heritage College Dictionary. 4th ed. Boston: Houghton, 2002.

Anderson, Philip Roger. "A Linguistic Study of the Third Person Generic Pronoun: Singular *They.*" MA thesis. St. Cloud State U, 1995.

Angelou, Maya. *Gather Together in My Name.* New York: Bantam, 1974.

Angier, Natalie. *Woman: An Intimate Geography.* Boston: Houghton, 1999.

Aristotle. *The Rhetoric and the Poetics of Aristotle.* 1954. Trans. W. Rhys Roberts. New York: Modern Library, 1984.

The Associated Press Stylebook and Briefing on Media Law. Ed. Norm Goldstein. Cambridge: Perseus, 2002.

Bain, Alexander. *A Higher English Grammar.* New York: Holt, 1879.

Barry, John M. *Rising Tide: The Great Mississippi Flood of 1927 and How It Changed America.* New York: Simon, 1997.

Bates, Marston. *The Forest and the Sea.* New York: Random, 1960. New York: Time, 1964.

Beardsley, Monroe C. "Style and Good Style." *Contemporary Essays on Style.* Ed. Glen A. Love and Michael Payne. Glenview IL: Scott, 1969. 3–15.

Beason, Larry. "Ethos and Error: How Business People React to Errors." *College Composition and Communication* 53.1 (Sept. 2001): 33–64.

Beckmann, Petr. *A History of Pi.* New York: St. Martin's, 1971.

Bernstein, Peter L. *Against the Gods: The Remarkable Story of Risk.* New York: Wiley, 1996.

Bickel, Lennard. *Mawson's Will.* 1977. South Royalton VT: Steerforth P, 2000.

Bishop, Wendy. "Suddenly Sexy: Creative Nonfiction Rear-ends Composition." *College English* 65.3 (Jan. 2003): 257–75.

Boorstin, Daniel J. *Cleopatra's Nose: Essays on the Unexpected.* New York: Vintage-Random, 1994.

Cahill, Thomas. *How the Irish Saved Civilization.* New York: Doubleday, 1999.

Carroll, James. *Constantine's Sword.* Boston: Houghton, 2001.

Carson, Rachel. *The Edge of the Sea.* New York: New Amer. Lib., 1955.

———. *The Sea around Us.* New York: Oxford UP, 1951.

———. *Silent Spring.* 1962. Boston: Houghton, 2002.

The Chicago Manual of Style. 15th ed. Chicago: U of Chicago P, 2003.

Christoph, Julie Nelson. "Reconceiving *Ethos* in Relation to the Personal." *College English* 64.6 (July 2002): 660–79.

The Compact Edition of the Oxford English Dictionary. New York: Oxford U, 1971.

Corbett, Edward P. J. *Classical Rhetoric for the Modern Student.* 4th ed. New York: Oxford UP, 1999.

Dateline NBC, NBC, 23 May 2000.

Dillard, Annie. *The Writing Life.* New York: Harper, 1989.

Dobrin, Sidney I., and Christian R. Weisser. "Breaking Ground in Ecocomposition: Exploring Relationships between Discourse and Environment." *College English* 64.5 (May 2002): 566–89.

Eubanks, Philip. "Understanding Metaphors for Writing: In Defense of the Conduit Metaphor." *College Composition and Communication* 53.1 (Sept. 2001): 92–118.

Fadiman, Anne. "Under Water." *New Yorker* 23 Aug. 1999: 65.

Foreman, Amanda. *Georgiana: Duchess of Devonshire.* New York: Random, 1998.

Frazier, Ian. *Great Plains*. New York: Picador-Farrar, 1989.

Fussell, Paul. *Doing Battle: The Making of a Skeptic*. Boston: Little, 1996.

Galbraith, John Kenneth. *The Great Crash 1929*. Boston: Houghton, 1954. New York: Time, 1962.

Geller, Jeffrey L. "The Stalemate of Reason." *Philosophy and Rhetoric* 30.4 (1997): 376–94.

Gibaldi, Joseph. *MLA Handbook for Writers of Research Papers*. 6th ed. New York: MLA, 2003.

Gibson, Walker. *Tough, Sweet and Stuffy*. Bloomington: Indiana University Press, 1966.

Gould, Stephen Jay. *The Lying Stones of Marrakech: Penultimate Reflections in Natural History*. New York: Harmony, 2000.

Hamilton, Edith. *The Greek Way*. New York: Norton, 1930. New York: Time, 1963.

Harris, Joseph. "Meet the New Boss, Same as the Old Boss: Class Consciousness in Composition." *College Composition and Communication* 52.1 (Sept. 2000): 43–68.

Harvey, Miles. *The Island of Lost Maps*. New York: Broadway-Random, 2000.

Hay, John. *The Great Beach*. New York: Ballantine, 1963.

Heilbrun, Carolyn G. *The Last Gift of Time*. New York: Ballantine, 1997.

Hillocks, George Jr. "Fighting Back: Assessing the Assessments." *English Journal* 92.4 (Mar. 2003): 63.

Hjortshoj, Keith. *Understanding Writing Blocks*. New York: Oxford UP, 2001.

Imhoff, Edgar Allen. *Always of Home: A Southern Illinois Childhood*. Carbondale: Southern Illinois UP, 1993.

Junger, Sebastian. *The Perfect Storm*. New York: Norton, 1997.

Kaplan, Robert D. *Balkan Ghosts*. New York: Vintage-Random, 1993.

Keegan, John. *The First World War*. New York: Vintage-Random, 1998.

Kennedy, John F. Inaugural Address, January 20, 1961.

Kerr, Walter. *The Decline of Pleasure*. New York: Simon, 1962. New York: Time, 1966.

Krakauer, Jon. *Into Thin Air*. New York: Villard, 1997.

Kraushaar, Jack J., and Robert A. Ristinen. *Energy and Problems of a Technical Society*. New York: Wiley, 1988.

Lamott, Anne. *Bird by Bird*. New York: Anchor-Doubleday, 1995.

Lanham, Richard A. *Style: An Anti-Textbook*. New Haven: Yale, 1974.

Lansing, Alfred. *Endurance: Shackleton's Incredible Voyage*. New York: Carroll, 1959.

Larson, Erik. *Isaac's Storm: The Drowning of Galveston*. London: Fourth Estate, 1999.

Leopold, Aldo. *A Sand County Almanac*. New York: Oxford UP, 1949.

Lessing, Doris. *Particularly Cats*. New York: Signet-Simon, 1967.

Lester, Toby. "Oh, Gods!" *Atlantic Monthly* Feb. 2002: 37–45.

Lippmann, Walter. *A Preface to Morals*. New York: Macmillan, 1929. New York: Time, 1964.

Manchester, William. *A World Lit Only by Fire*. Boston: Little, 1992.

Manguel, Alberto. *A History of Reading*. New York: Penguin, 1996.

Matthiessen, Peter. "Burning Bright." *Outside* Oct. 2002: 134–45.

McCullough, David G. *The Johnstown Flood*. New York: Touchstone-Simon, 1968.

McPhee, John. *Coming into the Country*. New York: Bantam, 1979.

———. *The Pine Barrens*. New York: Noonday Press, 1967.

Milic, Louis T. "Rhetorical Choice and Stylistic Option: The Conscious and Unconscious Poles." *Literary Style: A Symposium*. Ed. Seymour Chatman. London: Oxford UP, 1971. 77–94.

Miller, Casey, and Kate Swift. *Words and Women: New Language in New Times*. 1976. New York: Harper, 1991.

Miller, Judith, Stephen Engelberg, and William Broad. *Germs: Biological Weapons and America's Secret War*. New York: Simon, 2002.

Minnesota Department of Human Services. *A New Financial Worker's Guide to the CAF II*, St. Paul: Minnesota Department of Human Services, 15 Jan. 1993.

Morison, Samuel Eliot. *Admiral of the Ocean Sea: A Life of Christopher Columbus*. 1942. Vol. 1. Boston: Little, New York: Time, 1962.

———. *John Paul Jones: A Sailor's Biography*. Boston: Little, 1959. New York: Time, 1964.

National Council of Teachers of English. *Guidelines for Gender-Fair Use of Language*. NCTE Position and Guidelines. 7 Nov. 2002 <http://www.ncte.org/positions/gender.shtml>

Nystrand, Martin, Stuart Green, and Jeffrey Wiemelt. "Where Did Composition Studies Come From?" *Written Communication* 10.3 (July 1993): 267–333.

Packard, Jerrold, M. *Victoria's Daughters*. New York: Griffin-St. Martin's, 1998.

Pagels, Elaine. *The Origin of Satan*. New York: Random, 1995.

Pence, R. W., and D. W. Emery. *A Grammar of Present-Day English*. London: Macmillan, 1963.

Perkins, David. *Archimedes' Bathtub: The Art and Logic of Breakthrough Thinking*. New York: Norton, 2000.

Pinker, Steven. *The Blank Slate*. New York: Viking, 2002.

Pirsig, Robert M. *Zen and the Art of Motorcycle Maintenance*. New York: Bantam, 1974.

Publication Manual of the American Psychological Association. 5th ed. Washington, DC: 2001.

Quarterly Review of Doublespeak 24.3 (April 1998): 3.

Quintilian. *Institutes of Oratory*. Trans. Rev. John Selby Watson. 1856. Ed. James J. Murphy. New York: Library of Liberal Arts, 1965.

Rankin, Elizabeth. *The Work of Writing*. San Francisco: Jossey, 2001.

Ravitch, Diane. *The Language Police*. New York: Knopf, 2003.

Remnick, David. *Resurrection: The Struggle for a New Russia*. New York: Random, 1997.

Root, Robert L. Jr. "Naming Nonfiction." *College English* 65.1 (Jan. 2003): 242–56.

Rossiter, Clinton. *The American Presidency*. New York: Harcourt, 1956. New York: Time, 1963.

Russell, Franklin. *Watchers at the Pond*. New York: Knopf, 1961. New York: Time, 1966.

Sagan, Carl. *The Dragons of Eden*. New York: Ballantine, 1977.

St. Cloud State University Graduate Bulletin. St. Cloud, MN, 1993.

Seagrave, Sterling. *The Soong Dynasty*. New York: Harper, 1985.

Smith, Frank. "Reading like a Writer." *Joining the Literacy Club: Further Essays into Education*. Portsmouth, NH: Heinemann, 1988. 17–31.

———. *Writing and the Writer*. New York: Holt, 1982.

Smith, Gene. *When the Cheering Stopped: The Last Years of Woodrow Wilson*. New York: Morrow, 1964. New York: Time, 1966.

Strunk, William Jr., and E. B. White. *The Elements of Style,* 4th ed. Boston: Allyn, 2000.

Thomas, Lewis. *Et Cetera, Et Cetera.* New York: Penguin, 1990.

Tower, Cathy. "The Power of Text Characteristics." *Research in the Teaching of English* 37.1 (Aug. 2002): 55–88.

Tuchman, Barbara. *The March of Folly.* New York: Ballantine, 1984.

———. *Practicing History.* New York: Ballantine, 1981.

Tuckman, Bruce W. *Conducting Educational Research.* 4th ed. Orlando: Harcourt, 1994.

Vygotsky, Lev Semenovich. *Thought and Language.* Trans. Eugenia Hansfmann and Gertrude Vakar. Cambridge: MIT, 1962.

Walker, Barbara G. *The Crone: Woman of Age, Wisdom, and Power.* New York: Harper, 1985.

Weathers, Winston, and Otis Winchester. *Copy and Compose: A Guide to Prose Style.* Englewood Cliffs: Prentice-Hall, 1969.

Wedgwood, C. V. *A Coffin for King Charles.* New York: Macmillan, 1964. New York: Time, 1966.

West, Rebecca. *The New Meaning of Treason.* New York: Viking, 1964. New York: Time, 1966.

Wills, Garry. *Lincoln at Gettysburg.* New York: Touchstone-Simon, 1992.

Wilson, Edward O. *Consilience: The Unity of Knowledge.* New York: Knopf, 1998.

Winchester, Simon. *Krakatoa: The Day the World Ended.* New York: Harper, 2003.

———. *The Professor and the Madman.* New York: Harper, 1998.

Winik, Jay. *April 1865: The Month That Saved America.* New York: Harper, 2001.

Wollman-Bonilla, Julie E. "Does Anybody Really Care?" *Research in the Teaching of English* 36.3 (Feb. 2002): 311–26.

Woolf, Virginia. *A Room of One's Own.* 1929. San Diego: Harcourt, 1957.

Wurtzel, Elizabeth. *Bitch: In Praise of Difficult Women.* New York: Doubleday, 1998.

Zinsser, William. *On Writing Well.* New York: Harper, 1995.

Credits

Barn illustrations by Luke Eidenschenk.

Index

Abbreviations, 193–194
Absolute phrase, 65–66
Academic style, 2, 4–5, 87–89, 105,
    194–196
Action
  infinitive for, 161
  obscuring agent of, 111
Adams, Henry, 65
Address, comma enclosing, 188
Adjective
  hyphen and, 220
  indefinite, 232, 244–245
  as modifier, 60
  as subordinate element, 19
Adjective clause
  introduced by *who, where, that,* and
    which, 21–22
  as modifier, 61
  reduced as appositive, 65
Adjective complement, 39
Adjective phrase, 20, 64
Adverb
  hyphen and, 220

  as modifier, 60
  as subordinate element, 19
  transitional, 69, 81
Adverb clause
  introduced by *while,* 22
  as modifier, 61
all
  as singular or plural, 246
  subject-verb agreement with, 228
Alliteration, 87, 97–98
Allusion, 96–97
although
  to indicate concession, 121
  as subordinating conjunction, 119
Anaphora, 96
Anastrophe, 96
and
  beginning paragraph with, 114
  beginning sentence with, 113, 114
  comma with, 189–190
  with independent clause, 15, 16
  with infinitive phrase, 16
  joining nouns or pronouns, 251

and (*continued*)
omission of, 100–101
omitting from series, 45
pronoun-antecedent agreement
and, 242–243
repeating, 101–103
subject-verb agreement and,
230–231
Anderson, Philip Roger, 143
and yet, 117
Angelou, Maya, 87, 94, 101, 250
Angier, Natalie, 38, 86, 87, 89, 95, 97,
165, 170, 176, 187, 207
Antecedent, 235–236
collective, 243–244
compound, 242–243
distant, 243
generic, 244–245
pronoun as, 242
unknown gender of, 140
any, 246
anybody, 141
anyone, 239
Apostrophe, 213–217
to indicate omissions, 215
with possessive plural nouns,
214–215
with possessive singular nouns,
213–214
in pronouns, 249
Appositive, 33, 251
explanation as, 200
modifier as, 64–66
sentence fragment as, 129
Aristotle, 266, 271
Asyndeton, 100–102

Bain, Alexander, 142
Balance
comma splice for, 134–135
semicolon for, 208–209
Barry, John M., 69, 71, 94, 97, 137,
191, 198, 245, 247, 258
Bashevis, Isaac, 22, 37, 60, 115, 146,
154, 243, 245, 264

Beardsley, Monroe C., 265, 270
Beason, Larry, 151
Beckmann, Petr, 203, 205, 214, 223
Beginning sentence. *See* Sentence,
beginning
Bernstein, Peter L., 36, 46, 52, 57, 72,
90, 92, 150, 161, 164, 169, 194,
197, 197, 203, 249, 257, 261
between, 251–252
Bickel, Lennard, 54, 102, 213, 214
Bishop, Wendy, 127
Boorstin, Daniel J., 16–17, 45, 46, 67,
83, 98, 100, 129, 163, 175, 188,
190, 200, 244, 245, 251
but, 15
beginning sentence with, 113
comma with, 189–190
coordinated verb phrases joined
by, 45
by phrase
omitted for conciseness, 79
omitted from passive sentence, 108

Cahill, Thomas, 20, 27, 29, 36, 47–48,
50, 51, 55, 58, 62, 69, 82, 94, 96,
97, 114, 117, 186, 250, 253
Carroll, James, 35, 203, 209
Carson, Rachel, 3, 5, 6, 15, 35, 36, 38,
40, 51, 62, 71–72, 83, 85, 86, 96,
100, 116, 167, 172, 185, 193, 205,
221, 223, 227, 228, 229, 237
Case. *See* Pronoun case
Cause-and-effect process, 26
Christoph, Julie Nelson, 122, 149
Clarity, 266
comma splices and, 136
parallelism and, 29, 44
repetition for, 78, 174–175
rules and, 225
sentence variety and, 43
Clause
adjective, 21–22
nonrestrictive, *which* for, 163–166
noun, 22
paired, 41

restrictive, 188–189
restrictive, *that* for, 163, 189
subordinate, 14–17, 19
Coherence, 11
connected ideas, 73
connecting words, 68–70
consistent subjects, 69–70
flow and, 71–72
forecasting and, 72–73
key word repetition and, 70–71
modifiers and, 63
parallelism and, 44
passive voice for, 109–110
repetition and, 174–175
restating ideas and, 71–72
Collective antecedent, 243–244
Collective noun, verb after, 231–232
Colon, 204–207
complete statement following, 205
comma splice vs., 134
explanation and, 204–206
flexibility with, 206–207
with independent clause, 205–206
list following, 28
quotation and, 206
with series, 204
word following, 206
Colorful language, 11, 266
Comma
with addresses, 188
with *and*, 189–190
with *but*, 189–190
with dates, 188
final nonrestrictive modifiers and,
    186
independent clause and, 15, 185
interruptions with, 33–34
with introductory sentence
    elements, 185–186
items in series and, 186–187,
    189–190
misleading, 188
nonrestrictive interruptions and, 187
omission following, 196
omission preceding, 195

parallelism and, 45
parentheses and, 190
with quotation, 187, 189
restrictive element and, 188–189
as troublesome, 184
Comma splice, 133–138
for balance, 134–135
sentence ambiguity and, 135–136
Complement, 38
subject-verb agreement and,
    228–229
Compound antecedent, 242–243
Compound noun, 251–252
Compound pronoun, 251–252
Compound subject, verb with,
    230–231
Compound word, hyphen with,
    219–220
Concession, clauses of, 121
Concise writing, 76–84
metadiscourse and, 81–84
objects and, 79–81
redundancies vs., 77–79
subjects and, 79–81
verbs and, 79–81
Conjunction
beginning sentence with, 113–118
coordinating, 17
with independent clause, 15, 185
omitting, 100–103
parallelism and, 45
repeating, 100–103
subordinating, 119
Connecting words, 68–70
Connections, making. *See* Coherence
Contraction, 153–157
ain't, 155–156
emphasis for sentence-opening
    with, 155
for informality, 153–154
with *not*, 153
with pronouns and verbs, 153
for rhythm and emphasis, 155
Convention, freedom of choice vs.,
    1–6, 263, 266–267

Coordinated adjective phrases, 20
Coordinating conjunction
    after semicolon, 209
    omitting, 17, 100–103
    repeating, 100–103
Coordination, 14–18
    coordinated phrases, 16–17
    coordinated words, 16–17
    independent clauses, 15–16
    parallel structure, 44–49
Corbett, Edward P. J., 96
Cumulative ideas, subordinating,
    19–23
Cumulative sentence, 21

Dangling modifier, 64, 255–261
    gerund phrase, 257–258
    infinitive phrase, 258
    passive voice and, 258
    past participle, 256–257
Dash, 199–203
    comma splice vs., 134
    for emphasis, 57
    for explanation, 199–201
    with interpolation, 201
    to mark interruption, 33, 200
    as pause for emphasis, 201–202
Date, comma enclosing, 188
Declarative statements, 24
Dillard, Annie, 264, 265, 268–269
Direct object, 38. *See also* Object
Distant antecedent, 243
Dobrin, Sidney I., 152

Editing, avoiding early, 265,
    269–270
Ellipsis, periods for, 194–196
Ellison, Ralph, 264
Emphasis
    in academic style, 88
    contraction for, 155
    dash for, 57, 201
    exclamation point for, 57
    with exclamations, 42
    in independent clause, 56

    interruption for, 54
    italics for, 56–57
    passive voice for, 109–110
    placement of modifiers and, 62
    punctuation for, 56–57
    repetition for, 57, 175–176
    rhythm and, 50–58, 62–63. *See
        also* Rhythm
    sentence fragment for, 126
    subordinating for, 20–22
    transformation for, 55
    varied sentence length for, 53
    weighted end of sentence and,
        51–53
Ending, brief, 31
Eubanks, Philip, 152
Euphuism, 93. *See also* Figurative
    language
everyone, 141
    pronoun-antecedent agreement
        and, 244–245
    subject-verb agreement and, 232
Exclamation, emphasis with, 42
Exclamation point, 57, 194
Explanation, as appositive, 200
Expletive *there*, 38, 229–230

Fadiman, Anne, 177
Faulkner, William, 264
Fielding, Henry, 142
Figurative language, 93–98
    alliteration, 97–98
    allusion, 96–97
    anaphora, 96
    anastrophe, 96
    asyndeton, 100–102
    metaphor, 94–95
    metonymy, 97
    personification, 95–96
    polysyndeton, 100–102
    simile, 95
First-person pronoun, 146–149
    I, 146–148, 238–239
    we, 148–149
Flow, 68, 71

for
  beginning sentence with, 117
  followed by noun or pronoun,
    251–252
  at sentence end, 170
Forecasting sentence, 72–73
Foreman, Amanda, 167, 214, 229,
    237, 241
Formality
  contractions and, 153–154
  inverted sentences and, 40
  semicolon and, 211
  sentence-ending prepositions and,
    169–170
Foundation of writing, 11
Fragment. *See* Sentence fragment
Frazier, Ian, 99, 102, 213, 215, 217
Fussell, Paul, 5, 33, 101, 110, 161,
    194, 236

Galbraith, John Kenneth, 2, 23, 30,
    31, 40, 41, 53, 94, 111, 116, 184,
    188, 189, 253
Geller, Jeffery L., 122, 147
Gender-specific pronouns, 140
Generic noun, 244–245
Gerund, 257
Gerund phrase, 257–258
Gibaldi, Joseph, 194
Gibson, Walker, 265, 270
Gould, Stephen Jay, 49, 96, 97, 114,
    115, 154, 157, 201, 215, 216, 258
Green, Stuart, 159

had clause, 47
Hamilton, Edith, 5, 6, 21, 33, 40, 44,
    45, 55, 63, 116, 129, 133, 134,
    175, 185, 187
Hanson, Chris, 83, 84
Harris, Joseph, 159
Harvey, Miles, 36, 37, 95, 116, 127,
    146, 147, 150, 201, 217
Hay, John, 242
he, 139–142
he/she, 141, 146

Heilbrun, Carolyn G., 102, 124, 134,
    138, 164, 165, 174, 236, 249,
    251, 252
Hemingway, Earnest, 264
Hillocks, George, Jr., 148
him/her, 146
himself, 250
his/her, 141
Hjortshoj, Keith, 265, 266, 269–270
however, 69, 81, 82, 136
Humor, understated, 53
Hyphen
  in compound word, 219–220
  with divided word, 221
  with number, 220
  for omission in word, 221–222
  with prefix, 220–221

I, 146–148, 238–239
Imhoff, Edgar Allen, 42, 119, 154,
    187, 190, 256
Imperative verb, 25
Indefinite adjective
  generic antecedents and, 244–245
  subject-verb agreement with, 232
Indefinite pronoun
  generic antecedents and, 244–245
  subject-verb agreement with, 232
Independent clause
  in asyndeton series, 102
  colon with, 205
  commas separating, 185
  coordinated, 15–16
  emphasis in, 56
Infinitive, 16
  for action, 161
  at end of sentence, 170
  expressing parallel ideas through,
    44–49
  splitting, 158–162
Infinitive phrase, 16
  as dangling modifier, 258
  series of, 102
Informality, contractions for, 153–154
Informal voice, 86–87

-ing phrase, 256
Intensifier, 81–82
Interpolation, dash with, 201
Interruption
   dash for, 200
   for emphasis, 54
   nonrestrictive, comma enclosing, 187
   sentence, 32–34
Inversion. *See* Sentence, reversed word order in
it
   antecedent for, 235
   beginning sentence with, 55, 236
   as third-person pronoun, 146
Italics for emphasis, 56–57
it's/its, 154, 155, 215

Junger, Sebastian, 2, 16, 27, 29, 32, 41, 45, 49, 50, 51, 54, 57, 62, 86, 87, 96, 101, 107, 108, 109, 111, 124, 134, 149, 154, 173, 178, 183, 185, 238

Kaplan, Robert D., 41, 65, 67, 115, 120, 124, 164, 188, 190, 210, 216
Keegan, John, 30, 39, 53, 89, 94, 110, 121, 130, 147, 160, 175, 179, 192, 193, 256, 258
Kennedy, John F., 12, 24
Kerr, Walter, 145, 189
Krakauer, Jon, 5, 39, 64, 70, 147, 177, 185, 197, 211, 212, 220, 257
Kraushaar, Jack J., 16, 56, 74, 88, 90, 93, 148, 149, 212, 260

Lamott, Anne, 21, 28–29, 57, 114, 200, 205, 211, 215, 217
Lanham, Richard A., 263, 266
Lansing, Alfred, 32, 69, 95, 97, 115, 117, 126, 127, 168, 189, 193, 201–202, 235
Larson, Erik, 82, 128, 206
Leclerc, Georges Louis, 264, 269
Length of writing, 11

Leopold, Aldo, 3, 81, 102, 134, 135, 138, 171, 235, 246, 249, 252
Lessing, Doris, 66
Lester, Toby, 70, 71, 73
let's, 154
Lippman, Walter, 145

Making connections. *See* Coherence
Manchester, William, 17, 25, 26, 53, 54, 63, 66, 75, 89, 93, 109, 117, 123, 160, 161, 204, 208, 209, 210, 217, 256, 258
Manguel, Alberto, 55, 56, 217, 240, 242, 244, 249, 253, 254
Matthiessen, Peter, 22
McCullough, David G., 54, 66, 160, 169, 229, 239, 245, 246, 247
McPhee, John, 15, 26, 29, 40, 56, 95, 130–131, 157, 168, 201, 223, 228, 254

Metadiscourse, 81–84
Metaphor, 94–95, 266, 271
Metonymy, 87, 97
Milic, Louis T., 265, 269
Miller, Casey, 156, 186, 189, 199, 214, 216
Miller, Judith, 231
Modifier, 19, 60–64
   absolute, 65–66
   adjective as, 60–61
   adverb as, 60–61
   appositive, 64–66
   comma separating final nonrestrictive, 186
   dangling, 64, 255–261
   with infinitives, 159–161
   as metadiscourse, 82
   negative, 40, 161
   opening, 63–64
   orienting, 63–64
   parallel series of, 25
   phrase as, 61
   placement of, 62
   rhythm and emphasis and, 62–63

sentence-ending, ambiguous, 259
sentence-opening, 63–64
Morison, Samuel Eliot, 2, 20, 34, 37,
    39, 61, 65, 94, 114, 127, 147, 188,
    193, 202, 243, 244, 253, 257
myself, 250

Narrative, passive voice in, 111
Negative modifier, 40
Nominalization, 52
Nominative case, 248
Nominative pronoun, 249
none, 245
Nonrestrictive clause
    because for, 123
    which for, 163–166
Nonrestrictive interruption, 187
no one, 245–246
nor, 116–117
not, contractions with, 153
Noun
    collective, verb after, 231–232
    compound, 251–252
    generic, as singular or plural,
        244–245
    nominalizations, 52
    as object of preposition *by,* 16
    possessive plural, apostrophe with,
        214–215
    possessive singular, apostrophe
        with, 213–214
    summary, 237
Noun clause, introduced by *that,* 22
Noun phrase, 17
Numbers
    apostrophe with, 215
    hyphenated, 220
    period with, 193
Nystrand, Martin, 159

Object
    in active voice, 108
    direct, 38, 40
    hidden, 79–81
    of prepositions, 169

Objective case, 248
Occasion constraints, 13
Omission
    apostrophe to indicate, 215
    following comma, 196
    preceding comma, 195
    in quotation, 195
    in sentence, 195–196
    in word, hyphen for, 221–222
one . . . that, 230
one . . . who, 230
Opening modifiers, 63–64, 255–258
or
    beginning sentences with, 116
    introducing multiple clauses with,
        45
    joining nouns or pronouns,
        230–231, 251
Orienting modifiers, 63–64, 69
our, 148

Packard, Jarrold M., 22, 120, 121,
    154, 194

Padding, 76–77
Pagels, Elaine, 56, 120, 122, 202, 214,
    249, 251
Paragraph
    beginning with *and,* 114
    beginning with *but,* 114–116
    as building materials for writing, 11
    coherence and, 68–74
    consistent subject throughout, 70
    question at end of, 37
Parallelism, 21
    commas and, 45
    conjunctions and, 45
    craft and, 47–48
    parallel periods, 46–47
    repeated phrases, 174–175
    in sentences, 44–49
Parentheses
    comma omitted before, 190
    interruptions with, 34
    period with, 194

Participial phrase, 20
  as dangling modifier, 255–260
  as modifier, 61
  opening sentences with, 64
  punctuation in, 258–259
Participle
  in absolutes, 65–66
  omitting coordinating conjunction
    with three, 17
  present and past forms, 256–257
Passive sentence, 108
Passive verb, 107–112. *See also* Passive
    voice
  be verb in, 108
  for emphasis and rhythm, 52–53
Passive voice. *See also* Passive verb
  for coherence, 109–110
  dangling modifier and, 258
  defined, 108
  for emphasis, 109–110
  for missing agents, 110–111
  in narratives, 111
Past participle, 256–257
Period, 192–198
  in abbreviations, 193–194
  in ellipsis, 194–196
  ending fragments with, 192–193
  ending sentences with, 192–193
  with numbers, 193
  parallel, 46–47
Periodic sentence, 26–27
Perkins, David, 206, 215
Personification, 95–96
Phrase
  absolute, 65–66
  in asyndeton series, 102
  confusing, 259
  coordinated, 14, 16–17
  coordinated adjective, 20
  as dangling modifier, 255–260
  infinitive, 16
  noun, 17
  participial, 20, 64
  prepositional, 20, 27–28, 40
  prepositional *of,* 16

restrictive, 188–189
subordinate, 14, 19
verb, parallel series of, 27
Pinker, Steven, 79, 109, 193, 203,
  212, 220
Pirsig, Robert M., 22, 164, 166, 169,
  171, 229, 238
Plural noun, apostrophe with
  possessive, 214–215
Polysyndeton, 100–102
Possessive case, 248
Prefix, hyphen with, 220–221
Preposition
  ending sentences with, 168–172
  objects of, 16, 169
Prepositional phrase, 40
  as modifier, 61
  orienting, 20
  progression of, 27–28
Pronoun
  agreement with. *See* Pronoun
    agreement
  ambiguities with, 236–238
  as antecedent, 235–236, 242
  apostrophe in, 215, 249
  appositive, 251. *See also* Appositive
  case. *See* Pronoun case
  compound, 251–252
  contractions with verbs and, 153
  epicene (neuter), 143
  first-person, 146–149, 238–239
  flexibility of, 234
  gender-specific, prohibition of, 140
  indefinite, 232, 244–245
  nominative, 249
  relative, 29
  second-person, 146, 238–239
  they as singular, 139–145
  third-person, 146
Pronoun agreement
  all, 246
  any, 246
  collective antecedent, 243–244
  compound antecedent, 242–243
  distant antecedent, 243

generic antecedent, 244–245
none, 245
no one, 245–246
some, 246
Pronoun case, 248–254
    after *than*, 252
    appositive pronouns, 251
    compounds, 251–252
    -self words, 250–251
    who/whom, 249–250
Punctuation
    apostrophe, 213–217
    colon, 204–207
    comma, 184–191
    dash, 199–203
    for emphasis, 56–57
    exclamation point, 194
    as feature of style, 183
    hyphen, 218–223
    in King James Bible, 182
    parentheses, 194
    with participial phrase, 258–259
    period, 192–198
    question mark, 194
    quotation mark, 194
    rules of, 182–183
    semicolon, 208–212

Qualifier, 82
Question, 35–38
    at end of paragraph, 37
    followed by sentence fragment,
        37
    functions of, 37–38
    preposition ending, 170
    rhetorical, 36
    as sentence fragment, 37
    as transition, 36
Question mark, 194
Quintilian, 266, 271
Quotation
    colon and, 206
    comma with, 187, 189
    with omission, 195
Quotation marks, 194

Rankin, Elizabeth, 142, 172
Ravitch, Diane, 55, 252
Reader
    adjustments for, 4–5
    constraints, 12–13
    relationship with writer, 270
"Read like a writer," 263, 267
Redundancies, 77–79
Reflexive case, 248
Relative pronouns, 29, 248–250
Remnick, David, 16, 17, 28, 29, 46,
        52, 60, 63, 64, 69, 78, 101, 121,
        128, 130, 175, 187, 203, 238,
        240, 246
Repetition, 173–179
    build up with, 42, 177
    for connections and clarity, 174–175
    for emphasis, 57, 175–176
    of key words, 70–71
    rhythm and, 45, 51, 176–177
    tedium of, 177
Response, sentence fragments for,
        128–130
Restrictive clause and phrase, 188–189
Rhetorical question, 36
Rhythm. *See also* Emphasis
    in academic style, 88
    contractions for, 155
    emphasis and, 50–58, 62–63
    repetition and, 45, 51, 176–177
    reversed sentence structure and, 39
Ristinen, Robert A., 16, 56, 88, 90, 93,
        148, 149, 154, 212, 260
Root, Robert L., Jr., 164
Rossiter, Clinton, 147, 162, 200, 203,
        205, 206
Rules for writing
    breaking, 2
    as conventions, 105
    learning, 226
    main purpose of, 225
Russell, Franklin, 66, 114, 145

Sagan, Carl, 32, 174, 209
Seagrave, Sterling, 28

Second-person pronoun, 146
  you as, 149–150, 238–239
-*self* words, 250–251
Semicolon, 208–212
  with cause-and-effect description,
    26
  comma splice vs., 134
  coordinating conjunction after, 209
  fragment after, 209
  with independent clause, 15
  need for, 136
  for separations in series, 210
  for shift from usual, 209–210
Sentence
  beginning. *See* Sentence, beginning
  as building materials for writing, 11
  cumulative, 21
  ending with preposition, 168–172
  forecasting, 72–78
  interrupting, 32–34
  long, 24–29
  omission in, 195–196
  paired clauses in, 41
  parallelism in, 44–49
  passive, 108
  period ending, 192–193
  periodic, 26–27
  question, 35–43
  reversed word order in, 38–41
  short, 29–32, 53
  transformation, 54–56
  variation in, 24–44
  varied length of, 53
  weighted end of, 51–53
Sentence, beginning
  with *because*, 119–120
  with conjunction, 113–118
  as emphatic position, 40
  with *it*, 55
  with modifier, 63, 255
  with participial phrase, 64,
    255–257
  with *since*, 120–121
  with *that* clause, 40–41, 42
  with *there*, 38–39, 55, 228–229

  with transitional word, 69
  with *what* clause, 54–55
  with *while*, 121–122
Sentence fragment, 125–132
  acceptability of, 129
  after semicolon, 209
  for emphasis, 126
  long, 130–131
  period ending, 192–193
  question as, 37
  question followed by, 37
  for response, 128–130
  for transition, 127
  which fragment, 127–128
Sentence order, normal, 38
Series
  asyndeton, 102
  colon with, 204
  comma with items in, 189–190
  comma for separation in, 186–187
  of infinitive phrases, 102
  semicolon for separation in, 210
  of verb phrases, 27
Setting of writing, 12–13
Shape of writing, 11
Shaw, George Bernard, 142
she. See *he/she*
Simile, 87, 95
since, 120–121
Singular noun, apostrophe with
    possessive, 213–214
Situational writing, 2–3
Smith, Frank, 263, 264, 266–267
Smith, Gene, 67, 114, 187, 214
so, 116
Special design features, 12
Strunk, William, Jr., 160, 266, 272
Style
  as abstract, 9
  changes in, 265, 270
  as conscious vs. unconscious, 13,
    265
  distinctive, 268
  as identity, 265, 266, 267, 269
  as persona or role, 3

Subject
in active and passive voice, 108
consistent, 69–70
coordinated adjective phrase with, 20
hidden, 79–81
implied "you," 25
that clause as, 40–41
what clause as, 42
writer's attitude toward, 5
Subject-verb agreement, 227–233
collective noun and, 231–232
compound subject and, 230–231
indefinite pronoun and adjective and, 232
inverted order and, 229–230
one . . . who (or *that*) and, 230
verb separated from subject, 227–229
Subordinate clause, 14–17
Subordinating conjunction, 119
Subordination, 14–18
to add details, 19–20
with cumulative ideas, 19–23
for emphasis, 20–22
Summary noun, 237
Summary words, 52
Swift, Kate, 156, 186, 189, 199, 214, 216

Thackeray, William, 142
that
adjective clause introduced by, 21
clause beginning with, 169
noun clause introduced by, 22
for restrictive clause, 163
that clause
embedded, 15
introductory, 42
parallel, 26
as sentence subject, 40–41
that which, 166
them, 146, 248
then, 136
there
beginning sentence with, 38–39, 55
expletive, 38

inverted subject-verb agreement with, 229–230
therefore, 69, 81, 136
they
as singular pronoun, 139–145
as third-person pronoun, 146
Third-person pronoun, 146
this, 128, 237–238
Thomas, Lewis, 2, 3, 4, 6, 17, 30, 32, 81, 110, 120, 125, 127, 132, 133, 134, 154, 155, 170, 186, 219, 221, 234, 236, 237, 241
Time and place orienter, 63–64
Topic sentence. *See* Forecasting sentence
Tower, Cathy, 147
Transformation, sentence, 54–55
Transition
paragraph, 117
question for, 35–36
sentence inversions for, 40
sentence fragment for, 127
Transitional adverb, 69, 81
comma splices and, 136
as nonrestrictive interruption, 187
published writers and, 210
Tuchman, Barbara, 15, 31, 33, 40, 42, 64, 65, 97, 101, 120, 124, 134, 135, 148, 162, 165, 166, 186, 193
Tuckman, Bruce W., 143

us, 148, 248
use/use of, 80

Verb
agreement with subject. *See* Subject-verb agreement
closely coordinated, 45
contractions with, 153
hidden, 79–81
imperative, 25, 150
metaphoric, 27
passive, 52–53, 107–110. *See also* Passive verb
Verbal, 161, 257

Verbal phrases, dangling modifier
   and, 255–260
Verb phrase, parallel series of, 27
Voice, 85–92
   droning, 90
   as indefinable, 91
   informal, 86–87
   passive. *See* Passive voice
   timbre, 90–91
   tone of, 87–89

Walker, Barbara G., 18, 52, 136,
   163–164, 168–169, 176, 200,
   213, 231, 237, 257
we, 148–149, 248
Weathers, Winston, 268, 264
Wedgwood, C. V., 61, 67, 253, 254
Weisser, Christian R., 152
West, Rebecca, 18, 30, 56, 99, 109,
   110, 115, 126, 133, 138, 162,
   242, 244
what, for *that which*, 166
what clause, 169
   beginning sentence with, 54–55
   as sentence subject, 42
   subject-verb agreement with,
      228–229
where, 21–22
which
   adjective clause introduced by, 21
   clauses beginning with, 169–170
   implied, 170
   for nonrestrictive clause, 163–166
which fragment, 127–128
while
   adverb clause introduced by, 22
   beginning sentences with, 121–122
White, E. B., 160, 266, 272
who, 21
who clause, 188
whom, 169

who/whom, 249–250
Wiemelt, Jeffrey, 159
Wills, Garry, 42, 116, 119, 121, 229,
   238
Wilson, Edward O., 75, 186, 195–196,
   230, 241, 259
Wilson, Woodrow, 67
Winchester, Otis, 264, 268
Word choice, 4–5, 11, 85–89, 270
Word order, reversing, 38–41
Words
   as building materials for writing, 11
   colorful, 11
   compound, hyphen in, 219–220
   connecting, 68–70
   coordinated, 14, 16–17
   divided, hyphen with, 221
   extra, 77
   key, repetition of, 70–71
   omissions in, hyphen for, 221–222
   prefixed, hyphens and, 220–221
   subordinate, 19
   summary, 52
   transitional, 69
   in voice, 85–89
Writer
   attitude toward subject, 5
   constraints, 12
   dialoguing with self, 37
   occasion for writing, 6
   reading like a, 267
   role of, 3
Writers, learning from, 2, 9, 267–268
Writers on style, 263–273

yet, beginning sentences with, 116, 117
"You"
   academic, 89
   as implied subject, 25
   as second-person pronoun, 146,
      149–150, 238–239, 248

Style and Difference